Anti-Inflammatory

Cookbook for Beginners 2022

500

Easy and Tasty Recipes with 21 Day Meal Plan to Lose Weight, Balance Hormones and Reverse Disease

Rosa Salisbury

CONTENTS

Chapter 6. Fish And Seafood... 52

Chapter 7. Soups & Stews..68

Chapter 8. Vegetarian Mains..83

Chapter 9. Salads 100

Chapter 10. Desserts...117

Introduction

This book guides you in understanding and following an easy anti-inflammatory diet. This way of eating is not really a diet, but a lifestyle, a way of consuming energy-giving, delicious whole foods in their natural state. It's less about counting calories and more about knowing the nutrients within those calories. There are no empty calories or fluffy fillers here, only real ingredients that benefit the human body.

Proper nutrition is a significant health investment. When you eat poor-quality food, you dip into the nutrient reserves in your bones, soft tissues, organs, glands, skin—even hair! I'm a firm believer that you can teach an old dog new tricks, and that means relearning how to feed ourselves.

Eating in a way that heals inflammation does not have to be a time-consuming ordeal. The principles in this book will help you make shorter trips to the grocery store. You'll quickly choose foods that benefit your body over flashy sweets and treats that leave you depleted. Also, the recipes I provide in this book are easy: Meal prep and cooking times won't take up too much of your time, so even your busiest day will allow for healthy eating.

Let's get cooking today!

Chapter 1. Eating on the Anti-Inflammatory Diet

The Benefits of the Anti-Inflammatory Diet

Many people who make the switch to an anti-inflammatory diet experience some very unexpected but welcome benefits, such as:

1. Being hungry less often: Nutrient-dense food satiates the body and minimizes cravings.

2. Gradual weight loss: Unlike fad diets, where fast weight loss can happen, only to return, eating anti-inflammatory foods and eliminating processed toxic ingredients in your diet results in gradual long-term weight loss that stays off.

3. A sense of well-being through discipline: Every healthy meal you create, every time you repeat a healthy choice, you give your body the tools to thrive, and doing so is emotionally and physically rewarding.

4. Fresh breath: Anti-inflammatory diet foods are easier to digest, which means less undigested, processed toxic ingredients inflaming the gut and causing gas and burping. Anti-inflammatory diet foods freshen the alimentary canal.

5. Less stress over what to eat: Planning and preparing foods in advance and having the convenience of the Instant Pot for cooking foods reduces your chances of making poor dietary decisions and minimizes the time spent in the kitchen.

Following the Anti-Inflammatory Diet

It's important that you don't become overwhelmed when embarking on an anti-inflammatory diet. Here are four easy dietary guidelines to focus on as you begin your journey.

1. **Provide your body with unprocessed, nutrient-dense, healing foods that protect against inflammation.**

Choose antioxidant-rich organic produce; wild-caught, cold-water fish high in omega-3 fatty acids; grass-fed, antibiotic-free meat and animal products; nuts and seeds high in healthy fats, protein, and fiber; and alliums (onions, garlics, leeks) and herbs (basil, oregano, rosemary) packed with unique inflammation-fighting compounds.

2. **Avoid highly reactive foods that cause inflammation.**

Not everyone will have the same foods that trigger imbalance in the body, but a few common ones tend to inflame all of us to one degree or another, including wheat gluten, processed dairy, refined sugar, peanuts, processed corn, soy, feedlot animal products, caffeine, and alcohol. Some people are also sensitive to citrus fruits and produce in the nightshade family (such as tomatoes, potatoes, peppers, and eggplant), although these foods are otherwise generally beneficial.

3. **Add supplements and spices that combat inflammation.**

When buying supplements, choose natural, food-based ones that will be absorbed by your body more easily. Fermented cod liver oil is the perfect inflammation-fighting supplement. It's one of nature's richest sources of omega-3 fatty acids.

Anti-inflammatory spices, such as ginger, garlic, cinnamon, and turmeric, are wonderful additions to meals, or you can purchase them in capsule form as a whole food supplement. Each contains unique and powerful compounds. For example, garlic contains high levels of sulfur, which encourages the immune system to fight disease.

4. **Focus on gut healing.**

Take a supplemental probiotic—a substance that promotes the health and growth of beneficial intestinal flora (good bacteria naturally present in your intestines). Choose one that contains several strains of bacteria, in several billion CFUs (colony-forming units). Such a supplement is frequently needed because many things we ingest today kill these good bacteria, including NSAIDs (nonsteroidal anti-inflammatory drugs), birth control substances, antibiotics, and many processed foods.

Sip on bone broth, which contains amino acids that soothe and heal your gut's lining. Enjoy an array of fermented foods (such as sauerkraut, kimchi, traditionally fermented pickles, cultured yogurt, kombucha, and kefir) that deliver healthy gut bacteria straight to your digestive tract.

Foods to Eat and Foods to Avoid

Foods to Eat

An anti-inflammatory diet helps to calm down our body's immune response to allergic reactions. As a result, it combats the harmful effects triggered by the exposure of toxins, allergens, bacteria, viruses, and fungi. Following is the list of inflammation-fighting ingredients.

- Omega-3 fatty acids (healthy fats). They are found in eggs, wild-caught fish, and grass-fed or pasture-raised meat cuts.

- Nuts and seeds, sunflower seeds, pumpkin seeds, chia seeds, almonds, walnuts, cashews, pistachio.

- Onions, ginger, garlic, bell peppers, pumpkin, and leeks.

- Leafy vegetables such as spinach, cauliflower, broccoli, Kale, asparagus, Bok Choy, etc.

- Herbs such as rosemary, basil, oregano, parsley, etc.

- All types of berries, pineapple, apple, oranges, red grapes, etc.

- Whole grains such as brown rice, millets, quinoa, and oats.

- Healthy oils such as coconut oil, extra-virgin olive oil, avocado oil, and sesame oil.

- Lentils, beets, avocado, green tea, coconut, mushrooms, zucchini, and beans.

- Spices such as turmeric, cinnamon, black pepper, cumin, etc.

- Non-dairy milk products such as almond milk, coconut milk, etc.

- Red wine (In moderation).

- Honey, maple syrup, dark chocolate, and cacao powder.

Foods to Avoid

These are the following foods that trigger inflammation. Eliminate them from your everyday diet and clear them off your pantry shelves.

- Processed meats: They are loaded with saturated fats (sausage, hot dogs, burgers, steaks, etc.)

- Unhealthy fats including lard, margarine, and shortening.

- Sugar added products (except for natural fruits): All canned products with added sugars such as soups, canned fruits, yogurts, bars, etc.

- Unsweetened canned fruits, tomatoes, etc., should be consumed in moderation.

- Sugar-based commercial drinks, beverages, and fruit juices.

- All processed and packaged foods: They are high in additives, artificial colors, and preservatives.

- Refined carbohydrates, including white bread, white pasta, and noodles.

- Foods containing trans fats: Commercially processed foods, fried foods, candies, ice creams, and baked items (cookies, crackers, pastries, cakes, muffins, etc.)

- Alcoholic beverages.

Ways to Make the Anti-Inflammatory Diet Easier

1. Plan ahead for the week: Knowing exactly what meals are on the menu for the week makes shopping, cooking, and storing seamless.

2. Buy in bulk: Many anti-inflammatory foods, such as grains and legumes, are more affordable when purchased in bulk. Having a surplus of ingredients at home can keep you from reaching for inflammatory options and reduce trips to the grocery store.

3. Batch cook and freeze: Batch cooking and storing food makes it easier to prep and store meals that are ready to reheat and eat. This helps reduce prep time and cooking time and cuts down on waste.

4. Take meals on the go: "Bringing a lunch" is popular once again. Lunch and leftover storage containers are crucial to this plan. We recommend investing in a good glass set with easy-to-find matching lids. This makes storing and heating prepared meals easier to grab "on the go."

5. Get rid of unhealthy foods: Using the Stocking Your Anti-Inflammatory Kitchen lists, you can comb through your kitchen to remove items that you now know are inflammatory. If these foods are not in your kitchen, you won't eat them.

Budget time for cooking: The recipes in this book give you total cooking and preparation times, making it easy to carve out the expected amount of time needed for each recipe, especially the time needed to build pressure in the pot and release it after cooking

Chapter 2. Breakfast And Brunch

Scrambled Tofu With Garlic, Onions, And Mung Bean Sprouts

Servings: 4
Cooking Time: 8 Minutes
Ingredients:
- 3 tablespoon coconut oil or extra-virgin olive oil, fresh-pressed
- 3 green onions, white and green parts, thinly sliced on the bias
- 3 garlic cloves, peeled and thinly sliced
- one 15 ounces package firm tofu, drained and diced into half
- kosher salt
- 1 cup mung bean sprouts
- 2 tablespoon mint, chopped
- 2 tablespoon parsley, chopped
- 1 tablespoon lime juice, plus more as needed

Directions:
1. Place the coconut oil, white parts of the green onions, and garlic in a cold sauté pan. Turn the heat to low. For 4 minutes, stir occasionally until they are lightly browned and softened as the aromatics warm.
2. Add the tofu and a pinch of salt and turn the heat to medium. For 3 minutes, cook and stir occasionally until the tofu is well coated with the oil and warmed. Stir in the mung bean sprouts and warm for 1 minute. Add the green parts of the green onions and the mint, parsley, and lime juice. Stir to combine.
3. Serve the scramble on its own.

Nutrition Info:
- Per Serving: Calories: 555 ;Fat: 40g ;Protein: 39g ;Carbs: 14g .

Amazing Banana Oat Pancakes

Servings: 2
Cooking Time: 15 Minutes
Ingredients:
- 2 tsp ground cinnamon
- 2 eggs
- 1 egg white
- 1 banana
- 1 cup rolled oats
- 1 tbsp coconut oil
- 1 tsp vanilla extract
- ½ tsp sea salt

Directions:
1. Place the oats in a food processor and pulse until it gets a coarse flour. Add in cinnamon, eggs, egg white, banana, vanilla, and salt and blitz until smooth. Brush a frying pan with some coconut oil. Cook your pancakes for 4 minutes until the edges begin to brown. Flip and cook your pancake on the other side for about 3 minutes more. Serve warm with your favorite topping. Enjoy!

Nutrition Info:
- Per Serving: Calories: 305;Fat: 16g;Protein: 16g;Carbs: 18g.

Cranberry & Chia Pudding

Servings: 4
Cooking Time: 5 Minutes + Chilling Time
Ingredients:
- 2 ¼ cups coconut milk
- ¾ cup chia seeds
- ½ cup hemp seeds
- ½ cup dried cranberries
- ¼ cup pure maple syrup

Directions:
1. Stir the chia seeds, hemp seeds, coconut milk, cranberries, and maple syrup in a medium bowl. Cover the bowl and refrigerate overnight. In the morning, stir and serve.

Nutrition Info:
- Per Serving: Calories: 485;Fat: 40g;Protein: 9g;Carbs: 25g.

Pear & Kale Smoothie

Servings: 2
Cooking Time: 5 Minutes
Ingredients:
- 3 cups baby kale
- ¼ cup cilantro leaves
- 2 pears, peeled and chopped
- 2 cups sugar-free apple juice
- 1 tbsp grated ginger
- 1 cup crushed ice

Directions:
1. Place the kale, cilantro, pears, apple juice, ginger, and ice in a food processor and pulse until smooth. Serve.

Nutrition Info:
- Per Serving: Calories: 310;Fat: 2g;Protein: 2g;Carbs: 78g.

Chocolate-blueberry Smoothie

Servings: 2
Cooking Time: 5 Minutes
Ingredients:
- 2 cups plain rice milk
- 1 cup frozen wild blueberries
- 2 tbsp cocoa powder
- 1 packet stevia
- ¼ tsp turmeric
- 1 cup crushed ice

Directions:

1. Place the rice milk, blueberries, cocoa powder, stevia, turmeric, and ice in a food processor and pulse until smooth. Serve immediately.
Nutrition Info:
- Per Serving: Calories: 100;Fat: 6g;Protein: 2g;Carbs: 17g.

Maple Coconut Pancakes

Servings: 4
Cooking Time: 55 Minutes
Ingredients:
- ½ cup coconut flour
- 4 eggs
- 1 cup coconut milk
- 1 tbsp pure maple syrup
- 1 tsp vanilla extract
- 1 tbsp melted coconut oil
- 1 tsp baking soda
- ½ tsp sea salt

Directions:
1. Beat the eggs, coconut milk, maple syrup, vanilla, and coconut oil in a large bowl. Stir to combine. Put the coconut flour, baking soda, and salt in a separate bowl; mix well. Add the egg mixture and whisk the batter well until smooth and no lump.
2. Heat a greased nonstick skillet over medium heat and cook your pancakes until the edges begin to brown. Flip halfway through the cooking time. Serve immediately.
Nutrition Info:
- Per Serving: Calories: 190;Fat: 10g;Protein: 8g;Carbs: 15g.

Mango Green Tea Smoothie

Servings: 2
Cooking Time: 5 Minutes
Ingredients:
- 1 tbsp fresh mint, chopped
- 2 cups mango, cubed
- 2 tsp turmeric powder
- 2 tbsp green tea powder
- 2 cups almond milk
- 2 tbsp honey
- 1 cup crushed ice

Directions:
1. Place the mint, mango, turmeric, green tea, almond milk, honey, and ice in a blender and pulse until smooth. Serve.
Nutrition Info:
- Per Serving: Calories: 290;Fat: 4g;Protein: 5g;Carbs: 69g.

Turkey Scotch Eggs

Servings: 2
Cooking Time: 35 Minutes
Ingredients:
- 1 clove garlic, chopped
- 4 eggs, boiled and peeled

- 16 oz ground turkey
- ½ tsp black pepper
- ½ tsp nutmeg
- ½ tsp cinnamon
- ½ tsp cloves
- ½ tsp dried tarragon
- ½ cup chopped parsley
- ½ tbsp dried chives

Directions:
1. Place your oven to 375ºF. Combine the turkey with the cinnamon, nutmeg, pepper, cloves, tarragon, chives, parsley, and garlic in a mixing bowl and mix with your hands until thoroughly mixed.
2. Divide the mixture into 4 circular shapes with the palms of your hands. Flatten each one into a pancake shape using the backs of your hands. Wrap the meat pancake around 1 egg until it's covered. Bake the Scotch Eggs in the oven for 25 minutes or until brown and crisp. Serve.
Nutrition Info:
- Per Serving: Calories: 500;Fat: 30g;Protein: 54g;Carbs: 4g.

Veggie Panini

Servings: 4
Cooking Time: 30 Minutes
Ingredients:
- 2 tbsp olive oil
- ½ lb sliced button mushrooms
- Sea salt and pepper to taste
- 1 ripe avocado, sliced
- 2 tbsp lemon juice
- ½ tsp pure maple syrup
- 8 whole-wheat bread slices
- 4 oz sliced Parmesan cheese

Directions:
1. Heat the olive oil in a medium skillet over medium heat and sauté the mushrooms until softened, 5 minutes. Season with salt and black pepper. Turn the heat off.
2. Preheat a panini press to medium heat, 3-5 minutes. Mash the avocado in a medium bowl and mix in the lemon juice, and maple syrup. Spread the mixture on 4 bread slices, divide the mushrooms and Parmesan cheese on top. Cover with the other bread slices and brush the top with olive oil. Grill the sandwiches one after another in the heated press until golden brown and the cheese is melted. Serve and enjoy!
Nutrition Info:
- Per Serving: Calories: 406;Fat: 25g;Protein: 19g;Carbs: 30.7g.

Tropical French Toasts

Servings: 4
Cooking Time: 55 Minutes
Ingredients:
- 2 eggs
- 1 ½ cups almond milk
- ½ cup almond flour
- 2 tbsp maple syrup
- 2 pinches of sea salt
- ½ tbsp cinnamon powder
- ½ tsp fresh lemon zest
- 1 tbsp fresh pineapple juice
- 8 whole-grain bread slices

Directions:
1. Preheat your oven to 400ºF. Lightly grease a roasting rack with olive oil. Set aside. In a medium bowl, whisk the eggs, then add the almond milk, almond flour, maple syrup, salt, cinnamon powder, lemon zest, and pineapple juice; stir well. Dip the bread in the almond milk mixture and allow sitting on a plate for 2-3 minutes.
2. Heat a large skillet over medium heat and grease with cooking oil. Place the bread in the pan. Cook until golden brown on the bottom side. Flip the bread and cook further until golden brown on the other side, 4 minutes in total. Transfer to a plate, drizzle some maple syrup on top and serve immediately.

Nutrition Info:
- Per Serving: Calories: 511;Fat: 33g;Protein: 14g;Carbs: 41g.

Flaky Eggs With Cabbage

Servings: 1
Cooking Time: 10 Minutes
Ingredients:
- 1 tablespoon coconut oil or avocado oil
- ½ medium head cabbage, sliced
- 2 slices prosciutto, ham, or bacon
- 2 large eggs
- ½ teaspoon fine Himalayan salt

Directions:
1. Heat an 8-inch skillet or griddle over medium heat. Melt the oil in the skillet when it's hot and swirl it around to grease the entire surface.
2. Add the cabbage, distributing it evenly over the whole skillet in one even layer. Let it cook undisturbed until the bottom of the cabbage browns for 5 minutes. Form a little mound by moving the cabbage to one side of the skillet.
3. On the other side of the skillet, put the prosciutto slices and cook for 2 to 3 minutes until crispy then flip it once. Then push the prosciutto to the side, snuggled up against the cabbage.
4. Into the remaining space in the skillet, crack the eggs and sprinkle everything with salt. For 2 to 3 minutes, let the eggs cook until the whites are no longer translucent and has crispy edges. Use a spatula to gently distribute the loose egg white over the cooked egg parts if the eggs look done except for little pools of raw white near the yolk, until they too are cooked.

Nutrition Info:
- Per Serving: Calories: 437 ;Fat: 33.6g ;Protein: 30.4g;Carbs: 8.7g .

Sausage With Turkey And Berries

Servings: 6
Cooking Time: 15 To 20 Minutes
Ingredients:
- 2 teaspoon organic canola oil, plus 2 tablespoons
- ½ cup yellow onion, finely chopped
- 11 ½ pounds turkey, ground
- ¾ cup dried berries
- ¼ cup flat-leaf parsley leaves, chopped
- 1 egg, lightly beaten
- 1 tablespoon fresh sage, minced
- 1 tablespoon thyme leaves
- 1 teaspoon lemon zest, grated
- 1 teaspoon kosher salt
- ½ teaspoon black pepper, ground
- ½ teaspoon allspice, ground

Directions:
1. Warm the 2 teaspoons canola oil in a small skillet over medium heat. Add the onion and cook, stirring frequently for 6 to 8 minutes until soft. Let cool.
2. Combine cooked onion, ground turkey, dried berries, parsley, egg, sage, thyme, lemon zest, salt, pepper, and allspice in a large bowl. Stir gently to combine. Do not to overmix. Cover and refrigerate the mixture for at least 1 hour, or up to overnight.
3. Shape the mixture into 12 patties, each about 2 ½ in wide and ½ in thick.
4. Warm the 2 tablespoons canola oil in a large nonstick skillet over medium-low heat. Arrange the patties in the pan so they are not touching and cook until they are browned and no longer pink in the center for 3 to 4 minutes per side. Serve immediately, or keep warm in a 200°F oven for up to 30 minutes.

Nutrition Info:
- Per Serving: Calories: 944 ;Fat: 71g ;Protein: 58g Carbs: 13g .

Sunflower Seed Granola

Servings: 6
Cooking Time: 55 Minutes
Ingredients:
- 1 ½ cups sunflower seeds
- 4 cups rolled oats
- ½ cup pure maple syrup
- ½ cup coconut oil
- 1 ½ tsp ground cinnamon

Directions:
1. Preheat your oven to 325ºF. In a large bowl, stir together the oats, sunflower seeds, maple syrup, coconut oil,

and cinnamon. Stir well until the oats and seeds are evenly coated with syrup, oil, and cinnamon.

2. Divide the granola mixture evenly between two foil-lined baking sheets. Place the sheets in the preheated oven and bake for 35-40 minutes, stirring every 10 minutes so everything browns evenly. Cool completely, then store in large glass jars with tight-fitting lids.

Nutrition Info:

- Per Serving: Calories: 400;Fat: 20g;Protein: 9g;Carbs: 47g.

Cherry & Coconut Oatmeal With Chia

Servings: 2
Cooking Time: 15 Minutes
Ingredients:

- 3 cups coconut milk
- 2 cups wholemeal oats
- 1 tbsp milled chia seeds
- 3 tsp raw cacao
- ½ tsp stevia
- 1 tsp coconut shavings
- 6 fresh cherries

Directions:

1. Place a pan over medium heat. Add the oats, cacao, stevia, and coconut milk and simmer them until the oats are fully cooked through, 5-10 minutes. Pour into your favorite breakfast bowl and sprinkle the coconut shavings, cherries, and milled chia seeds on top.

Nutrition Info:

- Per Serving: Calories: 653;Fat: 21g;Protein: 29g;Carbs: 87g.

Orange-bran Cups With Dates

Servings: 6
Cooking Time: 30 Minutes
Ingredients:

- 1 tsp avocado oil
- 3 cups bran flakes cereal
- 1 ½ cups whole-wheat flour
- ½ cup dates, chopped
- 3 tsp baking powder
- ½ tsp ground cinnamon
- ½ tsp sea salt
- ⅓ cup brown sugar
- ¾ cup fresh orange juice

Directions:

1. Preheat your oven to 400ºF. Grease a 12-cup muffin tin with avocado oil. Mix the bran flakes, flour, dates, baking powder, cinnamon, and salt in a bowl. In another bowl, combine the sugar and orange juice until blended. Pour into the dry mixture and whisk. Divide the mixture between the cups of the muffin tin. Bake for 20 minutes or until golden brown and set. Cool for a few minutes before removing from the tin and serve.

Nutrition Info:

- Per Serving: Calories: 256;Fat: 1g;Protein: 5.8g;Carbs: 57g.

Strawberry & Pecan Breakfast

Servings: 2
Cooking Time: 15 Minutes
Ingredients:

- 1 can coconut milk, refrigerated overnight
- 1 cup granola
- ½ cup pecans, chopped
- 1 cup sliced strawberries

Directions:

1. Drain the coconut milk liquid. Layer the coconut milk solids, granola, and strawberries in small glasses. Top with chopped pecans and serve right away.

Nutrition Info:

- Per Serving: Calories: 644;Fat: 79g;Protein: 23g;Carbs: 82g.

Tasteful Hash With Sweet Potato And Ground Turkey

Servings: 4
Cooking Time: 26 Minutes
Ingredients:

- 1½ pounds extra-lean ground turkey
- 1 sweet onion, chopped or 1 cup pre-cut packaged onion
- 2 teaspoons bottled garlic, minced
- 1 teaspoon ginger, ground
- 2 pounds sweet potatoes, peeled, cooked, and diced
- Pinch sea salt
- Pinch black pepper, freshly ground
- Pinch cloves, ground
- 1 cup kale, chopped

Directions:

1. Sauté the turkey for about 10 minutes, or until it is cooked through in a large skillet over medium-high heat.

2. Add the onion, garlic, and ginger. Sauté for 3 minutes.

3. Add the sweet potatoes, sea salt, pepper, and cloves. Lower the heat to medium. Sauté for about 10 minutes while stirring until the sweet potato is heated through.

4. Stir in the kale. Cook for about 3 minutes and stir until it has wilted.

5. Divide the hash among four bowls and serve.

Nutrition Info:

- Per Serving: Calories: 467 ;Fat: 14g ;Protein:34g;Carbs: 50g .

Spicy Quinoa Bowl With Black Beans

Servings: 4
Cooking Time: 25 Minutes
Ingredients:

- 1 cup brown quinoa, rinsed
- 3 tbsp Greek yogurt
- ½ lime, juiced
- 2 tbsp chopped cilantro

- 1 cup canned black beans
- 3 tbsp tomato salsa
- ¼ avocado, sliced
- 2 radishes, shredded
- 1 tbsp pepitas

Directions:

1. Cook the quinoa with 2 cups of salted water in a pot over medium heat or until the liquid absorbs, 15 minutes. Spoon the quinoa into serving bowls and fluff with a fork. In a small bowl, mix the yogurt, lime juice, cilantro, and salt. Divide this mixture on the quinoa and top with beans, salsa, avocado, radishes, and pepitas. Serve.

Nutrition Info:

- Per Serving: Calories: 340;Fat: 9g;Protein: 19.1g;Carbs: 49g.

Thyme Pumpkin Stir-fry

Servings: 2
Cooking Time: 25 Minutes
Ingredients:

- 1 cup pumpkin, shredded
- 1 tbsp olive oil
- ½ onion, chopped
- 1 carrot, chopped
- 2 garlic cloves, minced
- ½ tsp dried thyme
- 1 cup chopped kale
- Sea salt and pepper to taste

Directions:

1. Heat the olive oil in a skillet over medium heat. Add and sauté the onion and carrot for 5 minutes, stirring often. Add in garlic and thyme, cook for 30 seconds until the garlic is fragrant. Place in the pumpkin and cook for 10 minutes until tender. Stir in kale, cook for 4 minutes until the kale wilts. Season with salt and pepper. Serve hot.

Nutrition Info:

- Per Serving: Calories: 147;Fat: 7g;Protein: 3.1g;Carbs: 10.7g.

Sweet Kiwi Oatmeal Bars

Servings: 6
Cooking Time: 50 Minutes
Ingredients:

- 2 cups rolled oats
- 2 cups whole-wheat flour
- 1 ½ cups pure date sugar
- 1 ½ tsp baking soda
- ½ tsp ground cinnamon
- 1 cup almond butter, melted
- 4 cups kiwi, chopped
- ¼ cup organic cane sugar
- 2 tbsp arrowroot

Directions:

1. Preheat your oven to 380ºF. In a bowl, mix the oats, flour, date sugar, baking soda, salt, and cinnamon. Put in almond butter and whisk to combine. In another bowl,

combine the kiwis, cane sugar, and arrowroot until the kiwis are coated. Spread 3 cups of oatmeal mixture on a greased baking dish and top with kiwi mixture and finally put the remaining oatmeal mixture on top. Bake for 40 minutes. Allow cooling and slice into bars. Serve.

Nutrition Info:

- Per Serving: Calories: 482;Fat: 4g;Protein: 10.7g;Carbs: 101g.

Terrific Pancakes With Coconut And Banana

Servings: 4
Cooking Time: 10 Minutes
Ingredients:

- ½ cup almond flour
- ¼ cup coconut flour
- 1 teaspoon baking soda
- 3 eggs, beaten
- 2 bananas, mashed
- 1 teaspoon pure vanilla extract
- 1 tablespoon coconut oil

Directions:

1. Stir the almond flour, coconut flour, and baking soda together in a medium bowl until well mixed.
2. Make a well in the center and add the eggs, bananas, and vanilla. Beat together until well blended.
3. Place a large skillet over medium-high heat and add the coconut oil.
4. Pour ¼ cup of batter into the skillet, four per batch for each pancake. Cook for about 3 minutes, or until the bottom is golden and the bubbles on the surface burst. Flip and cook for about 2 minutes more until golden and cooked through. Transfer to a plate and repeat with any remaining batter.
5. Serve the pancake.

Nutrition Info:

- Per Serving: Calories: 218 ;Fat: 15g ;Protein: 8g;Carbs: 17g .

Blackberry Waffles

Servings: 4
Cooking Time: 15 Minutes
Ingredients:

- 1 ½ cups whole-wheat flour
- ½ cup old-fashioned oats
- ¼ cup date sugar
- 3 tsp baking powder
- ½ tsp sea salt
- 1 tsp ground cinnamon
- 2 cups soy milk
- 1 tbsp fresh lemon juice
- 1 tsp lemon zest
- ¼ cup coconut oil, melted
- ½ cup fresh blackberries

Directions:

1. Preheat your waffle iron. In a bowl, mix whole-wheat, oats, sugar, baking powder, salt, and cinnamon. Set aside. In

another bowl, combine milk, lemon juice, lemon zest, and coconut oil. Pour into the wet ingredients and whisk to combine. Add the batter to the hot greased waffle iron, using approximately a ladleful for each waffle. Cook for 3-5 minutes, until golden brown. Repeat the process until no batter is left. Serve topped with blackberries.

Nutrition Info:

- Per Serving: Calories: 439;Fat: 17g;Protein: 10.6g;Carbs: 62g.

Sweet Potato, Tomato, & Onion Frittata

Servings: 4
Cooking Time: 30 Minutes
Ingredients:

- 6 large eggs, beaten
- 1 tomato, chopped
- ¼ cup almond milk
- 1 tbsp tomato paste
- 1 tbsp olive oil
- 2 tbsp coconut flour
- 5 tbsp chopped onion
- 1 tsp minced garlic clove
- 2 shredded sweet potatoes

Directions:

1. Whisk the wet ingredients together in a bowl. Fold in the dry ingredients and stir to combine well. Place the mixture in a baking dish that will fit into the Instant Pot. Place a trivet in the pressure cooker and pour 1 cup of water inside. Place the baking dish in your pressure cooker on top of the trivet. Seal the lid and turn the sealing vent to "sealing". Cook for 18 minutes on "Manual" on High pressure. Once completed, let the pressure release naturally for 10 minutes and serve hot. Enjoy!

Nutrition Info:

- Per Serving: Calories: 190;Fat: 11g;Protein: 11g;Carbs: 12g.

Sweet Potato & Mushroom Hash

Servings: 4
Cooking Time: 30 Minutes
Ingredients:

- 2 cooked sweet potatoes, cubed
- 2 tbsp coconut oil
- ½ onion, thinly sliced
- 1 cup sliced mushrooms
- 1 garlic clove, thinly sliced
- 1 cup chopped Swiss chard
- ½ cup vegetable broth
- Sea salt and pepper to taste
- 1 tbsp chopped fresh thyme

Directions:

1. Melt the coconut oil in a large nonstick skillet over medium heat. Add the onion, mushrooms, and garlic. Sauté for 8 minutes, or until the onions and mushrooms are tender.

Add the sweet potatoes, Swiss chard, vegetable broth, salt, pepper, and thyme. Cook for 5 minutes. Serve.

Nutrition Info:

- Per Serving: Calories: 323;Fat: 7g;Protein: 30g;Carbs: 35g.

Granola With Maple And Cinnamon

Servings: 8-10
Cooking Time: 35-40 Minutes
Ingredients:

- 4 cups rolled oats, gluten-free
- 1 ½ cups sunflower seeds
- ½ cup maple syrup
- ½ cup coconut oil
- 1 ½ teaspoons cinnamon, ground

Directions:

1. Preheat the oven to 325°F.
2. Line two baking sheets with parchment paper.
3. Stir together the oats, sunflower seeds, maple syrup, coconut oil, and cinnamon in a large bowl. The oats and seeds must be evenly coated with syrup, oil, and cinnamon so stir it well.
4. Between two sheets, divide the granola mixture evenly.
5. For 35 to 40 minutes, place the sheets in the preheated oven while stirring it every 10 minutes so everything browns evenly.
6. Cool completely, then store it in a large glass jars with tight-fitting lids.

Nutrition Info:

- Per Serving: Calories: 400 ;Fat: 22g ;Protein: 9g ;Carbs: 47g .

Matcha Smoothie With Pear & Ginger

Servings: 2
Cooking Time: 5 Minutes
Ingredients:

- 1 tsp vanilla protein powder
- 1 tsp matcha powder
- 2 pears, peeled and chopped
- 2 tbsp honey
- 1 tsp ground ginger
- 2 cups almond milk
- 1 cup crushed ice

Directions:

1. Place the matcha powder, pears, honey, ginger, almond milk, vanilla powder, and ice in a food processor and pulse until smooth. Serve right away.

Nutrition Info:

- Per Serving: Calories: 210;Fat: 3g;Protein: 1g;Carbs: 50g.

Spicy Apple Pancakes

Servings: 4
Cooking Time: 30 Minutes
Ingredients:
- 2 cups almond milk
- 1 tsp apple cider vinegar
- 2 ½ cups whole-wheat flour
- 2 tbsp baking powder
- ½ tsp baking soda
- 1 tsp sea salt
- ½ tsp ground cinnamon
- ¼ tsp grated nutmeg
- ¼ tsp ground allspice
- ½ cup sugar-free applesauce
- 1 tbsp coconut oil

Directions:
1. Whisk the almond milk and apple cider vinegar in a bowl and set aside. In another bowl, combine the flour, baking powder, baking soda, salt, cinnamon, nutmeg, and allspice. Transfer the almond mixture to another bowl and beat with the applesauce and 1 cup of water. Pour in the dry ingredients and stir. Melt some coconut oil in a skillet over medium heat. Pour a ladle of the batter and cook for 5 minutes, flipping once until golden. Repeat the process until the batter is exhausted. Serve.

Nutrition Info:
- Per Serving: Calories: 596;Fat: 33g;Protein: 11g;Carbs: 67.2g.

Yummy Parfait With Yogurt, Berry, And Walnut

Servings: 2
Cooking Time: 0 Minute
Ingredients:
- 2 cups plain unsweetened yogurt, or plain unsweetened coconut yogurt or almond yogurt
- 2 tablespoons honey
- 1 cup blueberries, fresh
- 1 cup raspberries, fresh
- ½ cup walnut pieces

Directions:
1. Whisk the yogurt and honey in a medium bowl. Spoon into 2 serving bowls.
2. Top each with ½ cup blueberries, ½ cup raspberries, and ¼ cup walnut pieces.

Nutrition Info:
- Per Serving: Calories: 505 ;Fat: 22g ;Protein: 23g ;Carbs: 56g .

Maple Banana Oats

Servings: 4
Cooking Time: 35 Minutes
Ingredients:
- 1 cup steel-cut oats
- 2 bananas, mashed
- ¼ cup pumpkin seeds
- 2 tbsp maple syrup
- A pinch of sea salt

Directions:
1. Bring 3 cups of water to a boil in a pot, add in oats, and lower the heat. Cook for 20-30 minutes. Put in the mashed bananas, cook for 3-5 minutes more. Stir in maple syrup, pumpkin seeds, and salt. Serve and enjoy!

Nutrition Info:
- Per Serving: Calories: 167;Fat: 5g;Protein: 4.2g;Carbs: 28.6g.

Carrot-strawberry Smoothie

Servings: 2
Cooking Time: 5 Minutes
Ingredients:
- 1 cup diced carrots
- 1 cup strawberries
- 1 apple, chopped
- 2 tbsp maple syrup
- 2 cups almond milk

Directions:
1. Place in a food processor all the ingredients. Blitz until smooth. Pour in glasses and serve.

Nutrition Info:
- Per Serving: Calories: 708;Fat: 58g;Protein: 7g;Carbs: 53.4g.

Delightful Coconut With Cherries And Chia Seeds

Servings: 2
Cooking Time: 10 Minutes
Ingredients:
- 2 cups whole meal oats
- 1 tablespoon chia seeds, milled
- 3 cups milk, coconut
- 3 teaspoon raw cacao, optional
- ½ teaspoon stevia
- 1 teaspoon coconut shavings
- 6 cherries, fresh

Directions:
1. Mix the oats, cacao, stevia, and coconut milk in a pan mix
2. For 5 to 10 minutes, heat on a medium heat and simmer until the oats are fully cooked.
3. Pour it in a bowl and sprinkle on top the coconut shavings, cherries, and milled chia seeds.
4. Try adding cacao or a drizzle of honey if you prefer sweet food.

Nutrition Info:
- Per Serving: Calories: 455 ;Fat: 19g ;Protein: 28g;Carbs: 80g ;Sugar: 20g ;Fiber: 15g ;

Green Banana Smoothie

Servings: 2
Cooking Time: 5 Minutes
Ingredients:
- 2 cups flaxseed milk
- 2 cups spinach, chopped
- 2 bananas, peeled
- 1 packet stevia
- 1 tsp ground cinnamon
- 1 cup crushed ice

Directions:
1. Place the flaxseed milk, spinach, bananas, stevia, cinnamon, and ice in a food processor and pulse until smooth. Serve immediately.

Nutrition Info:
- Per Serving: Calories: 180;Fat: 5g;Protein: 4g;Carbs: 38g.

Almond, Blueberry & Coconut Rice

Servings: 4
Cooking Time: 40 Minutes
Ingredients:
- 2 dates, pitted and chopped
- 1 cup brown basmati rice
- 1 cup coconut milk
- 1 tsp sea salt
- ¼ cup slivered almonds
- ½ cup shaved coconut
- 1 cup fresh blueberries

Directions:
1. Place the basmati rice, dates, coconut milk, salt, and 1 cup of water in a saucepan. Stir well. Bring to a boil. Reduce the heat to low, then simmer for 30 minutes or until the rice is soft. Divide them into four bowls and serve with almonds, coconut, and blueberries on top.

Nutrition Info:
- Per Serving: Calories: 280;Fat: 9g;Protein: 7g;Carbs: 50g.

Delicate Rice With Coconut And Berries

Servings: 4
Cooking Time: 30 Minutes
Ingredients:
- 1 cup brown basmati rice
- 1 cup water
- 1 cup coconut milk
- 1 teaspoon salt
- 2 dates, pitted and chopped
- 1 cup blueberries, or raspberries, fresh and divided
- ¼ cup slivered almonds, toasted and divided
- ½ cup coconut, shaved and divided

Directions:
1. Combine the basmati rice, water, coconut milk, salt, and date pieces in a medium saucepan over high heat.

2. Stir until the mixture comes to a boil. For 20 to 30 minutes, lower the heat to simmer and cook, without stirring, or until the rice is tender.
3. Divide the rice among four bowls and top each serving with ¼ cup of blueberries, 1 tablespoon of almonds, and 2 tablespoons of coconut.

Nutrition Info:
- Per Serving: Calories: 281 ;Fat: 8g ;Protein: 6g ;Carbs: 49g .

Fresh Peach Smoothie

Servings: 2
Cooking Time: 5 Minutes
Ingredients:
- 1 avocado
- 2 cups baby spinach
- 1 cup peach chunks
- 2 cups almond milk
- Juice of 1 lime
- 2 tbsp maple syrup

Directions:
1. In a food processor, combine avocado, spinach, pear, milk, lime, and maple syrup. Purée until smooth to serve.

Nutrition Info:
- Per Serving: Calories: 886;Fat: 77g;Protein: 9g;Carbs: 53.9g.

Pecan & Pumpkin Seed Oat Jars

Servings: 4
Cooking Time: 10 Minutes + Chilling Time
Ingredients:
- 2 ½ cups old-fashioned rolled oats
- 5 tbsp pumpkin seeds
- 5 tbsp chopped pecans
- 5 cups soy milk
- 2 ½ tsp maple syrup
- Sea salt to taste
- 1 tsp ground cardamom
- 1 tsp ground ginger

Directions:
1. In a bowl, put oats, pumpkin seeds, pecans, soy milk, maple syrup, salt, cardamom, and ginger; toss to combine. Divide the mixture between mason jars. Seal the lids and place the jars in the fridge for about 10 hours. Serve.

Nutrition Info:
- Per Serving: Calories: 441;Fat: 16g;Protein: 18.4g;Carbs: 59g.

Baked Berry Millet With Applesauce

Servings: 6
Cooking Time: 65 Minutes
Ingredients:
- 2 cups blueberries
- 1 cup millet
- 2 cups sugar-free applesauce
- ⅓ cup coconut oil, melted

- 2 tsp grated fresh ginger
- 1 ½ tsp ground cinnamon

Directions:

1. Place your oven to 350ºF. Mix the millet, blueberries, applesauce, coconut oil, ginger, and cinnamon in a large bowl. Pour the mixture into a casserole dish. Cover with aluminum foil. Bake for 40 minutes. Remove the foil and bake for 10-15 minutes more until lightly crisp on top.

Nutrition Info:

- Per Serving: Calories: 325;Fat: 14g;Protein: 6g;Carbs: 48g.

Scrambled Eggs With Smoked Salmon

Servings: 4
Cooking Time: 15 Minutes

Ingredients:

- 2 chopped chives, chopped
- 2 tbsp olive oil
- 6 oz smoked salmon, flaked
- 8 eggs, beaten
- ¼ tsp ground black pepper

Directions:

1. Warm the olive oil in a skillet over medium heat and cook the salmon for 3 minutes, stirring often. Beat the eggs and pepper in a bowl, pour it over the salmon, and cook for 5 minutes, stirring gently until set. Top with chives and serve warm.

Nutrition Info:

- Per Serving: Calories: 240;Fat: 19g;Protein: 17g;Carbs: 1g.

Satisfying Eggs Benny

Servings: 4
Cooking Time: 15 Minutes

Ingredients:

- 8 slices bacon
- 12 spears asparagus, trimmed
- 4 cups water
- 1 tablespoon white vinegar
- 4 large eggs
- 4 Savory Flax Waffles
- ¼ to ½ cup Hollandaise

Directions:

1. Spaced the bacon slices about 1 inch apart and place them on a sheet pan. Distribute the asparagus around the bacon. Place the sheet pan in the oven and set it to 400°F. Cook until the oven comes to temperature, then for 10 to 15 more minutes.

2. Once the asparagus tips are lightly browned and the bacon is toasty on the edges, turn off the oven and crack the door a bit so everything stays warm. I like to put my waffles in there, too.

3. Begin poaching the eggs by lining a plate with paper towels. Heat the water in a small saucepan over medium heat. Add the vinegar and bring to a steady simmer. Crack each of the eggs into its own small ramekin.

4. Stir the water in the saucepan with a slotted spoon to create a whirlpool, then slowly add an egg to the center of the whirlpool. Stir gently the water around the edge of the pot for another 10 seconds, until the swirling motion of the water wraps the egg white around the yolk to create a neat poached egg. For 3 minutes, cook undisturbed until the white is opaque and the egg looks like a teardrop.

5. Remove the egg from the water with a slotted spoon and place it on the lined plate. Repeat with the remaining eggs.

6. Assemble the eggs benny like a waffle on the bottom, a layer of asparagus, 2 slices of bacon, a poached egg, and then 1 to 2 tablespoons of hollandaise.

7. You can store the rest of the meal by packing each component separately in an airtight container. They will keep in the fridge for up to 5 days.

Nutrition Info:

- Per Serving: Calories: 410 ;Fat: 30g ;Protein: 23g ;Carbs: 12g .

Almond Yogurt With Berries & Walnuts

Servings: 4
Cooking Time: 10 Minutes

Ingredients:

- 4 cups almond milk
- 2 cups Greek yogurt
- 2 tbsp pure maple syrup
- 2 cups mixed berries
- ¼ cup chopped walnuts

Directions:

1. In a medium bowl, mix the yogurt and maple syrup until well-combined. Divide the mixture into 4 breakfast bowls. Top with the berries and walnuts. Enjoy immediately.

Nutrition Info:

- Per Serving: Calories: 703;Fat: 63g;Protein: 13g;Carbs: 32.1g.

Amazing Breakfast Bowl With Kale, Pickled Red Onions, And Carne Molida

Servings: 1
Cooking Time: 7 Minutes

Ingredients:

- 1 large egg
- 1 tablespoon avocado oil
- 5 or 6 leaves curly or dinosaur kale, chopped
- ¼ teaspoon Himalayan salt, fine
- 2 tablespoons Coconut Yogurt
- ¼ cup Carne Molida
- 2 tablespoons Pickled Red Onions

Directions:

1. Bring a small pot of water to a rapid boil over high heat. Also, heat a large skillet over medium heat.

2. Gently add the egg when the water begins to boil. Set a timer for 6 minutes.

3. Pour the avocado oil into the skillet and add the kale while the egg cooks. Sprinkle with salt. Sauté, stir often,

until the kale wilts and begins to brown for 6 minutes. Remove from the heat and transfer the kale to a serving plate.

4. Remove the pot with the egg from the heat and drain the water then leave the egg in the pot. Fill the pot enough with cool water and ice to cover the egg. For 2 minutes, let the egg sit in the ice bath while preparing the rest of the dish.

5. Smear the yogurt on the plate across from the kale. Between the kale and the yogurt, spoon the carne molida and top with the pickled onions.

6. Tap the egg to crack the shell and submerge it under the water to peel it.

7. Place the egg on the yogurt. To make a vertical slit in it, use a paring knife by letting the yolk spill out over the yogurt.

8. Serve and dig in. Store this dish by storing the different components in separate airtight containers in the fridge for up to 5 days.

Nutrition Info:

*   Per Serving: Calories: 478| Fat: 31.3g ;Protein: 33.6g;Carbs: 12.5g.

Cherry & Cashew Pudding

Servings: 4
Cooking Time: 10 Minutes
Ingredients:

*   1 cup fresh raspberries
*   1 cup fresh blueberries
*   2 cups almond milk
*   ½ cup chia seeds
*   1 tsp vanilla extract
*   ¼ cup pure maple syrup
*   ½ cup chopped cashews
*   1 cup pitted cherries, chopped

Directions:

1. Place the almond milk, chia seeds, vanilla, and maple syrup in a mixing bowl. Stir well. Refrigerate overnight. Divide the almond milk mixture between four bowls, then serve with cashews and cherries on top.

Nutrition Info:

*   Per Serving: Calories: 270;Fat: 15g;Protein: 6g;Carbs: 38g.

Lemony Quinoa Muffins

Servings: 4
Cooking Time: 25 Minutes
Ingredients:

*   2 tbsp coconut oil melted
*   ¼ cup ground flaxseed
*   2 cups lemon curd
*   ½ cup pure date sugar
*   1 tsp apple cider vinegar
*   2 ½ cups whole-wheat flour
*   1 ½ cups cooked quinoa
*   2 tsp baking soda
*   A pinch of sea salt
*   ½ cup raisins

Directions:

1. Preheat your oven to 400ºF. In a bowl, combine the flaxseed and ½ cup water. Stir in the lemon curd, sugar, coconut oil, and vinegar. Add in flour, quinoa, baking soda, and salt. Put in the raisins, be careful not too fluffy.

2. Divide the batter between greased muffin tin and bake for 20 minutes until golden and set. Allow cooling slightly before removing it from the tin. Serve.

Nutrition Info:

*   Per Serving: Calories: 719;Fat: 11g;Protein: 19g;Carbs: 133g.

Organic Rhubarb Muffins

Servings: 2
Cooking Time: 25 Minutes
Ingredients:

*   2 tbsp crystallized ginger
*   ¼ cup brown rice flour
*   1 cup almond meal
*   3 tsp liquid stevia
*   1 tbsp ground linseed meal
*   ½ cup buckwheat flour
*   2 tbsp almond flour
*   2 tsp baking powder
*   ½ tsp ground cinnamon
*   1 cup sliced rhubarb
*   1 apple, peeled and diced
*   ⅓ cup almond milk
*   ¼ cup extra-virgin olive oil
*   1 free-range egg
*   1 tsp vanilla extract

Directions:

1. Place your oven to 350ºF. Put the almond meal, stevia, ginger, and linseed into a bowl. Sieve the flours over the mix along with the baking powder and spices, then stir. Add the rhubarb and the apple into the flour mixture.

2. In a separate bowl, beat the egg, vanilla, milk, and oil until combined. Fold the wet ingredients into the dry ingredients until smooth. Pour the batter into a greased muffin tin. Bake for 20 minutes or until risen and golden. Leave to cool. Serve.

Nutrition Info:

*   Per Serving: Calories: 690;Fat: 35g;Protein: 9g;Carbs: 90g.

Breakfast Ground Beef Skillet

Servings: 4
Cooking Time: 20 Minutes
Ingredients:

*   1 tablespoon olive oil
*   1 pound ground beef, lean
*   2 teaspoons bottled minced garlic
*   2 cups cauliflower, chopped
*   1 cup carrots, diced
*   1 zucchini, diced
*   2 scallions, white and green parts, chopped

- Sea salt
- Freshly ground black pepper
- 2 tablespoons fresh parsley, chopped

Directions:

1. Place a large skillet over medium-high heat and add the olive oil.

2. Add the ground beef and garlic. Sauté for about 8 minutes, or until cooked through.

3. Stir in the cauliflower, carrots, and zucchini. Sauté for about 10 minutes, or until tender.

4. Stir in the scallions and sauté for another minute.

5. Use sea salt and pepper to season the mixture. Serve topped with the parsley.

Nutrition Info:

- Per Serving: Calories: 214 ;Fat: 9g ;Protein: 26g;Carbs: 7g .

Almond & Raisin Granola

Servings: 6
Cooking Time: 20 Minutes
Ingredients:

- 5 ½ cups old-fashioned oats
- 1 ½ cups chopped walnuts
- ½ cup sunflower seeds
- 1 cup golden raisins
- 1 cup shaved almonds
- 1 cup pure maple syrup
- ½ tsp ground cinnamon
- ¼ tsp ground allspice
- A pinch of sea salt

Directions:

1. Preheat your oven to 325ºF. In a baking dish, mix the oats, walnuts, and sunflower seeds. Bake for 10 minutes. Remove and stir in the raisins, almonds, maple syrup, cinnamon, allspice, and salt. Bake for an additional 15 minutes. Allow cooling completely. Serve and enjoy!

Nutrition Info:

- Per Serving: Calories: 791;Fat: 34g;Protein: 21g;Carbs: 111g.

Marvellous Sausage Breakfast

Servings: 2
Cooking Time: 15 To 20 Minutes
Ingredients:

- 2 cups pork, lean ground
- 2 teaspoon sage leaves, freshly chopped
- 1 teaspoon thyme, chopped
- 1 teaspoon black pepper, ground
- ¼ teaspoon nutmeg, ground
- ¼ teaspoon cayenne pepper
- ¼ teaspoon rosemary, chopped
- 1 tablespoon extra-virgin olive oil

Directions:

1. Add all of the ingredients in a mixing bowl.

2. Use a spoon or blender to mix it until blended. Use the palms of your hands to shape and form 8 patties.

3. In a skillet, heat the oil over a medium heat. Cook the patties for 9 minutes one side and 9 on the other side until they're browned and cooked through.

Nutrition Info:

- Per Serving: Calories: 36 ;Fat: 3g ;Protein: 6g;Carbs: 2g .

Mango Rice Pudding

Servings: 4
Cooking Time: 30 Minutes
Ingredients:

- 1 cup brown rice
- 1 ½ cups non-dairy milk
- 3 tbsp pure date sugar
- 2 tsp pumpkin pie spice
- 1 mango, chopped
- 2 tbsp chopped walnuts

Directions:

1. In a pot over medium heat, add the rice, 2 cups water, milk, sugar, and pumpkin pie spice. Bring to a boil, lower the heat and simmer for 18-20 minutes until the rice is soft and the liquid is absorbed. Put in the mango and stir to combine. Top with walnuts. Serve and enjoy!

Nutrition Info:

- Per Serving: Calories: 312;Fat: 4.9g;Protein: 5g;Carbs: 64.6g.

Almond Waffles

Servings: 4
Cooking Time: 65 Minutes
Ingredients:

- 1 ½ cups almond milk
- 1 ½ cups buckwheat flour
- ½ cup brown rice flour
- 2 tsp baking powder
- ½ tsp sea salt
- 1 egg
- 2 tsp vanilla extract
- 1 tbsp pure maple syrup

Directions:

1. Sift the flours, baking powder, and salt in a bowl; mix. Whisk together the egg, vanilla, maple syrup, almond milk, and 1 cup of water in a separate bowl. Pour the egg mixture into the flour mixture and keep stirring until a smooth batter forms. Let it stand for 10 minutes.

2. Preheat the waffle iron and grease with cooking oil. Pour the batter in the waffle iron to cover ¾ of the bottom. Cook for 10-12 minutes or until golden brown and crispy. Flip the waffle halfway through the cooking time. The cooking time will vary depending on the waffle iron you use. Serve the waffles immediately.

Nutrition Info:

- Per Serving: Calories: 280;Fat: 5g;Protein: 8g;Carbs: 55g.

Amazing Yellow Smoothie

Servings: 4
Cooking Time: 5 Minutes
Ingredients:
- 1 banana
- 1 cup chopped mango
- 1 cup chopped apricots
- 1 cup strawberries
- 1 carrot, chopped
- 1 cup water

Directions:
1. Put the banana, mango, apricots, strawberries, carrot, and water in a food processor. Pulse until smooth; add more water if needed. Divide between glasses and serve.

Nutrition Info:
- Per Serving: Calories: 89;Fat: 0.6g;Protein: 1.6g;Carbs: 21.7g.

Appetizing Crepes With Berries

Servings: 4 To 6
Cooking Time: 5 Minutes
Ingredients:
- 1 cup buckwheat flour
- ½ teaspoon sea salt
- 2 tablespoons coconut oil (1 tablespoon melted)
- 1½ cups almond milk, or water
- 1 egg
- 1 teaspoon vanilla extract
- 3 cups fresh berries, divided
- 6 tablespoons Chia Jam, divided

Directions:
1. Whisk together the buckwheat flour, salt, 1 tablespoon of melted coconut oil, almond milk, egg, and vanilla in a small bowl until smooth.
2. Melt the remaining 1 tablespoon of coconut oil in a large (12-inch) nonstick skillet over medium-high heat. Tilt the pan, coating it evenly with the melted oil.
3. Into the skillet, ladle ¼ cup of batter. Tilt the skillet to coat it evenly with the batter.
4. Cook for 2 minutes, or until the edges begin to curl up. Flip the crêpe and cook for 1 minute on the second side using a spatula. Transfer the crêpe to a plate.
5. Continue to make crepes with the remaining batter. You should have 4 to 6 crêpes.
6. Place 1 crêpe on a plate, top with ½ cup of berries and 1 tablespoon of Chia Jam. Fold the crêpe over the filling. Repeat with the remaining crêpes and serve.

Nutrition Info:
- Per Serving: Calories: 242 ;Fat: 11g ;Protein: 7g ;Carbs: 33g .

Sautéed Cherry Tomatoes With Scrambled Herb

Servings: 2
Cooking Time: 10 Minutes

Ingredients:
- 4 eggs
- 2 teaspoons fresh oregano, chopped
- 1 tablespoon extra-virgin olive oil
- 1 cup cherry tomatoes, halved
- ½ garlic clove, sliced
- ½ avocado, sliced

Directions:
1. Beat the eggs until well combined and whisk in the oregano in a medium bowl.
2. Place a large skillet over medium heat. Add the olive oil once the pan is hot.
3. Pour the eggs into the skillet and use either a heat-resistant spatula or wooden spoon to scramble the eggs. Transfer the eggs to a serving dish.
4. For 2 minutes, add the cherry tomatoes and garlic to the pan and sauté. Spoon the tomatoes over the eggs and top the dish with the avocado slices.

Nutrition Info:
- Per Serving: Calories: 310 ;Fat: 26g ;Protein: 13g ;Carbs: 10g .

Mediterranean Coconut Pancakes

Servings: 4
Cooking Time: 5 Minutes
Ingredients:
- 4 eggs
- 1 cup coconut or almond milk, plus additional as needed
- 1 tablespoon melted coconut oil, or almond butter, plus additional
- 1 tablespoon maple syrup
- 1 teaspoon vanilla extract
- ½ cup coconut flour
- 1 teaspoon baking soda
- ½ teaspoon sea salt

Directions:
1. Mix together the eggs, coconut milk, coconut oil, maple syrup, and vanilla in a medium bowl with an electric mixer.
2. Stir together the coconut flour, baking soda, and salt in a small bowl. Add these dry ingredients to the wet ingredients and beat well, until smooth and lump free.
3. Add additional liquid to thin to the consistency of traditional pancake batter if the batter is too thick.
4. Lightly grease a large skillet with coconut oil. Place it over medium-high heat.
5. Add the batter in ½-cup scoops and cook for about 3 minutes, or until golden brown on the bottom. Flip and cook for about 2 minutes more.
6. Stack the pancakes on a plate and continue to cook the remaining batter which makes about 8 pancakes.

Nutrition Info:
- Per Serving: Calories: 193 ;Fat: 11g ;Protein: 9g ;Carbs: 15g .

Zesty Frittata With Sweet Potato And Zucchini

Servings: 2
Cooking Time: 30 Minutes
Ingredients:

- 1 tablespoon coconut or extra virgin olive oil
- 4 free range eggs
- 1 sweet potato, peeled and sliced
- 1 zucchini, peeled and sliced
- 2 teaspoon parsley
- 1 teaspoon black pepper, cracked

Directions:

1. Preheat broiler on a medium heat.
2. In a skillet, heat the oil under the broiler until hot.
3. Across the skillet, spread the potato slices and cook for 8 to 10 minutes or until soft.
4. Add the zucchini to the skillet and cook for 5 minutes more.
5. In a separate bowl, whisk the eggs and parsley and season to taste before pouring mixture over the veggies.
6. For 10 minutes, cook on a low heat until golden.
7. Remove and turn over onto a plate or serving board.

Nutrition Info:

- Per Serving: Calories: 32 ;Fat: 3g ;Protein: 9g;Carbs: 1g .

Sweet And Savoury Breakfast Quinoa With Nutmeg And Cherry

Servings: 2
Cooking Time: 20 Minutes
Ingredients:

- ½ cup quinoa
- ½ cup cherries, unsweetened fresh
- 1 cup water
- ¼ teaspoon nutmeg, ground
- ½ teaspoon vanilla extract

Directions:

1. Combine all of the ingredients in a pan. Cook over medium to high heat until it boils.
2. Once it boils, cover and simmer for 15 minutes or until the quinoa is soft and the liquid has been absorbed.
3. Pour into serving bowls.

Nutrition Info:

- Per Serving: Calories: 183 ;Fat: 3g ;Protein: 6g ;Carbs: 33g .

Coconut Oat Bread

Servings: 4
Cooking Time: 50 Minutes
Ingredients:

- 4 cups whole-wheat flour
- ¼ tsp sea salt
- ½ cup rolled oats
- 1 tsp baking soda
- 1 ¾ cups coconut milk, thick

- 2 tbsp pure maple syrup

Directions:

1. Preheat your oven to 450ºF. In a bowl, mix flour, salt, oats, and baking soda. Add in coconut milk and maple syrup and whisk until dough forms. Dust your hands with some flour and knead the dough into a ball. Shape the dough into a circle and place on a baking sheet.
2. Cut a deep cross on the dough and bake in the oven for 15 minutes. Reduce the heat to 400ºF and bake further for 20-25 minutes or until a hollow sound is made when the bottom of the bread is tapped. Slice and serve.

Nutrition Info:

- Per Serving: Calories: 761;Fat: 27g;Protein: 17g;Carbs: 115g.

Cheesy Spinach Frittata

Servings: 4
Cooking Time: 25 Minutes
Ingredients:

- 2 cups fresh baby spinach
- 2 tbsp extra-virgin olive oil
- 8 eggs, beaten
- 1 tsp garlic powder
- Sea salt and pepper to taste
- 3 tsp grated Parmesan cheese

Directions:

1. Place your oven to 360ºF. Warm the olive oil in a large skillet. Add the spinach and cook for about 3 minutes, stirring occasionally. In a medium bowl, whisk the eggs, garlic powder, salt, and pepper. Carefully pour the egg mixture over the spinach and cook the eggs for about 3 minutes until they begin to set around the edges. Using a rubber spatula, gently pull the eggs away from the edges of the pan. Tilt the pan to let the uncooked egg flow into the edges. Cook for 2-3 minutes until the edges set. Sprinkle with the Parmesan cheese and put the skillet under the broiler. Broil for about 3 minutes until the top puffs. Cut into wedges to serve. Enjoy!

Nutrition Info:

- Per Serving: Calories: 200;Fat: 15g;Protein: 13g;Carbs: 2g.

Simple Apple Muffins

Servings: 6
Cooking Time: 40 Minutes
Ingredients:

- 1 egg
- 2 cups whole-wheat flour
- 1 cup pure date sugar
- 2 tsp baking powder
- ¼ tsp sea salt
- 2 tsp cinnamon powder
- 1/3 cup melted coconut oil
- 1/3 cup almond milk
- 2 apples, chopped
- ½ cup almond butter, cubed

Directions:

1. Preheat your oven to 400°F. Grease 6 muffin cups with cooking spray. In a bowl, mix 1 ½ cups of whole-wheat flour, ¾ cup of the date sugar, baking powder, salt, and 1 tsp of cinnamon powder. Whisk in the melted coconut oil, egg, and almond milk and fold in the apples. Fill the muffin cups two-thirds way up with the batter.

2. In a bowl, mix the remaining flour, remaining date sugar, and cold almond butter. Top the muffin batter with the mixture. Bake for 20 minutes. Remove the muffins onto a wire rack, allow cooling, and dust them with the remaining cinnamon powder. Serve and enjoy!

Nutrition Info:

- Per Serving: Calories: 463;Fat: 18g;Protein: 8.2g;Carbs: 71g.

Mexican Burrito Brunch

Servings: 2
Cooking Time: 20 Minutes
Ingredients:

- 2 garlic cloves
- 2 tablespoon extra-virgin olive oil
- 1 tablespoon chipotle chili powder
- 1 tablespoon apple cider vinegar
- juice of 1 lime
- 2 teaspoon pepper
- 1 teaspoon paprika
- ½ teaspoon oregano
- 2 chicken breasts, skinless
- Cilantro quinoa:
- 2 cups quinoa
- juice of 1 lime
- juice of ½ lemon
- 2 tablespoon chopped cilantro
- ½ iceberg or equivalent lettuce
- 1 beef tomato, chopped

Directions:

1. Take the garlic, chipotle powder, vinegar, lime juice, olive oil, salt, pepper, paprika, and oregano and blend in a blender or pestle and mortar.

2. Marinate the chicken in this mix for as long as possible.

3. Heat the broiler to medium-high heat.

4. Grill the chicken for 10-15 minutes or until cooked through.

5. Remove and chop the chicken into cubes.

6. Boil a pan of water on medium to high heat and add quinoa before covering and turning down the heat. Allow simmering for 15-20 minutes with the lid on. Check it's fully cooked. It will soak up most of the water and will appear translucent.

7. Serve quinoa with the oil, lime, lemon juices, and chicken and shredded lettuce, and tomatoes on top.

Nutrition Info:

- Per Serving: Calories: 1234 ;Fat: 44g ;Protein: 87g ;Carbs: 124g .

Gluten-free And Dairy-free Little Fruit Muffins

Servings: 2
Cooking Time: 20 Minutes
Ingredients:

- 1 cup almond meal
- 3 teaspoon stevia
- 2 tablespoon ginger, chopped and crystalized
- 1 tablespoon linseed meal, ground
- ½ cup buckwheat flour
- ¼ cup brown rice flour
- 2 tablespoon corn flour, organic
- 2 teaspoon baking powder, gluten-free
- ½ teaspoon cinnamon, ground
- 1 cup rhubarb, sliced
- 1 peeled and diced apple
- ⅓ cup almond milk
- ¼ cup extra virgin olive oil
- 1 free range egg
- 1 teaspoon vanilla extract

Directions:

1. Preheat the oven to 350°F. Line muffin tins using a baking brush or kitchen towel with coconut or olive oil. Into a bowl, put the almond meal, stevia, ginger, and linseed.

2. Sieve the flours over the mix along with the baking powder and spices and stir. Into the flour mixture, add the rhubarb and apple.

3. Beat the egg, vanilla, milk, and oil in a separate bowl until fully combined. Fold the wet ingredients into the dry ingredients until smooth.

4. Into the muffin tin, pour batter and leave a 1 cm gap at the top so that the muffin can rise. For 20 minutes, bake it until risen and golden. Remove then place on a cooling rack before serving.

Nutrition Info:

- Per Serving: Calories: 535 ;Fat: 15g ;Protein: 8g ;Carbs: 97g .

Chapter 3. Smoothies

Fantastic Fruity Smoothie

Servings: 1
Cooking Time: 0 Minutes
Ingredients:
- 2 cups carrots, peeled and sliced
- 2 cups filtered water
- 1 apple, peeled and sliced
- 1 banana, peeled and sliced
- 1 cup fresh pineapple, peeled and sliced
- ½ tablespoon ginger, grated
- ¼ teaspoon turmeric, ground
- 1 tablespoon lemon juice
- 1 cup almond or soy milk

Directions:
1. Blend carrots and water to make a puréed carrot juice.
2. Pour into a Mason jar or sealable container, cover and place in the fridge.
3. Add the rest of the smoothie ingredients once done to a blender or juicer until smooth.
4. Add the carrot juice in at the end, blending thoroughly until smooth.
5. Serve with or without ice.

Nutrition Info:
- Per Serving: Calories: 367 ;Fat: 5g ;Protein: 6g ;Carbs: 80g.

Salad-like Green Smoothie

Servings: 1
Cooking Time: 0 Minutes
Ingredients:
- ¾ to 1 cup water
- 1 cup spinach leaves, lightly packed
- 2 kale leaves, thoroughly washed
- 2 romaine lettuce leaves
- ½ avocado
- 1 pear, stemmed, cored, and chopped

Directions:
1. Combine the water, spinach, kale, romaine lettuce, avocado, and pear in a blender.
2. Blend until smooth and serve.

Nutrition Info:
- Per Serving: Calories: 180 ;Fat: 10g ;Protein: 4g ;Carbs: 23g .

Nut-free Green Smoothie Bowl

Servings: 2
Cooking Time: 0 Minutes
Ingredients:
- 3 cups packed baby spinach
- 1 green apple, cored
- 1 small ripe banana
- ½ ripe avocado

- 1 tablespoon maple syrup
- ½ cup mixed berries
- ¼ cup slivered almonds, toasted
- 1 teaspoon sesame seeds

Directions:
1. Combine the spinach, apple, banana, avocado, and maple syrup in a blender and blend until smooth. The mixture should be thick.
2. Divide the mixture between two bowls. Top with the berries, almonds, and sesame seeds, then serve.

Nutrition Info:
- Per Serving: Calories: 280 ; Fat: 14g ;Protein: 6g ;Carbs: 38g .

Fresh Berry Smoothie With Ginger

Servings: 2
Cooking Time: 0 Minutes
Ingredients:
- 2 cups blackberries, fresh
- 2 cups almond milk, unsweetened
- 1 to 2 packets stevia, or to taste
- One 1 inch piece fresh ginger, peeled and roughly chopped
- 2 cups ice, crushed

Directions:
1. Combine the blackberries, almond milk, stevia, ginger, and ice in a blender. Blend until smooth.

Nutrition Info:
- Per Serving: Calories: 95 ;Fat: 3g ;Protein: 3g ;Carbs: 16g.

Fancy Cold Soup Smoothie

Servings: 1
Cooking Time: 15 Minutes
Ingredients:
- Frozen Veggie Mix:
- 2 cups butternut squash, diced
- 1 cup broccoli florets
- 1 cup onions, diced
- 4 cloves garlic, peeled
- 3 cups water
- Smoothie:
- 1 bag steamed and then frozen mixed veggies
- 1½ cups bone broth or water
- 2 tablespoons collagen peptides
- 1 tablespoon MCT oil or MCT oil powder
- 2 teaspoons apple cider vinegar
- ½ teaspoon thyme or oregano, dried
- ½ teaspoon Himalayan salt, fine
- ½ teaspoon turmeric powder

Directions:
1. Make the frozen veggie mix. Place all of the veggies in a large skillet with a tight-fitting lid. Add the water and

bring to a boil. Cover and steam for 15 minutes or until the butternut squash is fork-tender. Remove from the heat, drain, and let cool.

2. Divide the cooled vegetables into five resealable plastic bags, about 1 cup per bag. Seal and pop in the freezer for 1 hour before making your smoothie.

3. Place 1 bag of frozen veggies in a blender when you're ready to make a smoothie and add the smoothie ingredients then blend until smooth. Drink. Store any leftovers in the fridge in an airtight container for up to 4 days.

Nutrition Info:

- Per Serving: Calories: 304 ;Fat: 18g ;Protein: 20g;Carbs: 9g.

Smoothie That Can Soothe Inflammation

Servings: 1
Cooking Time: 0 Minutes
Ingredients:

- 1 pear, cored and quartered
- ½ fennel bulb
- 1 thin slice ginger, fresh
- 1 cup packed spinach
- ½ cucumber, peeled if wax-coated or not organic
- ½ cup water
- Ice

Directions:

1. Combine the pear, fennel, ginger, spinach, cucumber, water, and ice in a blender. Blend until smooth.

Nutrition Info:

- Per Serving: Calories: 147 ;Fat: 1g ;Protein: 4g ;Carbs: 37g .

Mediterranean Green On Green Smoothie

Servings: 1
Cooking Time: 0 Minutes
Ingredients:

- 1 cup packed baby spinach
- ½ green apple
- 1 tablespoon maple syrup
- ¼ teaspoon cinnamon, ground
- 1 cup almond milk, unsweetened
- ½ cup ice

Directions:

1. Combine all the ingredients in a blender and blend until smooth. Serve.

Nutrition Info:

- Per Serving: Calories: 130 ;Fat: 4g ;Protein: 2g ;Carbs: 23g .

Lovable Smoothie With Coconut And Ginger

Servings: 1
Cooking Time: 0 Minutes

Ingredients:

- ½ cup coconut milk
- ½ cup coconut water
- ¼ avocado
- ¼ cup coconut shreds or flakes, unsweetened
- 1 teaspoon raw honey or maple syrup
- 1 thin slice ginger, fresh
- Pinch ground cardamom
- Ice

Directions:

1. Combine in a blender the coconut milk, coconut water, avocado, coconut, honey, ginger, cardamom, and ice. Blend until smooth.

Nutrition Info:

- Per Serving: Calories: 238 ;Fat: 18g ;Protein: 5g ;Carbs: 16g .

Great Watermelon Smoothie

Servings: 1
Cooking Time: 0 Minutes
Ingredients:

- 1 cup watermelon chunks
- 2 cups mixed berries, frozen
- 1 cup coconut water
- 2 tablespoons chia seeds
- ½ cup tart cherries

Directions:

1. Blend ingredients in a blender or juicer until puréed.
2. Serve immediately and enjoy.

Nutrition Info:

- Per Serving: Calories: 1134 ;Fat: 26g ;Protein: 16g ;Carbs: 218g.

Vegetarian Mango Smoothie With Green Tea And Turmeric

Servings: 2
Cooking Time: 0 Minutes
Ingredients:

- 2 cups mango, cubed
- 2 teaspoons turmeric powder
- 2 tablespoons matcha powder
- 2 cups almond milk
- 2 tablespoons honey
- 1 cup ice, crushed

Directions:

1. Combine in a blender the mango, turmeric, matcha, almond milk, honey, and ice. Blend until smooth.

Nutrition Info:

- Per Serving: Calories: 285 ;Fat: 3g ;Protein: 4g ;Carbs: 68g .

Tropical And Extra Red Smoothie

Servings: 2
Cooking Time: 0 Minutes
Ingredients:

- 1 cup coconut water
- ½ cup pineapple juice, unsweetened
- 1 banana
- ½ cup fresh raspberries
- ½ cup shredded coconut, unsweetened
- 3 ice cubes

Directions:

1. Combine the coconut water, pineapple juice, banana, raspberries, and coconut in a blender. Blend until smooth.
2. Add the ice and blend until thick.

Nutrition Info:

- Per Serving: Calories: 209 ;Fat: 10g ;Protein: 3g;Carbs: 31g .

Minty Juice With Pineapple And Cucumber

Servings: 3 ½
Cooking Time: 0 Minutes
Ingredients:

- 1 large, ripe pineapple, skin removed and core intact
- ¼ cup mint leaves
- 1 cucumber

Directions:

1. Cut the pineapple in long strips that will fit through the juicer feed tube. Process the pineapple, adding the mint leaves in between pieces, on the proper setting of the juicer. Juice the cucumber, then stir. Serve immediately.

Nutrition Info:

- Per Serving: Calories: 9 ;Fat: 5g;Protein: 1g ;Carbs: 2g .

Fabolous Minty Green Smoothie

Servings: 2
Cooking Time: 0 Minutes
Ingredients:

- 1 cup canned lite coconut milk
- 1 cup fresh spinach
- 1 banana, cut into chunks
- ½ avocado
- ½ English cucumber, cut into chunks
- 2 tablespoons fresh mint, chopped
- 1 tablespoon lemon juice, freshly squeezed
- 1 tablespoon raw honey
- 3 ice cubes

Directions:

1. Combine the coconut milk, spinach, banana, avocado, cucumber, mint, lemon juice, and honey in a blender. Blend until smooth.
2. Add the ice and blend until thick.

Nutrition Info:

- Per Serving: Calories: 482 ;Fat: 40g ;Protein: 6g;Carbs: 37g.

Organic Berry Smoothie

Servings: 1
Cooking Time: 0 Minutes
Ingredients:

- ¾ to 1 cup water
- ½ cup raspberries, frozen
- ½ cup strawberries, frozen
- ¼ cup blackberries, frozen
- 2 tablespoons nut butter or seed butter

Directions:

1. Combine the water, raspberries, strawberries, blackberries, and nut butter in a blender.
2. Blend until smooth and serve.

Nutrition Info:

- Per Serving: Calories: 186 ;Fat: 9g ;Protein: 4g ;Carbs: 24g.

Delightful Smoothie With Apple And Honey

Servings: 2
Cooking Time: 0 Minutes
Ingredients:

- 1 cup canned lite coconut milk
- 1 apple, cored and cut into chunks
- 1 banana
- ¼ cup almond butter
- 1 tablespoon raw honey
- ½ teaspoon cinnamon, ground
- 4 ice cubes

Directions:

1. Combine the coconut milk, apple, banana, almond butter, honey, and cinnamon in a blender. Blend until smooth.
2. Add the ice and blend until thick.

Nutrition Info:

- Per Serving: Calories: 434 ;Fat: 30g ;Protein: 4g;Carbs: 46g .

Southern Smoothie With Sweet Potato

Servings: 2
Cooking Time: 0 Minutes
Ingredients:

- ½ cup almond milk, unsweetened
- ½ cup orange juice, freshly squeezed
- 1 cup sweet potato, cooked
- 1 banana
- 2 tablespoons pumpkin seeds
- 1 tablespoon pure maple syrup
- ½ teaspoon pure vanilla extract
- ½ teaspoon cinnamon, ground
- 3 ice cubes

Directions:

1. In a blender, combine the almond milk, orange juice, sweet potato, banana, pumpkin seeds, maple syrup, vanilla, and cinnamon. Blend until smooth.

2. Add the ice and blend until thick.
Nutrition Info:
- Per Serving: Calories: 235 ;Fat: 4g ;Protein: 5g ;Carbs: 43g .

Cheery Cherry Smoothie

Servings: 1
Cooking Time: 0 Minutes
Ingredients:
- 1 cup frozen pitted cherries, no-added-sugar
- ¼ cup fresh, or frozen, raspberries
- ¾ cup coconut water
- 1 tablespoon raw honey or maple syrup
- 1 teaspoon chia seeds
- 1 teaspoon hemp seeds
- Drop vanilla extract
- Ice

Directions:
1. Combine in a blender the cherries, raspberries, coconut water, honey, chia seeds, hemp seeds, vanilla, and ice. Blend until smooth.

Nutrition Info:
- Per Serving: Calories: 266 ;Fat: 2g ;Protein: 3g ;Carbs: 52g.

Fresh Minty Punch With Peach

Servings: 4
Cooking Time: 0 Minutes
Ingredients:
- One 10 ounces bag frozen no-added-sugar peach slices, thawed
- 3 tablespoons lemon juice, freshly squeezed
- 3 tablespoons raw honey or maple syrup
- 1 tablespoon lemon zest
- 2 cups coconut water
- 2 cups sparkling water
- 4 fresh mint sprigs, divided
- Ice

Directions:
1. Combine in a food processor the peaches, lemon juice, honey, and lemon zest. Process until smooth.
2. Stir together the peach purée and coconut water in a large pitcher. Chill the mixture in the refrigerator.

3. Fill four large (16 ounces) glasses with ice when ready to serve. Add 1 mint sprig to each glass. Add ¾ cup peach mixture to each glass and top each with sparkling water.
Nutrition Info:
- Per Serving: Calories: 81 ;Carbs: 18g ;Fat: 3g;Protein: 32g;Carbs: 5g.

Super Sweet Strawberry Smoothie

Servings: 2
Cooking Time: 30 Minutes
Ingredients:
- 1 stalk of celery, chopped
- ½ cup of kale
- ½ cup of spinach
- 1 cup strawberries
- 1 lime wedge
- 1 cup coconut water

Directions:
1. Take all of the ingredients and blend until smooth.
2. Serve over ice.
Nutrition Info:
- Per Serving: Calories: 113 ;Fat: 1g ;;Protein: 4g ;Carbs: 25g .

Mixed Berry Smoothie With Acai

Servings: 3 ½
Cooking Time: 0 Minutes
Ingredients:
- One 3 ½ ounces pack frozen acai purée
- 1 cup frozen mango chunks, 1204
- 1 cup frozen berries, 120g
- 2 cups Cinnamon Cashew Milk or Almond Milk, 480ml
- 1 to 2 teaspoons maple syrup or honey

Directions:
1. Defrost the acai pack to soften under hot water. Place the acai, mango, and berries in a blender, along with the nut milk. Start on a low setting, purée the mixture until it begins to break up, stopping and scraping down the sides if needed. Slowly turn the blender speed to high and purée until there are no lumps for 1 to 2 minutes. Taste and blend in the maple syrup, if preferred. Serve immediately.
Nutrition Info:
- Per Serving: Calories: 273 ; Fat: 7g ;Protein: 8g ;Carbs: 47g .

Chapter 4. Sauces, Condiments, And Dressings

Delicious Pesto With Kale

Servings: 1
Cooking Time: 0 Minutes
Ingredients:
- 2 cups chopped kale leaves, thoroughly washed and stemmed
- ½ cup almonds, toasted
- 2 garlic cloves
- 3 tablespoons lemon juice, freshly squeezed
- 3 tablespoons extra-virgin olive oil
- 2 teaspoons lemon zest
- 1 teaspoon salt
- ½ teaspoon black pepper, freshly ground
- ¼ teaspoon red pepper flakes

Directions:
1. Combine in a food processor the kale, almonds, garlic, lemon juice, olive oil, lemon zest, salt, black pepper, and red pepper flakes then process until smooth.
2. Refrigerate in an airtight container for up to one week.

Nutrition Info:
- Per Serving: Calories: 91 ;Fat: 8g ;Protein: 2g;Carbs: 4g .

Creamy Dressing With Sesame

Servings: ¾
Cooking Time: 0 Minutes
Ingredients:
- ½ cup canned coconut milk, full-fat
- 2 tablespoons tahini
- 2 tablespoons lime juice, freshly squeezed
- 1 teaspoon minced garlic, bottled
- 1 teaspoon fresh chives, minced
- Pinch sea salt

Directions:
1. Whisk in a small bowl the coconut milk, tahini, lime juice, garlic, and chives until well blended. You can also prepare this in a blender.
2. Season with sea salt and transfer the dressing to a container with a lid. Refrigerate for up to 1 week.

Nutrition Info:
- Per Serving: Calories: 40 ;Fat: 4g ;Protein: 1g;Carbs: 2g .

To Die For Homemade Mayonnaise

Servings: 1
Cooking Time: 0 Minutes
Ingredients:
- 3 tablespoons coconut vinegar
- 1 teaspoon thyme leaves, dried
- ½ teaspoon garlic, granulated
- ½ teaspoon mustard, dry
- ½ teaspoon Himalayan salt, fine
- 3 large egg yolks
- 1 cup avocado oil

Directions:
1. Place the vinegar and seasonings in a 16 ounces measuring cup or quart-sized mason jar. Add gently the egg yolks and the avocado oil.
2. Insert the immersion blender into the mixture and turn it on high then move it up and down slightly until the mix is completely emulsified. Scrape all of the mayonnaise off of the blender by using a spatula and then transfer the mayonnaise to a jar or other container with a tight-fitting lid.
3. Store in the refrigerator for up to 10 days.

Nutrition Info:
- Per Serving: Calories: 262 ;Fat: 30g ;Protein: 1g;Carbs: 4g.

Simple Garlic Confit

Servings: ½
Cooking Time: 60 Minutes
Ingredients:
- Garlic cloves, peeled
- Olive oil or avocado oil
- Himalayan salt
- Fresh herb sprigs

Directions:
1. Preheat the oven to 250°F.
2. Put as many garlic cloves as you like in a small baking dish with a lid leaving at least an inch of space at the top.
3. Pour in the olive oil until the garlic is just submerged. Sprinkle in a little salt and place a few sprigs of herbs on top. Cover with the lid and place on a sheet pan to prevent a mess.
4. Pop it in the oven and bake for an hour or until you can easily pierce the garlic cloves with a fork. Remove from the oven and let it cool to room temperature.
5. Transfer all of the garlic with the oil and herbs to an airtight glass or ceramic storage container. Store in the fridge for up to 3 months. Use a clean spoon to remove garlic cloves or oil.

Nutrition Info:
- Per Serving: Calories: 169 ;Fat: 19g ;Protein: 46g;Carbs: 2g.

Colourful And Sweet Spread With Carrot

Servings: 2
Cooking Time: 0 Minutes
Ingredients:
- 3 carrots, peeled and cut into chunks
- ½ cup almonds
- 2 tablespoons lemon juice, freshly squeezed
- 1 tablespoon pure maple syrup
- ½ teaspoon cardamom, ground

- Sea salt

Directions:

1. Pulse the carrots until very finely chopped in a food processor.
2. Add the almonds, lemon juice, maple syrup, and cardamom then process until smooth.
3. Season the spread with sea salt and transfer to a lidded container. Refrigerate for up to 6 days.

Nutrition Info:

- Per Serving: Calories: 26 ;Fat: 2g ;Protein: 1g;Carbs: 3g ,

Garlicky Sauce With Tahini

Servings: 1
Cooking Time: 0 Minutes
Ingredients:

- ½ cup tahini
- 1 garlic clove, minced
- Juice of 1 lemon
- Zest of 1 lemon
- ½ teaspoon salt, plus additional as needed
- ½ cup warm water, plus additional as needed

Directions:

1. Stir together in a small bowl the tahini and garlic.
2. Add the lemon juice, lemon zest, and salt. Stir well.
3. Whisk in ½ cup of warm water, until fully mixed and creamy. Add more water if the sauce is too thick.
4. Taste and adjust the seasoning if needed.
5. Refrigerate in a sealed container.

Nutrition Info:

- Per Serving: Calories: 180 ;Fat: 16g ;Protein: 5g ;Carbs: 7g .

Marinated Greek Dressing

Servings: 1 ½
Cooking Time: 0 Minutes
Ingredients:

- 3 cloves garlic, minced
- 1 cup extra-virgin olive oil or avocado oil
- Juice of 3 lemons, ½ cup
- 2 tablespoons fresh oregano leaves, minced
- 1 teaspoon black pepper, ground
- 1 teaspoon onion powder
- ½ teaspoon Himalayan salt, fine

Directions:

1. In a blender, place all of the ingredients and blend on medium speed until the dressing has emulsified and has a light-brown appearance and the garlic is almost smooth.
2. Store in an airtight container in the fridge for up to 10 days. Shake or stir before using since this. dressing separates very quickly

Nutrition Info:

- Per Serving: Calories: 150 ;Fat: 17g ;Protein: 46g;Carbs: 1g .

Fragrant Peach Butter

Servings: 2
Cooking Time: 3 Hours
Ingredients:

- Eight 3 pounds peaches, peeled, pitted, and chopped, or about 6 cups frozen, sliced peaches
- Water
- ¼ cup raw honey

Directions:

1. Combine in a large saucepan over high heat the peaches with enough water to cover the fruit by about 1 inch. Bring the liquid to a boil.
2. Reduce the heat to low and simmer for 3 hours while stirring frequently until the mixture appears a thick applesauce.
3. Stir in the honey. Simmer for 30 minutes until the mixture starts to caramelize. Remove the peach butter from the heat and let it cool for 30 minutes.
4. Spoon the mixture into a container and cool completely before covering. Keep refrigerated for up to 2 weeks.

Nutrition Info:

- Per Serving: Calories: 46 ;Fat: 15g;Protein: 1g;Carbs: 11g .

Game Changer Pickled Red Onions

Servings: 4
Cooking Time: 10 Minutes
Ingredients:

- 2 cups water, filtered
- 1 cup apple cider vinegar
- 1 teaspoon Himalayan salt, fine
- 1 teaspoon granulated erythritol or another low-carb sweetener
- 2 bay leaves
- 2 red onions, thinly sliced and cut into half-moons

Directions:

1. Combine the water, vinegar, salt, erythritol, and bay leaves in a small saucepan over medium heat. Bring to a light simmer and cook for 8 minutes. Stir to make sure the salt and sweetener have dissolved.
2. In a jar, put all the onion slices with the bay leaves and then pour the hot brine over the onions until fully submerged. Let the onions steep for 30 minutes at room temperature before using. Seal the jar and store it in the fridge for up to a month.

Nutrition Info:

- Per Serving: Calories: 5 ;Fat: 7g ;Protein: 6g;Carbs: 2g

Decadent And Simple Alfredo With Cauliflower

Servings: 2
Cooking Time: 12 Minutes
Ingredients:

- 3 cups cauliflower, florets
- 5 cloves garlic, peeled
- 1 cup coconut milk, full-fat

- 3 tablespoons salted butter, ghee, or lard
- 1 tablespoon fish sauce
- 1 tablespoon red wine vinegar
- 1 teaspoon Himalayan salt, fine
- 1 teaspoon black pepper, ground

Directions:

1. Fill a saucepan with about an inch of water and add the cauliflower and garlic. Heat the pan over medium-high heat and bring to a boil with the lid on. Cook for 8 minutes until the cauliflower is fork-tender. Remove from the heat and drain.
2. In a blender, place the cauliflower, garlic, and remaining ingredients. Purée until smooth.
3. Store in an airtight container in the fridge for up to 10 days. Bring to a simmer in a saucepan over medium heat to reheat.

Nutrition Info:

- Per Serving: Calories: 250 ;Fat: 24g ;Protein: 4g ;Carbs: 9g .

Goddess And Vibrant Green Dressing

Servings: 2
Cooking Time: 0 Minutes
Ingredients:

- 4 cloves garlic, peeled
- ½ cup fresh chives or green onions, minced
- ¼ cup lemon juice
- 2 tablespoons coconut aminos
- 1 tablespoon Dijon mustard
- 1½ teaspoons Himalayan salt, fine
- 1 teaspoon chia seeds
- 1 teaspoon black pepper, ground
- 1 teaspoon poppy seeds
- 1 teaspoon hemp seeds, shelled
- 5 drops liquid stevia
- 1 cup avocado oil

Directions:

1. Place all of the ingredients except the oil in a blender and pulse to combine. Drizzle slowly in the avocado oil while the blender runs until the sauce comes creamy and smooth.
2. Store in an airtight container in the refrigerator for up to 10 days. Shake before using.

Nutrition Info:

- Per Serving: Calories: 128 ;Fat: 14g ;Protein: 4g;Carbs: 1g.

Fantastic On Hand Marinara Sauce

Servings: 6
Cooking Time: 7 To 8 Hours
Ingredients:

- 2 cans diced tomatoes, 28 ounces
- 3 tablespoons tomato paste
- 1 yellow onion, diced
- 1 carrot, minced
- 1 celery stalk, minced

- 2 bay leaves
- 1 tablespoon basil leaves, dried
- 2 teaspoons oregano, dried
- 1½ teaspoons garlic powder
- 1 teaspoon sea salt
- Pinch red pepper flakes
- Freshly ground black pepper

Directions:

1. Combine in your slow cooker the tomatoes, tomato paste, onion, carrot, celery, bay leaves, basil, oregano, garlic powder, salt, and red pepper flakes, and season with black pepper.
2. Cover the cooker and set it to low. Cook for 7 to 8 hours.
3. Remove and discard the bay leaves. Blend using an immersion blender the sauce to your preferred consistency or leave it naturally chunky.

Nutrition Info:

- Per Serving: Calories: 71 ;Fat: 5g;Protein: 3g ;Carbs: 17g .

Commercial And Mild Curry Powder

Servings: ¼
Cooking Time: 0 Minutes
Ingredients:

- 1 tablespoon turmeric, ground
- 1 tablespoon cumin, ground
- 2 teaspoons coriander, ground
- 1 teaspoon cardamom, ground
- 1 teaspoon cinnamon, ground
- 1 teaspoon ginger, ground
- ½ teaspoon fenugreek powder
- ½ teaspoon cloves, ground

Directions:

1. Stir together in a small bowl the turmeric, cumin, coriander, cardamom, cinnamon, ginger, fenugreek, and cloves until fully blended.
2. Store the curry powder in an airtight container for up to 1 month.

Nutrition Info:

- Per Serving: Calories: 6 ;Fat: 15g;Protein: 46g;Carbs: 1g.

Buttery Slow Cooked Ghee

Servings: 2
Cooking Time: 2 Hours
Ingredients:

- 1 pound unsalted butter, 4 sticks

Directions:

1. Add the butter in the slow cooker. Set the slow cooker to high and leave it uncovered.
2. White foam should appear in 45 minutes. Over time, from 1 to 2 hours, the foam will turn golden brown and give off a nutty smell.
3. Turn off the slow cooker once the foam has turned brown.

4. Line a strainer with a triple thickness of cheesecloth and place the strainer over a wide-mouth jar.

5. Skim off as much of the brown foam as possible using a large spoon or ladle and discard it. Carefully ladle the remaining ghee into the cheesecloth-lined strainer.

6. Discard the cheesecloth once all the ghee has been strained and let the ghee come to room temperature before covering the jar with an airtight lid and refrigerating it. It will last for three months.

Nutrition Info:
- Per Serving: Calories: 102 ;Fat: 12g ;Protein: 46g;Carbs: 4g.

Excellent Tapenade With Green Olive

Servings: 1
Cooking Time: 0 Minutes
Ingredients:
- 1 cup pitted green olives
- 2 garlic cloves
- ¼ cup extra-virgin olive oil
- ¼ cup lemon juice, freshly squeezed
- Pinch dried rosemary
- Salt
- Freshly ground black pepper

Directions:
1. Combine the olives, garlic, olive oil, lemon juice, and rosemary in a food processor. Season with salt and pepper. Process until the mixture is almost smooth and a little chunky is okay.
2. Refrigerate in an airtight container. The tapenade will keep for several weeks.

Nutrition Info:
- Per Serving: Calories: 73 ;Fat: 8g ;Protein: 6g;Carbs: 2g ;

Herbaceous Dressing With Creamy Coconut

Servings: 1
Cooking Time: 0 Minutes
Ingredients:
- 8 ounces coconut yogurt, plain
- 2 tablespoons lemon juice, freshly squeezed
- 2 tablespoons fresh parsley, chopped
- 1 tablespoon fresh chives, snipped
- ½ teaspoon salt
- Pinch freshly ground black pepper

Directions:
1. Whisk together the yogurt, lemon juice, parsley, chives, salt, and pepper in a medium bowl.
2. Refrigerate in an airtight container.

Nutrition Info:
- Per Serving: Calories: 14 ;Fat: 1g ;Protein: 6g;Carbs: 2g.

Feels Like Summer Chutney With Mint

Servings: 2
Cooking Time: 0 Minutes

Ingredients:
- One 10 ounces bag frozen no-added-sugar peach chunks, thawed, drained, coarsely chopped, juice reserved
- ½ medium red onion, diced
- ¼ cup dried cherries, coarsely chopped
- 2 tablespoons lemon juice, freshly squeezed
- 1 tablespoon raw honey or maple syrup
- 1 teaspoon apple cider vinegar
- ¼ teaspoon salt
- 1 tablespoon fresh mint leaves, chopped

Directions:
1. In a medium bowl, place the peach chunks.
2. Stir in the onion, cherries, lemon juice, honey, cider vinegar, and salt.
3. Let the mixture stand for 30 minutes before serving.
4. Stir in the mint when ready to serve.
5. Refrigerate in an airtight container for no more than three days.

Nutrition Info:
- Per Serving: Calories: 42 ;Fat: 2g ;Protein: 1g ;Carbs: 1g .

Must-have Ranch Dressing

Servings: 1 ½
Cooking Time: 0 Minutes
Ingredients:
- ½ cup water, filtered
- ½ cup coconut milk, full-fat
- ½ cup hemp seeds, shelled
- 2 tablespoons red wine vinegar
- 1 tablespoon coconut aminos
- 1 tablespoon Dijon mustard
- 2 teaspoons dill weed, dried
- 1 teaspoon parsley, dried
- 1 teaspoon Himalayan salt, fine
- 1 teaspoon fish sauce
- 1 teaspoon garlic powder
- 1 teaspoon onion powder
- 1 teaspoon black pepper, ground

Directions:
1. Place all of the ingredients in a blender and blend until smooth.
2. Store in an airtight glass or ceramic container in the fridge for up to 10 days. Before using, set out at room temperature to soften for a few minutes and shake or stir to mix well.

Nutrition Info:
- Per Serving: Calories: 225 ;Fat: 18g ;Protein: 11g;Carbs: 4g.

Tasty And Fiery Tunisian Vinaigrette

Servings: 1 ¼
Cooking Time: 0 Minutes
Ingredients:
- ¾ cup olive oil
- ¼ cup apple cider vinegar
- 1 tablespoon lemon juice, freshly squeezed
- ¼ cup fresh parsley, chopped
- 1 teaspoon minced garlic, bottled
- 1 teaspoon cumin, ground
- ¼ teaspoon coriander, ground
- Pinch sea salt

Directions:
1. Whisk the olive oil, cider vinegar, and lemon juice in a medium bowl until emulsified.
2. Whisk in the parsley, garlic, cumin, and coriander.
3. Season with sea salt.
4. Refrigerate the vinaigrette in a sealed container for up to 2 weeks.

Nutrition Info:
- Per Serving: Calories: 133 ;Fat: 15g;Protein: 26g;Carbs: 4g.

Herbaceous Spread With Avocado

Servings: 2
Cooking Time: 0minutes
Ingredients:
- 1 avocado, peeled and pitted
- 2 tablespoons lemon juice, freshly squeezed
- 2 tablespoons fresh parsley, chopped
- 1 teaspoon fresh dill, chopped
- ½ teaspoon coriander, ground
- Sea salt
- Freshly ground black pepper

Directions:
1. Pulse the avocado in a blender until smoothly puréed.
2. Add the lemon juice, parsley, dill, and coriander. Pulse until well blended.
3. Season with sea salt and pepper.
4. Refrigerate the spread in a sealed container for up to 4 days.

Nutrition Info:
- Per Serving: Calories: 53 ;Fat: 5g ;Protein: 1g;Carbs: 2g .

Chapter 5. Poultry And Meats

Baked Basil Chicken

Servings: 4
Cooking Time: 45 Minutes
Ingredients:
- 2 garlic cloves, sliced
- 1 white onion, chopped
- 14 oz tomatoes, chopped
- 2 tbsp chopped rosemary
- Sea salt and pepper to taste
- 4 skinless chicken thighs
- 1 lb peeled pumpkin, cubed
- 1 tbsp extra virgin olive oil
- 2 tbsp basil leaves

Directions:
1. Preheat your oven to 375°F. Warm the olive oil in a skillet over medium heat. Add the garlic and onion and sauté for 5 minutes or until fragrant. Add the tomatoes, rosemary, salt, and pepper and cook for 15 minutes or until slightly thickened. Arrange the chicken thighs and pumpkin cubes on a baking sheet, then pour the mixture in the skillet over the chicken and sweet potatoes. Stir to coat well. Pour in enough water to cover the chicken and sweet potatoes. Bake in for 20 minutes. Top with basil.

Nutrition Info:
- Per Serving: Calories: 295;Fat: 9g;Protein: 21g;Carbs: 32g.

Port Wine Garlicky Lamb

Servings: 4
Cooking Time: 30 Minutes
Ingredients:
- 2 lb lamb shanks
- 1 tbsp olive oil
- ½ cup Port wine
- 1 tbsp tomato paste
- 10 peeled whole garlic cloves
- ½ cup chicken broth
- 1 tsp balsamic vinegar
- ½ tsp dried rosemary
- 1 tbsp olive oil

Directions:
1. Heat the oil in the Instant Pot on "Sauté" and brown the lamb shanks on all sides. Add the garlic and cook until lightly browned, no more than 2 minutes. Stir in the rest of the ingredients, except the oil and vinegar. Seal the lid and cook for 20 minutes on "Manual" on high. When cooking is complete, release the pressure naturally for 10 minutes. Remove the lamb shanks and let the sauce boil for 5 minutes

with the lid off. Stir in the vinegar and butter. Serve the gravy poured over the shanks.

Nutrition Info:

- Per Serving: Calories: 620;Fat: 35g;Protein: 60g;Carbs: 9g.

Korean Chicken Thighs

Servings: 4
Cooking Time: 4 Hours 10 Minutes
Ingredients:

- 8 boneless, skinless chicken thighs
- ¼ cup miso paste
- 2 tbsp coconut oil, melted
- 1 tbsp honey
- 1 tbsp rice wine vinegar
- 2 garlic cloves, sliced
- 1 tsp minced ginger root
- 2 red chilies, sliced
- 1 cup chicken broth
- 2 scallions, sliced
- 1 tbsp sesame seeds

Directions:

1. Place the miso, coconut oil, honey, rice wine vinegar, garlic, chilies, and ginger root in your slow cooker and mix well. Add the chicken. Cover and cook on "High" for 4 hours. Top with scallions and sesame seeds. Serve.

Nutrition Info:

- Per Serving: Calories: 315;Fat: 14g;Protein: 31g;Carbs: 17g.

Spicy Lime Pork Tenderloins

Servings: 4
Cooking Time: 7 Hours 15 Minutes
Ingredients:

- 2 lb pork tenderloins
- 1 cup chicken broth
- ¼ cup lime juice
- 3 tsp chili powder
- 2 tsp garlic powder
- 1 tsp ginger powder
- ½ tsp sea salt

Directions:

1. Combine chili powder, garlic powder, ginger powder, and salt in a bowl. Rub the pork all over with the spice mixture and put it in your slow cooker. Pour in the broth and lime juice around the pork. Cover with the lid and cook for 7 hours on "Low". Remove the pork from the slow cooker and let rest for 5 minutes. Slice the pork against the grain into medallions before serving.

Nutrition Info:

- Per Serving: Calories: 260;Fat: 6g;Protein: 49g;Carbs: 5g.

Authentic Chicken Curry With Coconut

Servings: 6

Cooking Time: 35 Minutes
Ingredients:

- 3 cups coconut milk
- 2 cups water
- 1 to 2 tablespoons curry powder
- 2 pounds boneless skinless chicken thighs, cut into cubes
- 1 teaspoon salt
- 3 bunches Swiss chard, washed, stemmed, and roughly chopped

Directions:

1. Combine the coconut milk, water, curry powder, chicken, and salt in a large pot. Bring to a boil over high heat. Reduce the heat to low. Cover and simmer for 30 minutes.
2. Add the Swiss chard to the pot. Cook for 5 minutes or until the chard wilts.

Nutrition Info:

- Per Serving: Calories: 581 ;Fat: 40g ;Protein: 48g ;Carbs: 10g .

Rosemary Turkey With Mushrooms

Servings: 4
Cooking Time: 20 Minutes
Ingredients:

- 1 ½ lb boneless, skinless turkey breasts, cubed
- 3 tbsp olive oil
- 1 cup mushrooms, sliced
- 1 onion, chopped
- 2 tbsp chopped rosemary
- Sea salt and pepper to taste
- 3 garlic cloves, minced

Directions:

1. Warm the olive oil in a skillet over medium heat. Add the mushrooms, garlic, onion, turkey, salt, and pepper and stir-fry for 7-10 minutes until the meat is cooked through and the veggies are tender. Garnish with rosemary. Serve.

Nutrition Info:

- Per Serving: Calories: 310;Fat: 15g;Protein: 3g;Carbs: 16g.

Hot & Spicy Shredded Chicken

Servings: 4
Cooking Time: 1 Hour
Ingredients:

- 1 ½ lb boneless and skinless chicken breast
- 2 cups diced tomatoes
- ½ tsp oregano
- 2 green chilies, chopped
- ½ tsp paprika
- 2 tbsp coconut sugar
- ½ cup salsa
- 1 tsp cumin
- 2 tbsp olive oil

Directions:

1. In a small bowl, combine the oil with all of the spices. Rub the chicken breast with the spicy marinade. Place the meat in your Instant Pot. Add the diced tomatoes.

2. Close the lid and cook for 25 minutes on "Manual". Transfer the chicken to a cutting board and shred it. Return the shredded meat to the Instant Pot. Choose the "Slow Cook" setting and cook for 30 more minutes.

Nutrition Info:

- Per Serving: Calories: 310;Fat: 10g;Protein: 38g;Carbs: 12g.

Sicilian Chicken Bake

Servings: 4
Cooking Time: 30 Minutes
Ingredients:

- 1 cup sliced cremini mushrooms
- 4 garlic cloves, minced
- 4 chicken breasts
- 2 tbsp avocado oil
- 1 cup chopped spinach
- 1 fennel bulb, sliced
- 20 cherry tomatoes, halved
- ½ cup chopped fresh basil
- ½ red onion, thinly sliced
- 2 tsp balsamic vinegar

Directions:

1. Preheat your oven to 400°F. Arrange the chicken breasts on a baking dish and brush them generously with avocado oil. Mix together the mushrooms, spinach, fennel, tomatoes, basil, red onion, garlic, and balsamic vinegar in a medium bowl and toss to combine. Top the breasts with the vegetable mixture. Bake in the oven for about 20 minutes, or until the juices run clear when pierced with a fork. Allow the chicken to rest for 5-10 minutes before slicing. Serve and enjoy!

Nutrition Info:

- Per Serving: Calories: 225;Fat: 8g;Protein: 27g;Carbs: 7g.

Cumin Lamb Meatballs With Aioli

Servings: 4
Cooking Time: 30 Minutes
Ingredients:

- 1 tsp ground cumin
- 2 tbsp chopped cilantro
- 1 ½ lb ground lamb
- 1 tbsp dried oregano
- 1 tsp onion powder
- 1 tsp garlic powder
- Sea salt and pepper to taste
- ½ cup garlic aioli

Directions:

1. Preheat your oven to 400°F. Combine the ground lamb, cumin, cilantro, rosemary, oregano, onion powder, garlic powder, salt, and pepper in a bowl. Shape 20 meatballs out of the mixture and transfer to a parchment-lined baking

sheet. Bake for 15 minutes until the meat reaches an internal temperature of 140°F. Serve warm with aioli.

Nutrition Info:

- Per Serving: Calories: 450;Fat: 24g;Protein: 2g;Carbs: 11g.

Cute Tiny Chicken Burgers

Servings: 4
Cooking Time: 30 Minutes
Ingredients:

- ¼ cup quinoa flour, brown rice flour, or chickpea flour
- 1 pound chicken, ground
- 4 scallions, finely sliced
- ¾ teaspoon salt
- 2 to 4 tablespoons coconut oil, divided

Directions:

1. Cover a large plate with parchment paper.

2. Mix together in a medium bowl the quinoa flour and chicken. Fold in the scallions and add the salt.

3. Take about 2 tablespoons of the chicken mixture and roll into a ball with wet hands. Flatten into a patty and place it on the prepared plate. Repeat with the remaining mixture.

4. Heat 2 tablespoons of coconut oil in a large sauté pan set over medium heat.

5. Add the patties and work in batches. Cook for 8 to 10 minutes per side. Add more oil to the pan, if necessary, for additional batches. Fully cooked patties should register at least 165°F on a meat thermometer.

6. Serve hot.

Nutrition Info:

- Per Serving: Calories: 365 ;Fat: 23g ;Protein: 37g ;Carbs: 3g .

Potted Rump Steak

Servings: 4
Cooking Time: 30 Minutes
Ingredients:

- 3 tbsp olive oil
- 2 bay leaves
- 1 lb rump steak
- 2 cups diced celery
- 1 tsp sea salt
- 3 onions, chopped
- 2 cups sliced mushrooms
- 18 oz canned tomato paste
- 10 ½ oz beef broth
- 1 ½ cups dry red wine

Directions:

1. Heat the oil in your Instant Pot on "Sauté" and brown the steak on all sides. Add the vegetables and stir in all of the seasonings. Combine the paste with the wine and broth. Add this mixture to the cooker. Seal the lid and cook for 35 minutes on "Manual" on high pressure. Check the meat and cook for a little bit more if you don't like the density or you want your meat overcooked. When the cooking is over, do a quick release. Serve and enjoy.

Creamy Beef Tenderloin Marsala

Servings: 4
Cooking Time: 25 Minutes
Ingredients:
- 4 beef tenderloin fillets
- Sea salt and pepper to taste
- 2 tbsp olive oil
- 1 shallot, finely minced
- ½ cup Marsala wine
- 2 cups fresh blueberries
- 3 tbsp cold butter, cubed

Directions:
1. Pound the beef with a rolling pin to ¾-inch thickness. Sprinkle with salt and pepper. Warm the olive oil in a skillet over medium heat. Add the beef and brown for 10 minutes on both sides. Set aside covered with foil.
2. Place the shallot, Marsala wine, blueberries, salt, and pepper in the skillet, and using a wide spatula, scrape any brown bits from the bottom. Bring to a simmer, then low the heat, and simmer for 4 minutes, until blueberries break down and the liquid has reduced by half. Add in butter cubed, one piece at time, and put the beef back to the skillet; toss to coat. Serve and enjoy!

Nutrition Info:
- Per Serving: Calories: 550;Fat: 33g;Protein: 2g;Carbs: 15g.

Ground Turkey & Spinach Stir-fry

Servings: 4
Cooking Time: 20 Minutes
Ingredients:
- 2 tbsp olive oil
- 1 ½ lb ground turkey
- 2 cups chopped spinach
- 4 green onions, sliced
- 2 tbsp fresh thyme
- Sea salt and pepper to taste
- 2 garlic cloves, minced

Directions:
1. Warm the olive oil in a skillet over medium heat. Brown the turkey, breaking apart with a wide spatula for about 6 minutes. Add the spinach, green onions, garlic, thyme, salt, and pepper. Cook for 3-5 minutes, stirring often.

Nutrition Info:
- Per Serving: Calories: 420;Fat: 21g;Protein: 2g;Carbs: 8g.

Worth It Glazed Chicken Thighs With Cauliflower

Servings: 4
Cooking Time: 35 To 40 Minutes
Ingredients:
- ½ cup balsamic vinegar
- ¼ cup extra-virgin olive oil
- 2 tablespoons maple syrup
- 8 bone-in chicken thighs, 2 to 3 ounces
- 2 cauliflower heads, broken or cut into florets
- Salt

Directions:
1. Whisk together the balsamic vinegar, olive oil, and maple syrup in a small bowl.
2. Combine in a medium dish the chicken thighs and vinegar-maple mixture. Marinate the chicken for 30 minutes in the refrigerator.
3. Preheat the oven to 350°F.
4. Cover the chicken with aluminum foil and place it in the preheated oven. Bake for 30 to 35 minutes, or until the chicken is cooked through. The internal temperature should be 165°F.
5. Leave the chicken in the oven uncovered if you've left the skin on the chicken for 10 minutes more to crisp the skin.
6. Fill a large pot with 2 inches of water and insert a steamer basket. Bring to a boil over high heat. Add the cauliflower then cover and steam for 8 minutes.
7. Serve the chicken with the cauliflower. Drizzle the extra marinade from the casserole dish over the cauliflower, and season with salt, if necessary.

Nutrition Info:
- Per Serving: Calories: 535 ;Fat: 38g ;Protein: 33g ;Carbs: 14g .

Sumac Chicken Thighs

Servings: 4
Cooking Time: 55 Minutes
Ingredients:
- 6 bone-in chicken thighs
- 2 sweet potatoes, cubed
- 2 tbsp extra-virgin olive oil
- 2 shallots, sliced thin
- Sea salt and pepper to taste
- 1 tsp sumac
- ½ tsp ground cinnamon
- 1 cup chicken broth

Directions:
1. Preheat your oven to 425°F. In a large baking dish, stir together the oil, shallots, salt, cumin, cinnamon, pepper, and chicken broth. Add the chicken and sweet potatoes. Stir to coat with the spices. Place the dish in the preheated oven and bake for 35-45 minutes, or until the chicken is cooked through and the sweet potatoes are tender. Serve.

Nutrition Info:
- Per Serving: Calories: 520;Fat: 32g;Protein: 32g;Carbs: 22g.

Awesome Herbaceous Roasted Chuck And Scrummy Vegetable

Servings: 4
Cooking Time: 7 Hours
Ingredients:

- 16 ounces chuck roast, lean
- 1 teaspoon pepper
- 2 onions cut, peeled and quartered
- 8 baby carrots, peeled and quartered
- 1 stalk of celery, sliced
- 1 bay leaf
- 10 cups water
- 1 cauliflower, cut into florets
- 5 cherry tomatoes
- Seasoning:
- 1 tablespoon cayenne pepper
- 2 tablespoons rosemary, dried or fresh

Directions:
1. Use a sharp knife to trim any fat from the chuck roast.
2. Season with herbs and spices.
3. Put the onions, carrots, and celery into the crockpot or slow cooker, then the meat, and finally add the bay leaf and water.
4. Cook on low for 5 to 7 hours or until the meat is tender.
5. You can add the cauliflower and cherry tomatoes for the last 15 minutes or until cooked through.
6. Serve hot.

Nutrition Info:

- Per Serving: Calories: 170 ;Fat: 5g ;Protein: 22g ;Carbs: 10g.

Sweet Gingery & Garlicky Chicken Thighs

Servings: 4
Cooking Time: 45 Minutes
Ingredients:

- 2 lb chicken thighs
- ½ cup honey
- 3 tsp grated ginger
- 2 garlic cloves, minced
- 5 tbsp brown sugar
- 1 ¾ cup chicken broth
- ½ cup low-sodium soy sauce
- ½ cup hoisin sauce
- 4 tbsp sriracha sauce
- 2 tbsp olive oil

Directions:
1. Place the chicken on the bottom of your Instant Pot. Combine the remaining ingredients in a bowl. Pour the sauce over the chicken. Seal the lid and cook for 40 minutes on "Manual" on high pressure. Once it goes off, do a quick pressure release and open up. Remove the chicken and transfer to a plate. Serve and enjoy!

Nutrition Info:

- Per Serving: Calories: 790;Fat: 20g;Protein: 74g;Carbs: 80g.

Thyme Pork Loin Bake

Servings: 4
Cooking Time: 90 Minutes
Ingredients:

- 1 lb boned pork loin
- 1 fennel bulb, sliced
- ½ celeriac, diced
- 2 tbsp olive oil
- 1 tbsp pure maple syrup
- 1 lemon, zested
- A pinch of sea salt
- 1 tsp chopped thyme

Directions:
1. Preheat your oven to 375°F. Toss the fennel, celeriac, 1 tablespoon of olive oil, maple syrup, lemon zest, and sea salt in a baking dish. Warm the remaining olive oil in a large skillet over medium heat and add the pork loin. Brown it on all sides, turning, for about 15 minutes total. Place the browned pork on top of the vegetables and sprinkle with thyme. Roast the pork for about 1 hour until cooked through, but still juicy. Transfer the roast and vegetables to a serving platter and pour any pan juices over the top. Serve and enjoy!

Nutrition Info:

- Per Serving: Calories: 405;Fat: 22g;Protein: 32g;Carbs: 15g.

Spicy Beef Fajitas

Servings: 4
Cooking Time: 15 Minutes
Ingredients:

- 1 ½ lb flank steak, cut into strips
- ½ tsp ancho chili powder
- 3 tbsp olive oil
- 2 green bell peppers, sliced
- 1 onion, sliced
- 1 cup store-bought salsa
- 1 tsp garlic powder
- ½ tsp Fajita seasoning

Directions:
1. Warm the olive oil in a skillet over medium heat. Stir-fry the flank steak strips, bell peppers, and onion for 6 minutes until browned. Stir in ancho chili powder, salsa, garlic powder, and fajita seasoning and cook for 3 minutes, stirring often. Serve right away.

Nutrition Info:

- Per Serving: Calories: 480;Fat: 26g;Protein: 3g;Carbs: 13g.

Chicken A La Tuscana

Servings: 4
Cooking Time: 25 Minutes
Ingredients:
- 2 cups cherry tomatoes
- 4 chicken breast halves
- 1 tsp garlic powder
- Sea salt and pepper to taste
- 2 tbsp extra-virgin olive oil
- ½ cup sliced green olives
- 1 eggplant, chopped
- ¼ cup dry white wine

Directions:
1. Pound the chicken breasts with a meat tenderizer until half an inch thick. Rub them with garlic powder, salt, and ground black pepper. Warm the olive oil in a skillet over medium heat. Add the chicken and cook for 14-16 minutes, flipping halfway through the cooking time. Transfer to a plate and cover with aluminum foil. Add the tomatoes, olives, and eggplant to the skillet and sauté for 4 minutes or until the vegetables are soft. Add the white wine to the skillet and simmer for 1 minute. Remove the aluminum foil and top the chicken with the vegetables and their juices, then serve warm.

Nutrition Info:
- Per Serving: Calories: 170;Fat: 10g;Protein: 7g;Carbs: 8g.

Tomato & Lentil Lamb Ragù

Servings: 4
Cooking Time: 40 Minutes
Ingredients:
- 1 red onion, chopped
- 4 garlic cloves, minced
- 1 lb ground lamb
- 14 oz canned diced tomatoes
- 1 cup chicken broth
- 2 tbsp extra-virgin olive oil
- ½ cup green lentils
- Sea salt and pepper to taste
- 1 tsp ginger powder
- 1 tsp ground cumin

Directions:
1. Warm the olive oil in a large pan over high heat. Add the onion and garlic sauté for 3 minutes. Add the ground lamb, breaking it up with a spoon. Brown for 3-4 minutes. Stir in the tomatoes, chicken broth, lentils, salt, ginger powder, cumin, and pepper. Simmer for 20 minutes, or until the lentils are cooked and most of the liquid has evaporated. Serve and enjoy!

Nutrition Info:
- Per Serving: Calories: 400;Fat: 15g;Protein: 40g;Carbs: 23g.

Magical Ramen And Pork Char Siu

Servings: 6

Cooking Time: 30 Minutes
Ingredients:
- Char Siu:
- 1½ to 2 pounds pork tenderloin
- 1 teaspoon fine Himalayan salt
- ½ cup blackberries
- 4 tablespoons coconut aminos, divided
- 3 tablespoons lard, bacon fat, or ghee
- 2 tablespoons coconut vinegar
- 1 tablespoon Dijon mustard
- 1 tablespoon fish sauce
- 2 teaspoons ginger powder
- 1 teaspoon Chinese five-spice powder
- 1 teaspoon garlic powder
- 2 teaspoons sweetener, granulated erythritol or other low-carb
- Ramen:
- 6 cups bone broth
- 4 cloves garlic, minced
- 1 inch piece fresh ginger, peeled and minced
- 2 tablespoons sesame oil
- 1 teaspoon coconut aminos
- 1 teaspoon fish sauce
- 1 teaspoon fine Himalayan salt
- 6 cups shirataki noodles
- 6 large eggs
- ½ ounce fresh cilantro or basil, trimmed

Directions:
1. Place the pork tenderloin in a freezer bag or airtight container. Sprinkle with the salt.
2. Heat a small saucepan over medium heat in the saucepan. Combine the blackberries, 2 tablespoons of the coconut aminos, lard, vinegar, mustard, fish sauce, ginger powder, Chinese five-spice powder, and garlic powder. Bring to a simmer and cook while stirring occasionally for 8 to 10 minutes. Mash when the blackberries turned red.
3. In a fine-mesh sieve, pour the sauce into a small bowl using a spoon to mash the berries and scraping the sieve to get as much out as possible. Let the sauce cool to room temperature.
4. Add the sauce to the pork and rub it all over, then seal the bag or container. Place in the fridge to marinate for 3 hours or up to overnight.
5. Set the pork out to come to room temperature 30 minutes before cooking. Preheat the oven to 350°F. Line a sheet pan with parchment paper and place a baking rack on it.
6. Remove the pork loin from the marinade and place it on the rack, reserving the marinade. Mix the marinade with the remaining 2 tablespoons of coconut aminos and the erythritol.
7. Place the pork on the middle rack of the oven and roast for 15 minutes and spoon half of the marinade over it. Roast for another 7 to 10 minutes, until the internal temperature is

145°F. Spoon the remaining marinade all over it. Broil for 2 minutes.

8.   Remove the pork from the oven and let it rest for 5 minutes, then cut it into ¼-inch-thick slices.

9.   Prepare the ramen while the pork roasts. Mix in a large pot the broth with the garlic, ginger, sesame oil, coconut aminos, fish sauce, and salt. Bring to a simmer and cook for 8 minutes. Reduce the heat and keep warm until the pork is done.

10. In a fine-mesh sieve, rinse the shirataki noodles and drain then set aside.

11. Bring a large pot of water to a rapid boil if you're including hard-boiled eggs. Add the eggs to the water one at a time. Boil for 7 minutes, then quickly drain all the water from the pot and cover the eggs with ice and cold water. Let them sit for 2 minutes. Peel the eggs under the cold water or under a fine stream of running water. Make sure to remove that fine film under the shell to ensure the egg whites won't break off.

12. Assemble the ramen bowls. Place 1 cup of noodles in each of six bowls, then add 1 cup of hot broth to each bowl. Add a hard-boiled egg, a few sprigs of cilantro, and three or four slices of char siu pork. Serve hot and dig in.

13. Store in a separate airtight container. The pork will keep in the fridge for 3 to 4 days, the broth a week, and the eggs 5 days. Prepare the noodles to order.

Nutrition Info:

- Per Serving: Calories: 499 ;Fat: 22g ;Protein: 52g;Carbs: 7g .

Miso Chicken With Sesame

Servings: 4 To 6
Cooking Time: 4 Hours
Ingredients:

- ¼ cup white miso
- 2 tablespoons coconut oil, melted
- 2 tablespoons honey
- 1 tablespoon rice wine vinegar, unseasoned
- 2 garlic cloves, thinly sliced
- 1 teaspoon fresh ginger root, minced
- 1 cup chicken broth
- 8 boneless, skinless chicken thighs
- 2 scallions, sliced
- 1 tablespoon sesame seeds

Directions:

1.   Combine the miso, coconut oil, honey, rice wine vinegar, garlic, and ginger root in a slow cooker. Mix it well.

2.   Add the chicken and toss to combine. Cover and cook on high for 4 hours.

3.   Transfer the chicken and sauce to a serving dish. Garnish with the scallions and sesame seeds and serve.

Nutrition Info:

- Per Serving: Calories: 320 ;Fat: 15g ;Protein: 32g Carbs: 17g.

Mustardy Leg Of Lamb

Servings: 4

Cooking Time: 6 Hours 15 Minutes
Ingredients:

- 1 lamb leg
- ½ cup white wine
- 1 ½ cups chicken broth
- 1 onion, roughly chopped
- Sea salt and pepper to taste
- 1 tsp garlic powder
- 1 tsp dried rosemary
- 1 tsp Dijon mustard

Directions:

1.   Make a paste in a small bowl by stirring together mustard, garlic powder, rosemary, salt, and pepper. Rub the paste evenly onto the lamb and put it in your slow cooker. Pour in broth, white wine, and onion around the lamb. Cover with the lid and cook for 6 hours on "Low". Serve.

Nutrition Info:

- Per Serving: Calories: 780;Fat: 40g;Protein: 92g;Carbs: 3g.

Smoked Turkey

Servings: 4
Cooking Time: 4 Hours 15 Minutes
Ingredients:

- 2 lb turkey breast
- 2 tsp smoked paprika
- 1 tsp liquid smoke
- 1 tbsp Dijon mustard
- 3 tbsp honey
- 2 garlic cloves, minced
- 4 tbsp olive oil
- 1 cup chicken broth

Directions:

1.   Brush the turkey breast with olive oil. Set your Instant Pot to "Sauté" and heat the oil. Add the turkey and brown it on all sides. Place ½ cup chicken broth and all of the remaining ingredients in a bowl. Stir to combine well. Pour the mixture over the meat. Seal the lid, set to "Manual", and cook for 30 minutes on High. Let the pressure release naturally for at least 10 minutes. Let sit for at least 5 minutes before slicing. Serve and enjoy!

Nutrition Info:

- Per Serving: Calories: 910;Fat: 50g;Protein: 95g;Carbs: 15g.

Holiday Turkey

Servings: 4
Cooking Time: 6 Hours 15 Minutes
Ingredients:

- 1 lb turkey breast strips
- 1 celery stalk, minced
- 1 carrot, minced
- 1 shallot, diced
- ½ red bell pepper, chopped
- 1 tbsp extra-virgin olive oil
- 6 tbsp tomato paste

- 2 tbsp apple cider vinegar
- 1 tbsp pure maple syrup
- 1 tsp Dijon mustard
- 1 tsp chili powder
- ½ tsp garlic powder
- ½ tsp sea salt
- ½ tsp dried oregano

Directions:

1. Blend the olive oil, turkey, celery, carrot, shallot, red bell pepper, tomato paste, vinegar, maple syrup, mustard, chili powder, garlic powder, salt, and oregano in your slow cooker. Using a large spoon, break up the turkey into smaller chunks as it combines with the other ingredients. Cover the cooker and set to "Low". Cook for 6 hours.

Nutrition Info:

- Per Serving: Calories: 250;Fat: 12g;Protein: 23g;Carbs: 13g.

Tempting And Tender Beef Brisket

Servings: 4
Cooking Time: 4 Hours
Ingredients:

- 16 oz beef brisket, 100% grass-fed and fat trimmed
- 2 cloves garlic, minced
- 1 sprig of thyme
- 1 sprig of rosemary
- 1 tablespoon mustard
- ¼ cup extra virgin olive oil
- ¼ teaspoon pepper, ground
- 1 onion, sliced
- 1 cup carrots, sliced
- 2 cups tomatoes, chopped

Directions:

1. Heat oven to 300°F.
2. Use a fork to mash the mustard, thyme, and rosemary with the garlic for the paste before mixing in the oil and pepper.
3. Pour the mixture over the brisket.
4. Onto the bottom of a baking dish, place half of the veggies.
5. Place the beef on top of the vegetables and cover with the rest of the vegetables and chopped tomatoes.
6. Bake in the oven or slow cooker for about 3 to 4 hours, or until tender, and serve with your favorite side.

Nutrition Info:

- Per Serving: Calories: 297 ;Fat: 23g ;Protein: 18g ;Carbs: 4g .

Leftover Chicken Salad Sandwiches

Servings: 4
Cooking Time: 10 Minutes
Ingredients:

- 2 cups leftover cooked, skinless chicken, pulled
- 1 spring onion, finely sliced
- ¼ cup paleo mayonnaise
- 1 red bell pepper, sliced

- 2 tbsp chopped tarragon
- 2 tsp Dijon mustard
- ½ tsp sea salt
- 8 slices whole-wheat bread

Directions:

1. Combine chicken, mayonnaise, red bell pepper, tarragon, mustard, spring onion, and salt in a bowl. To make the sandwiches, spread one side of 4 bread slices with the mixture and top with the remaining bread. Serve.

Nutrition Info:

- Per Serving: Calories: 320;Fat: 10g;Protein: 4g;Carbs: 31g.

A Fresh Lean Beef Burger That You Can Truly Enjoy

Servings: 2
Cooking Time: 25 Minutes
Ingredients:

- 8 ounces lean ground beef, 100% grass-fed
- 1 teaspoon black pepper
- 1 teaspoon garlic powder
- 1 teaspoon coconut oil
- 1 onion, sliced
- 1 avocado, sliced
- 2 tablespoons balsamic vinegar
- 1 large tomato, cut into 6 slices

Directions:

1. Mix the ground beef with pepper and garlic powder.
2. Heat a skillet on medium to high heat and add the coconut oil.
3. Sauté the onions for 5 to 10 minutes until it appears brown.
4. Add in the balsamic vinegar and sauté for 5 minutes more.
5. Using the palms of your hands, form burger shapes with the ground beef and add to the skillet. Sauté on each side for about 5 to 6 minutes then remove.
6. Let them sit on a tray to cool slightly and then assemble your burger on your serving plate by adding your sliced tomato, avocado, and onions on the top.
7. You can serve a bunless burger with salad or with a 100% whole grain burger bun as you preferred.

Nutrition Info:

- Per Serving: Calories: 583 ;Fat: 51g ;Protein: 19g ;Carbs: 14g .

Robust Herbed Lamb With Zucchini Boats

Servings: 6
Cooking Time: 40 Minutes
Ingredients:

- 6 zucchinis, ends trimmed, halved lengthwise
- 1 onion, finely diced
- 2 tablespoons water
- 1 pound lamb, ground

- 1 to 2 tablespoons fresh rosemary, minced
- ½ teaspoon salt

Directions:

1. Preheat the oven to 350°F.
2. Line a baking sheet with parchment paper.
3. Gently hollow out about 1 inch of space along the length of the inside of the zucchini halves with a small spoon.
4. Sauté the onion in the water for 5 minutes or until soft in a large pan set over medium heat.
5. Add the ground lamb, rosemary, and salt. Cook for 10 minutes and break up the lamb with a spoon. Remove from the heat.
6. Place the zucchini on the prepared sheet, hollow-side up.
7. Fill each zucchini with equal amounts of the lamb mixture.
8. Place the sheet in the preheated oven and bake for 25 minutes or until the lamb is fully cooked and the zucchini are tender.

Nutrition Info:

- Per Serving: Calories: 183 ;Fat: 6g ;Protein: 24g ;Carbs: 98g .

Mustardy Beef Steaks

Servings: 4
Cooking Time: 60 Minutes
Ingredients:

- ½ cup olive oil
- 2 tbsp Dijon mustard
- ½ cup balsamic vinegar
- 2 garlic cloves, minced
- 1 tsp rosemary, chopped
- 4 (½-inch thick) beef steaks
- Sea salt and pepper to taste

Directions:

1. Combine the olive oil, mustard, vinegar, garlic, rosemary, salt, and pepper in a bowl. Add in steaks and toss to coat. Let marinate covered for 30 minutes. Remove any excess of the marinade from the steaks and transfer them to a warm skillet over high heat and cook for 4-6 minutes on both sides. Let sit for 5 minutes and serve.

Nutrition Info:

- Per Serving: Calories: 480;Fat: 3g;Protein: 48g;Carbs: 4g.

Chili Pork Ragout

Servings: 4
Cooking Time: 8 Hours And 15 Minutes
Ingredients:

- 1 cup spinach, minced
- 1 lb pork tenderloin
- 1 yellow onion, diced
- 1 red bell pepper, diced
- 1 can diced tomatoes
- 2 tsp chili powder
- 1 tsp garlic powder
- ½ tsp ground cumin

- 1 tsp fennel seeds
- ¼ tsp red pepper flakes

Directions:

1. Add the pork, onion, bell pepper, tomatoes, chili powder, garlic powder, cumin, fennel seeds, red pepper flakes, and spinach in your slow cooker. Cover the cooker and set to "Low". Cook for 7-8 hours. Transfer the pork loin to a cutting board and shred with a fork. Return it to the slow cooker, stir it into the sauce, and serve.

Nutrition Info:

- Per Serving: Calories: 290;Fat: 10g;Protein: 35g;Carbs: 15g.

Classic Pork Chops And Creamy Green Beans

Servings: 4
Cooking Time: 40 Minutes
Ingredients:

- Creamy Green Beans:
- 1 medium head cauliflower, roughly chopped
- 1½ cups bone broth
- ¼ cup Garlic Confit or 4 cloves garlic, peeled
- 2 tablespoons cooking fat
- 2 cups fresh green beans, trimmed
- 1 red onion, sliced
- 2 teaspoons fine Himalayan salt, divided
- 2 large egg yolks
- Pork Chops:
- 2 teaspoons Himalayan salt, fine
- 1 teaspoon garlic powder
- 1 teaspoon black pepper, ground
- 1 teaspoon onion powder
- 5 sprigs thyme, fresh
- 4 thick-cut pork chops, boneless
- 2 tablespoons avocado oil
- ¼ cup bone broth
- 2 tablespoons coconut aminos
- 2 tablespoons red wine vinegar

Directions:

1. Make the creamy green beans. In a medium-sized pot, place the cauliflower, broth, and garlic confit and bring to a simmer over medium heat. Cover and cook until the cauliflower is fork-tender for 20 minutes.
2. Heat a large skillet over medium heat. Heat the cooking fat in the skillet when it's hot. Add the green beans, red onion slices, and 1 teaspoon of the salt. Sauté and stir occasionally for 10 minutes until the beans appear brown and the onions are tender and translucent. Reduce the heat to medium-low.
3. Transfer it and all of the broth to a blender, add the remaining teaspoon of salt, and blend until smooth. Open the lid vent while the blender is running and drop in the egg yolks one at a time.
4. Pour the cauliflower cream over the green beans and onions once well combined in the skillet. Stir, cover, and

remove from the heat, but keep the pan on the stove or in the oven so it stays warm.

5. Prepare the pork chops. Heat a large skillet over medium heat. Combine the salt, garlic powder, pepper, onion powder, and thyme sprigs in a small bowl while the skillet heats. Rub the seasoning mixture all over the pork chops, making sure they are evenly coated.

6. Melt the oil in the hot skillet. Add the chops and space them. Cook undisturbed for 5 minutes then flip the chops over and cook for 3 minutes on the other side.

7. Add the broth, coconut aminos, and vinegar to the skillet with the pork chops. Cover and cook for 3 minutes. Gently press on the center of a chop by using your finger. It should be firm when it's done but with a little give and the internal temperature should be 165°F. Remove from the heat.

8. Let the pork chops rest for a few minutes then pour the pan sauce over the chops. Serve with the creamy green beans.

9. Store leftovers in an airtight container in the fridge for up to 5 days. Reheat in a large skillet, covered, over medium-low heat for 8 to 10 minutes.

Nutrition Info:
- Per Serving: Calories: 563 ;Fat: 28g ;Protein: 59g;Carbs: 18g .

Delightful Stuffed Lamb With Peppers

Servings: 6
Cooking Time: 60 Minutes
Ingredients:
- 1 onion, finely diced
- 2 tablespoons water, plus additional for cooking
- 1½ pounds lamb, ground
- 1 cup grated zucchini
- ¼ cup fresh basil, minced
- 1 teaspoon salt
- 6 bell peppers, any color, seeded, ribbed, tops removed and reserved

Directions:
1. Preheat the oven to 350°F.
2. Sauté the onion in the water in a large pan set over medium heat for 5 minutes, or until soft.
3. Add the ground lamb and zucchini. Cook for 10 minutes by breaking up the meat with a spoon.
4. Stir in the basil and salt. Remove from the heat.
5. Fill a casserole dish with 1½ inches of water.
6. Stuff each pepper with an equal amount of the lamb mixture and place them into the dish. Cap each pepper with its reserved top.
7. Place the dish in the preheated oven and bake for 45 to 50 minutes.

Nutrition Info:
- Per Serving: Calories: 258 ;Fat: 9g Protein: 348g ;;Carbs: 10g.

Cherry Tomato & Basil Chicken Casserole

Servings: 4
Cooking Time: 30 Minutes
Ingredients:
- 8 small chicken thighs
- ½ cup green olives
- 1 lb cherry tomatoes
- A handful of basil leaves
- 1 ½ tsp minced garlic
- 1 tsp dried oregano
- 1 tbsp olive oil

Directions:
1. Heat the olive oil in your Instant Pot on "Sauté". Cook the chicken for about 2 minutes per side. Place the tomatoes in a plastic bag and smash them with a meat pounder. Remove the chicken from the cooker. Combine tomatoes, garlic, 1 cup of water, and oregano in the pot. Top with the browned chicken. Close the lid and cook for 15 minutes on "Manual" on high pressure. Let the pressure release naturally for at least 10 minutes, then release the rest of the pressure and take the lid off. Stir in the basil and olives. Stir and serve immediately.

Nutrition Info:
- Per Serving: Calories: 337;Fat: 21g;Protein: 27g;Carbs: 12g.

Dairy Free Chicken Alfredo

Servings: 6
Cooking Time: 4 To 8 Hours
Ingredients:
- Sauce:
- 1 large cauliflower head, broken or cut into florets
- Heaping ½ cup cashews, soaked in water for 4 hours
- 1 teaspoon salt
- ¼ cup water, reserved from cooking the cauliflower
- Chicken:
- 6 bone-in skinless chicken thighs, 2 to 3 ounces
- 4 cups spinach

Directions:
1. Fill a large pot with 2 inches of water and insert a steamer basket. Bring to a boil over high heat.
2. Add the cauliflower to the steamer basket. Cover and steam for 10 to 12 minutes or until very tender. Reserve ¼ cup of the cooking liquid.
3. Drain and rinse the cashews in a colander.
4. Combine in a blender the cooked cauliflower, cashews, salt, and ¼ cup of the cauliflower cooking liquid. Blend until smooth and creamy.
5. Place the chicken thighs in a slow cooker.
6. Pour the sauce over the chicken.
7. Cook on high for 3 to 4 hours, or on low for 7 to 8 hours.
8. Transfer the chicken to a work surface. Remove and discard the bones and gristle. Shred the meat.
9. Return the chicken meat to the cooker.

10. Stir in the spinach. Cook for 5 minutes or until the spinach wilts.

Nutrition Info:

- Per Serving: Calories: 286 ;Fat: 18g ;Protein: 27g ;Carbs: 12g .

Ragù Dish With Pork

Servings: 4 To 6

Cooking Time: 7 To 8 Hours

Ingredients:

- 1 pound pork tenderloin
- 1 medium yellow onion, diced
- 1 red bell pepper, diced
- 1 can diced tomatoes, 28 ounces
- 2 teaspoons chili powder
- 1 teaspoon garlic powder
- ½ teaspoon cumin, ground
- ½ teaspoon smoked paprika
- Dash red pepper flakes
- 1 cup fresh spinach leaves, minced

Directions:

1. Combine the pork, onion, bell pepper, tomatoes, chili powder, garlic powder, cumin, paprika, red pepper flakes, and spinach in your slow cooker.
2. Cover the cooker and set to low. Cook for 7 to 8 hours.
3. In a cutting board, transfer the pork loin and shred with a fork. Return it to the slow cooker and stir it into the sauce then serve.

Nutrition Info:

- Per Serving: Calories: 292 ;Fat: 10g ;Protein: 36g ;Carbs: 15g.

Herby Green Whole Chicken

Servings: 6

Cooking Time: 1 Hour 45 Minutes

Ingredients:

- 1 sweet onion, quartered
- 1 whole chicken
- 2 lemons, halved
- 4 garlic cloves, crushed
- 4 fresh thyme sprigs
- 4 fresh rosemary sprigs
- 4 fresh parsley sprigs
- 3 bay leaves
- 2 tbsp olive oil
- Sea salt and pepper to taste

Directions:

1. Preheat your oven to 400ºF. Put the chicken in a greased pan. Stuff it with lemons, onion, garlic, thyme, rosemary, parsley, and bay leaves into the cavity. Brush the chicken with olive oil, and season lightly with sea salt and pepper. Roast the chicken for about 1 ½ hours until golden brown and cooked through. Remove the chicken from the oven and let it sit for 10 minutes. Remove the lemons, onion, and herbs from the cavity and serve.

Nutrition Info:

- Per Serving: Calories: 260;Fat: 9g;Protein: 39g;Carbs: 6g.

Gingered Beef Stir-fry With Peppers

Servings: 4

Cooking Time: 15 Minutes

Ingredients:

- 2 tbsp olive oil
- 1 lb ground beef
- 2 green garlic stalks, minced
- 6 scallions, chopped
- 2 red bell peppers, chopped
- 2 tbsp grated fresh ginger
- ½ tsp sea salt
- 2 tbsp tarragon, chopped

Directions:

1. Warm the olive oil in a skillet over medium heat and place the ground beef. Cook for 5 minutes until browns. Stir in scallions, green garlic, bell peppers, ginger, and salt and cook for 4 more minutes until the bell peppers are soft. Top with tarragon and serve immediately.

Nutrition Info:

- Per Serving: Calories: 600;Fat: 20g;Protein: 2g;Carbs: 10g.

Garlicky Steak With Mustard

Servings: 4

Cooking Time: 10 Minutes

Ingredients:

- ½ cup extra-virgin olive oil
- ½ cup balsamic vinegar
- 2 tablespoons Dijon mustard
- 2 garlic cloves, minced
- 1 teaspoon fresh rosemary, chopped
- 1 teaspoon salt
- ¼ teaspoon black pepper, freshly ground
- 4 boneless grass-fed steaks, 6 ounces and ½ inch thick

Directions:

1. Whisk together in a shallow baking dish the olive oil, balsamic vinegar, Dijon, garlic, rosemary, salt, and pepper.
2. Add the steaks and turn them to coat well with the marinade. Cover and let the steaks marinate for 30 minutes at room temperature or up to 2 hours in the refrigerator.
3. Heat a large skillet over high heat.
4. Remove the steaks from the marinade and blot them with a paper towel to remove the excess marinade.
5. Cook the steaks and flip it once until nicely browned 2 to 3 minutes on each side.
6. Before serving, let the steaks rest for 5 minutes.

Nutrition Info:

- Per Serving: Calories: 480 ;Fat: 31g ;Protein: 48g ;Carbs: 3g .

Apple-glazed Whole Chicken

Servings: 4
Cooking Time: 60 Minutes
Ingredients:
- 1 whole chicken, cut into 8 pieces
- 1 cup sugar-free apple juice
- 1 tbsp brown rice flour
- Sea salt and pepper to taste
- ½ tsp ground cinnamon
- 1 tsp ground cumin
- 2 tsp sweet paprika
- ½ tsp garlic powder

Directions:
1. Preheat your oven to 375°F. Place the chicken pieces in a baking pan. In a small bowl, combine the brown rice flour, salt, ground cinnamon, cumin, paprika, garlic powder, and pepper. Rub the spice mix onto the chicken pieces. Carefully pour the apple juice into the pan. Place the pan in the oven and bake for 35-45 minutes, or until the chicken is golden brown and cooked through. Serve.

Nutrition Info:
- Per Serving: Calories: 370;Fat: 20g;Protein: 38g;Carbs: 10g.

Mumbai-inspired Chicken

Servings: 6
Cooking Time: 30 Minutes
Ingredients:
- 2 chicken breasts, cubed
- 2 carrots, diced
- 1 white onion, diced
- 1 tbsp minced fresh ginger
- 6 garlic cloves, minced
- 1 cup sugar snap peas, diced
- 1 can coconut cream
- 2 tbsp coconut oil, divided
- 1 tbsp sugar-free fish sauce
- 1 cup chicken broth
- ½ cup diced tomatoes
- ½ tsp garam masala
- Sea salt and pepper to taste
- ¼ tsp cayenne pepper

Directions:
1. Warm the coconut oil in a skillet over medium. Add the chicken breasts and cook for 15 minutes, stirring occasionally; reserve. Add the carrots, onion, ginger, and garlic to the same skillet and sauté for 5 minutes or until fragrant and the onion is translucent. Add the peas, coconut cream, fish sauce, chicken broth, tomatoes, garam masala, salt, cayenne pepper, pepper, and ¼ cup of water. Stir. Bring to a boil. Reduce the heat and simmer for 10 minutes. return the cooked chicken and cook for 2 more minutes. Serve immediately.

Nutrition Info:
- Per Serving: Calories: 220;Fat: 15g;Protein: 13g;Carbs: 9g.

Italian-style Chicken

Servings: 4
Cooking Time: 25 Minutes
Ingredients:
- 1 tbsp Italian seasoning
- 2 tbsp parsley, chopped
- 4 chicken breast halves
- 1 tsp garlic powder
- 2 tbsp olive oil
- 1 zucchini, chopped
- 2 cups cherry tomatoes
- ½ cup sliced green olives
- ¼ cup dry white wine

Directions:
1. Pound the chicken breasts with a rolling pin to ½-inch thickness. Sprinkle them with Italian seasoning and garlic powder. Warm the olive oil in a skillet over medium heat and place in the breasts. Sear for 14-20 minutes on all sides until slightly browned. Set aside covered with foil.
2. Place the zucchini, tomatoes, and olives in the skillet and cook for 4 minutes until the zucchini is tender. Pour in wine and scrape any brown bits from the bottom and simmer for 1 minute. Add the chicken back to the pot and gently stir to coat in the sauce. Garnish with parsley.

Nutrition Info:
- Per Serving: Calories: 170;Fat: 12g;Protein: 2g;Carbs: 9g.

Sweet Balsamic Chicken

Servings: 4
Cooking Time: 30 Minutes
Ingredients:
- 1 shallot, minced
- 1 tsp sea salt
- 2 tbsp honey
- ¼ cup balsamic vinegar
- 4 chicken breasts

Directions:
1. Preheat your oven to 350°F. Mix the shallot, salt, honey, and vinegar in a baking dish until the honey dissolves. Add in chicken breast and toss to coat and bake for 20 minutes. Let rest for 5 minutes and serve.

Nutrition Info:
- Per Serving: Calories: 232;Fat: 5g;Protein: 35g;Carbs: 13g.

Fiery Pork Loin With Lime

Servings: 4 To 6
Cooking Time: 6 To 7 Hours
Ingredients:
- 3 teaspoons chili powder
- 2 teaspoons garlic powder
- 1 teaspoon cumin, ground
- ½ teaspoon sea salt
- 2 pork tenderloins, 1-pound
- 1 cup broth of choice
- ¼ cup lime juice, freshly squeezed

Directions:
1. Stir together in a small bowl the chili powder, garlic powder, cumin, and salt. Rub the pork all over with the spice mixture and put it in the slow cooker.
2. Pour the broth and lime juice around the pork in the cooker.
3. Cover the cooker and set to low. Cook for 6 to 7 hours.
4. Remove the pork from the slow cooker and let rest for 5 minutes. Before serving, slice the pork against the grain into medallions.

Nutrition Info:
- Per Serving: Calories: 259 ;Fat: 5g ;Protein: 50g ;Carbs: 5g .

Pecan-dusted Pork Tenderloin Slices

Servings: 4
Cooking Time: 20 Minutes
Ingredients:
- 1 lb pork tenderloin, sliced
- Sea salt and pepper to taste
- ½ cup pecans
- 1 cup full-fat coconut milk
- 2 tbsp olive oil

Directions:
1. Preheat your oven to 400°F. Pulse the pecans in your blender until a powder consistency is reached. Remove to a bowl and mix with salt and pepper. In another bowl, combine the coconut milk and olive oil. Dip the pork chops first in the coconut mixture, then in the pecan mix, and transfer to a parchment-lined baking sheet. Bake for 10 minutes until the meat reaches an internal temperature of 160°F. Serve immediately.

Nutrition Info:
- Per Serving: Calories: 440;Fat: 35g;Protein: 4g;Carbs: 7g.

Basic Poached Wrapped Chicken

Servings: 4 To 6
Cooking Time: 15 Minutes
Ingredients:
- 2 cups water, plus additional for soaking the wrappers
- 2 boneless skinless chicken breasts, 4 ounces
- 10 rice paper wrappers
- 1 small head romaine lettuce, sliced thin
- 2 cups lightly packed spinach, sliced thin
- ½ cup fresh dill, minced

Directions:
1. Bring the water to a boil in a shallow pan set over high heat. Reduce the heat to medium. Add the chicken breasts. Cover and cook for 15 minutes or until the chicken is cooked through and the internal temperature is at least 165°F. Remove the chicken from the pot. Let it cool and slice it thinly.
2. Place a cutting board on a flat surface with the fillings near you.
3. Fill a large, shallow bowl with warm water. The water should be hot enough to cook the wrappers but warm enough so you can comfortably touch it.
4. Soak one rice paper wrapper in the water, and place it on the cutting board.
5. Place ½ cup of romaine, ¼ cup of spinach, 1 teaspoon of dill, and a few chicken slices in the middle of the wrapper.
6. Fold the sides in over the fillings. Starting at the bottom, tightly roll up the wrapper burrito-style.
7. Repeat with the remaining wrappers, chicken, and vegetables.

Nutrition Info:
- Per Serving: Calories: 255 ;Fat: 5g ;Protein: 20g ;Carbs: 32g .

Smoky Lamb Souvlaki

Servings: 4
Cooking Time: 25 Minutes + Marinating Time
Ingredients:
- 1 lb lamb shoulder, cubed
- 2 tbsp olive oil
- 1 tbsp apple cider vinegar
- 2 tsp crushed fennel seeds
- 2 tsp smoked paprika
- Salt and garlic powder to taste

Directions:
1. Blend the olive oil, cider vinegar, crushed fennel seeds, smoked paprika, garlic powder, and sea salt in a large bowl. Stir in the lamb. Cover the bowl and refrigerate it for 1 hour to marinate. Preheat a frying pan over high heat. Thread 4-5 pieces of lamb each onto 8 skewers. Fry for 3-4 minutes per side until cooked through. Serve.

Nutrition Info:
- Per Serving: Calories: 275;Fat: 15g;Protein: 31g;Carbs: 1g.

Beef Skewers

Servings: 4
Cooking Time: 30 Minutes + Chilling Time
Ingredients:
- 1 lb beef ribeye steak, cut into 1 ½-inch pieces
- 1 red onion, quartered and separated into layers
- 1 red pepper, cut into chunks
- 8 button mushrooms
- 2 tbsp olive oil, divided
- 1 tbsp coconut aminos

- 1 tbsp apple cider vinegar
- 1 tbsp minced garlic
- 1 tbsp chopped cilantro
- Sea salt and pepper to taste

Directions:

1. Toss 1 tablespoon of olive oil, coconut aminos, cider vinegar, garlic, salt, pepper, and cilantro in a mixing bowl. Add the beef and stir to coat. Cover the bowl and refrigerate for 1 hour to marinate.

2. Preheat a grill pan over medium heat. Combine the vegetables in a bowl and toss with the remaining olive oil, salt, and pepper. Thread the meat and vegetables. Place the skewers on the hot grill pan and cook for 10 minutes, turning once or twice, or until the beef is cooked. Serve.

Nutrition Info:

- Per Serving: Calories: 320;Fat: 15g;Protein: 36g;Carbs: 10g.

Turkey Stuffed Bell Peppers

Servings: 6
Cooking Time: 30 Minutes
Ingredients:

- 6 bell peppers, tops removed and deseeded
- 3 tbsp avocado oil
- 1 lb ground turkey
- 1 onion, diced
- 2 garlic cloves, minced
- 16 oz canned tomatoes
- ½ tsp paprika
- ½ tsp ground cumin
- ½ tsp dried oregano
- Sea salt and pepper to taste

Directions:

1. Preheat your oven to 400°F. Warm the avocado oil in a skillet over medium heat and brown the ground turkey for 5 minutes. Add garlic and onion and cook for 2 minutes, stirring often. Stir in tomatoes, paprika, cumin, oregano, salt, and pepper. Spoon the mixture into the bell peppers. Arrange them on a greased baking dish. Bake for 20-25 minutes or until softened. Serve warm.

Nutrition Info:

- Per Serving: Calories: 190;Fat: 9g;Protein: 15g;Carbs: 10g.

Tangy Beef Carnitas

Servings: 4
Cooking Time: 30 Minutes
Ingredients:

- 1 tsp cayenne pepper
- 1 tsp paprika
- ¼ cup fresh cilantro leaves
- 6 tbsp olive oil
- 4 garlic cloves, minced
- 1 jalapeño pepper, chopped
- 1 ½ lb beef flank steak
- Sea salt and pepper to taste

- 1 cup guacamole

Directions:

1. Place cilantro, 4 tbsp of olive oil, garlic, cayenne pepper, paprika, and jalapeño in your food processor and pulse until it reaches a paste consistency. Reserve 1 tbsp of the paste. Rub the flank steak with the remaining paste. Warm the remaining olive oil in a skillet over medium heat. Sear the steak for 15 minutes on all sides until browned. Remove the meat to a cutting board and let it cool for 5 minutes. Cut it against the grain into ½-inch-thick slices. Put the beef in a bowl and add the reserved garlic paste; toss to combine. Serve with guacamole.

Nutrition Info:

- Per Serving: Calories: 720;Fat: 53g;Protein: 2g;Carbs: 13g.

Grilled Beef Burgers With Chipotle Aioli

Servings: 4
Cooking Time: 20 Minutes
Ingredients:

- 1 tbsp olive oil
- 4 beef burgers
- ½ cup chipotle aioli
- 4 tsp low-sodium soy sauce
- 2 tbsp brown sugar
- 2 tbsp chopped scallions

Directions:

1. Preheat your grill to medium-high heat. Cook the burgers on the grill to the desired doneness, about 10 minutes. Combine the aioli, soy sauce, brown sugar, and scallions in a bowl. Top each burger with the sauce and serve.

Nutrition Info:

- Per Serving: Calories: 340;Fat: 19g;Protein: 1g;Carbs: 14g.

Lettuce-wrapped Beef Roast

Servings: 4
Cooking Time: 8 Hours 15 Minutes
Ingredients:

- 2 lb beef chuck roast
- 1 shallot, diced
- 1 cup beef broth
- 3 tbsp coconut aminos
- 1 tbsp rice vinegar
- 1 tsp garlic powder
- 1 tsp olive oil
- ½ tsp ground ginger
- ¼ tsp red pepper flakes
- 8 romaine lettuce leaves
- 1 tbsp sesame seeds
- 1 scallion, diced

Directions:

1. Place the beef, shallot, broth, coconut aminos, vinegar, garlic powder, olive oil, ginger, and red pepper flakes in

your slow cooker. Cover the cooker and set to "Low". Cook for 8 hours. Scoop spoonfuls of the beef mixture into each lettuce leaf. Top with sesame seeds and scallion.

Nutrition Info:

- Per Serving: Calories: 425;Fat: 22g;Protein: 45g;Carbs: 12g.

Melt-in-your-mouth Chicken & Rice

Servings: 4
Cooking Time: 15 Minutes
Ingredients:

- 2 cups cooked brown rice
- 1 cup cooked chicken, cubed
- 4 oz snow peas, trimmed
- ½ cup chicken broth
- 1 tsp sea salt
- ½ tsp ground ginger
- 2 tbsp olive oil
- 1 tsp crushed chilies
- 2 scallions, sliced

Directions:

1. Warm the olive oil in a large skillet over medium heat. Add the rice and chicken. Sauté for about 2 minutes. Add the snow peas, chicken broth, salt, and ginger. Cover the pan, reduce the heat to low, and cook for 3 minutes, or until the snow peas turn bright green. Remove the pan from the heat. Stir in the crushed chilies and scallions.

Nutrition Info:

- Per Serving: Calories: 280;Fat: 6g;Protein: 14g;Carbs: 39g.

Marvellous Chocolate Chili

Servings: 4 To 6
Cooking Time: 45 Minutes
Ingredients:

- 1 tablespoon extra-virgin olive oil
- 1 pound lean ground beef
- 1 large onion, chopped
- 2 garlic cloves, minced
- 1 tablespoon cocoa, unsweetened
- 1½ teaspoons chili powder
- 1 teaspoon salt
- ½ teaspoon cumin, ground
- 2 cups chicken broth
- 1 cup tomato sauce

Directions:

1. Heat the oil over high heat in a Dutch oven. Add the ground beef and brown well for 5 minutes.
2. Add the onion, garlic, cocoa, chili powder, salt, and cumin and cook while stirring for a minute.
3. Add the chicken broth and tomato sauce and bring to a boil. Reduce the heat to a simmer, cover, and cook, stirring occasionally for 30 to 40 minutes. Add more chicken broth or water if the sauce becomes too thick as it cooks to thin it.
4. Ladle into bowls and serve.

Nutrition Info:

- Per Serving: Calories: 370 ;Fat: 27g ;Protein: 23g ;Carbs: 9g.

The Best General Tso's Chicken

Servings: 4
Cooking Time: 30 Minutes
Ingredients:

- 3 tbsp coconut aminos
- 1 tsp Shaoxing wine
- 1 tbsp arrowroot powder
- ½ tsp red pepper flakes
- 2 garlic cloves, minced
- 2 tbsp rice vinegar
- 3 tbsp coconut sugar
- ¼ tsp ground ginger
- 1 tbsp almond butter
- 1 lb chicken breasts, cubed
- 1 tbsp avocado oil
- 1 cup brown rice flour
- ¼ tsp garlic powder
- ¼ tsp sea salt

Directions:

1. Cook the ginger and almond butter in a saucepan over medium heat for 2 minutes. Add the coconut aminos, Shaoxing wine, arrowroot powder, red pepper flakes, garlic, vinegar, and coconut sugar to the saucepan. Stir to mix well. Bring to a boil. Reduce the heat t and simmer for 5 minutes or until the sauce is thickened.
2. Heat the avocado oil in a nonstick skillet over medium heat. Combine the rice flour, garlic powder, and sea salt in a small bowl. Mix well. Dip the chicken in the mixture, then place in the skillet and cook for 8 minutes or until golden brown and crispy. Flip the chicken halfway through the cooking time. Transfer the chicken thighs to a large plate and pour over it the sauce. Serve and enjoy!

Nutrition Info:

- Per Serving: Calories: 480;Fat: 20g;Protein: 32g;Carbs: 41g.

Lemon & Caper Turkey Scaloppine

Servings: 4
Cooking Time: 25 Minutes
Ingredients:

- 1 tbsp capers
- ¼ cup whole-wheat flour
- Sea salt and pepper to taste
- 4 turkey breast cutlets
- 2 tbsp olive oil
- 3 lemons, juiced
- 1 lemon, zested
- 1 tbsp chopped parsley

Directions:

1. Pound the turkey with a rolling pin to ¼-inch thickness. Combine flour, salt, and pepper in a bowl. Roll each cutlet piece in the flour, shaking off the excess. Warm the olive oil in a skillet over medium heat. Sear the cutlets for 4 minutes

on both sides. Transfer to a plate and cover with aluminium foil. Pour the lemon juice and lemon zest in the skillet to scrape up the browned bits that stick to the bottom of the skillet. Stir in capers and rosemary. Cook for 2 minutes until the sauce has thickened slightly. Drizzle the sauce over the cutlets. Serve.

Nutrition Info:
- Per Serving: Calories: 190;Fat: 14g;Protein: 2g;Carbs: 9g.

Chicken Piccata

Servings: 6
Cooking Time: 20 Minutes
Ingredients:
- 1 cup pimento olives, minced
- 6 chicken breast halves
- ¼ cup olive oil
- 2 tbsp lemon juice
- 1 tbsp sherry wine
- ½ cup whole-wheat flour
- 4 shallots, chopped
- 3 garlic cloves, crushed
- ¾ cup chicken broth
- 1 tsp dried basil
- 3 tsp grated Parmesan cheese
- ¼ cup plain yogurt
- ¼ tsp white pepper

Directions:
1. Heat the olive oil in your Instant Pot on "Sauté". Add the chicken and brown it on all sides. This will take 5 to 8 minutes. Remove the chicken from the cooker. Add the shallots and garlic, and stir-fry them for a couple of minutes. Add the sherry wine, broth, lemon juice, salt, olives, basil, and pepper. Return the chicken to the cooker. Seal the lid and cook on "Manual" on High Pressure for 10 minutes. Once ready, carefully open the lid. Stir in plain yogurt and Parmesan cheese. Close the lid again and cook for an additional minute. Serve hot.

Nutrition Info:
- Per Serving: Calories: 320;Fat: 20g;Protein: 19g;Carbs: 15g.

Jerk Chicken Drumsticks

Servings: 4
Cooking Time: 4 Hours 15 Minutes
Ingredients:
- 1 lb chicken drumsticks
- ¼ cup cilantro, chopped
- 3 tbsp lime juice
- ½ tsp garlic powder
- ½ tsp sea salt
- 1 tbsp jerk seasoning

Directions:
1. In a small bowl, stir together the cilantro, lime juice, garlic powder, salt, and jerk seasoning to form a paste. Put the drumsticks in your slow cooker. Spread the cilantro paste evenly on each drumstick. Cover the cooker and set to "High". Cook for 4 hours, or until the juices run clear. Leave to rest for 10 minutes. Serve and enjoy!

Nutrition Info:
- Per Serving: Calories: 415;Fat: 11g;Protein: 70g;Carbs: 1g.

Good For The Bones Stir Fried Sesame Chicken

Servings: 6
Cooking Time: 25 Minutes
Ingredients:
- ¾ cup warm water
- ½ cup tahini
- ¼ cup plus 2 tablespoons toasted sesame oil, divided
- 2 garlic cloves, minced
- ½ teaspoon salt
- 1 pound boneless skinless chicken breasts, cut into ½-inch cubes
- 6 cups lightly packed kale, thoroughly washed and chopped

Directions:
1. Whisk together in a medium bowl the warm water, tahini, ¼ cup of sesame oil, garlic, and salt.
2. Heat the remaining 2 tablespoons of sesame oil in a large pan set over medium heat.
3. Add the chicken and cook for 8 to 10 minutes while stirring.
4. Stir in the tahini-sesame sauce. Mix it well to coat the chicken. Cook for 6 to 8 minutes more.
5. Add the kale one handful at a time. When the first handful wilts, add the next. Continue until all the kale has been added. Serve hot.

Nutrition Info:
- Per Serving: Calories: 417 ;Fat: 30g ;Protein: 27g ;Carbs: 12g .

Chapter 6. Fish And Seafood

Cumin Salmon With Daikon Relish

Servings: 4
Cooking Time: 35 Minutes
Ingredients:
- 1 scallion, chopped
- 4 tangerines, chopped
- ½ cup chopped daikon
- 2 tbsp chopped cilantro
- 1 tsp lemon zest
- A pinch of sea salt
- 1 tsp ground cumin
- 1 tsp ground coriander
- 4 skin-on salmon fillets
- 1 tsp olive oil

Directions:
1. Stir together tangerines, daikon, scallion, cilantro, salt, and lemon zest in a mixing bowl. Set the relish aside. Preheat your oven to 425°F. In a small bowl, stir together the cumin and coriander. Rub the flesh side of the fillets with the spice mixture. Arrange the salmon in a baking dish in a single layer, skin-side up. Brush with olive oil. Bake for 15 minutes, or until just cooked through, and lightly golden. Spoon the relish over the fish. Serve.

Nutrition Info:
- Per Serving: Calories: 295;Fat: 11g;Protein: 33g;Carbs: 14g.

Lemon Sauce Salmon

Servings: 4
Cooking Time: 20 Minutes
Ingredients:
- 4 salmon fillets
- 1 tbsp honey
- ½ tsp cumin
- 1 tbsp hot water
- 1 tbsp olive oil
- 1 tsp smoked paprika
- 1 tbsp chopped parsley
- ¼ cup lemon juice

Directions:
1. Pour 1 cup of water into the Instant pot, then put the steamer rack in place. Place the salmon on the steamer rack skin side down. Seal the lid and cook for 3 minutes on "Manual". In a bowl, whisk together the remaining ingredients. Once the cooking is over, release the pressure quickly, and drizzle the sauce over the salmon. Seal the lid again and cook for 2 more minutes on "Manual". Then, perform a quick pressure release and serve immediately.

Nutrition Info:
- Per Serving: Calories: 495;Fat: 32g;Protein: 41g;Carbs: 6g.

Crusty And Nutty Tilapia With Kale

Servings: 2
Cooking Time: 15 Minutes
Ingredients:
- 2 teaspoon extra virgin olive oil
- 2 tablespoon low fat hard cheese, grated
- ½ cup roasted and ground brazil nuts/hazelnuts/hard nut
- ½ cup bread crumbs, 100% wholegrain
- 2 tilapia fillets, skinless
- 2 teaspoons mustard, whole grain
- 1 head of kale, chopped
- 1 tablespoon sesame seeds, lightly toasted
- 1 clove of garlic, mashed

Directions:
1. Preheat the oven to 350°F.
2. Lightly oil a baking sheet with 1 teaspoon extra virgin olive oil.
3. In a separate bowl, mix in the nuts, breadcrumbs, and cheese.
4. Spread a thin layer of the mustard over the fish and then dip into the breadcrumb mixture.
5. Transfer to a baking dish.
6. Bake for 12 minutes or until cooked through.
7. In a skillet, heat 1 teaspoon oil on a medium heat and sauté the garlic for 30 seconds, adding in the kale for 5 minutes more.
8. Mix in the sesame seeds.
9. Serve the fish at once with the kale on the side.

Nutrition Info:
- Per Serving: Calories: 451 ;Fat: 31g Protein: 35g ;;Carbs: 14g.

Saucy Tropical Halibut

Servings: 4
Cooking Time: 35 Minutes
Ingredients:
- ½ mango, diced
- 1 avocado, diced
- ½ cup chopped strawberries
- 1 tsp chopped fresh mint
- 1 lemon, juiced and zested
- 1 tbsp olive oil
- 4 boneless, skinless halibut fillets
- Sea salt and pepper to taste

Directions:
1. Mix avocado, mango, strawberries, mint, lemon juice, and lemon zest in a bowl; stir well. Set the sauce aside.
2. Warm the olive oil in a pan over medium heat. Lightly season the halibut with salt and pepper. Add the fish and fry for 3-4 minutes per side, turning once or until it is just cooked through. Top with avocado salsa and serve.

Nutrition Info:

- Per Serving: Calories: 355;Fat: 15g;Protein: 42g;Carbs: 12g.

Old Bay Crab Cakes

Servings: 4
Cooking Time: 30 Minutes
Ingredients:
- ½ cup shredded carrots
- 2 scallions, chopped
- 2 lb cooked lump crabmeat
- ½ cup shredded coconut
- ½ cup coconut flour
- 2 eggs
- 1 tsp Old Bay spice mix
- 1 tsp lemon zest
- 2 tbsp olive oil

Directions:
1. Mix together the crab, coconut, coconut flour, carrot, scallions, eggs, Old Bay spice mix, and lemon zest in a large bowl. Shape the mixture into 8 patties and flatten them until they are about 1 inch thick. Warm the olive oil in a skillet over medium heat. Add the crab cakes and sear for about 6 minutes per side until cooked through and golden on both sides, turning once. Serve.

Nutrition Info:
- Per Serving: Calories: 405;Fat: 20g;Protein: 49g;Carbs: 5g.

Southern Trout With Crusty Pecan

Servings: 4
Cooking Time: 15 Minutes
Ingredients:
- Extra-virgin olive oil, for brushing
- 4 large trout fillets, boneless
- Salt
- Freshly ground black pepper
- 1 cup pecans, finely ground, divided
- 1 tablespoon coconut oil, melted, divided
- 2 tablespoon fresh thyme leaves, chopped
- Lemon wedges

Directions:
1. Preheat the oven to 375°F.
2. Brush a rimmed baking sheet with olive oil.
3. Place the trout fillets on the baking sheet skin-side down. Season with salt and pepper.
4. Into the flesh of each fillet, press gently ¼ cup of ground pecans.
5. Drizzle the melted coconut oil over the nuts and then sprinkle the thyme over the fillets.
6. Give each fillet another sprinkle of salt and pepper.
7. Place the sheet in the preheated oven and bake for 15 minutes, or until the fish is cooked through.

Nutrition Info:
- Per Serving: Calories: 672 ;Fat: 59g ;Protein: 30g ;Carbs: 13g .

Appealing Lemon With Wild Salmon And Mixed Vegetables

Servings: 4
Cooking Time: 25 To 30 Minutes
Ingredients:
- Four 5 ounces wild salmon fillets
- 1 teaspoon salt, divided
- 1 lemon, washed and sliced thin
- 1 broccoli head, roughly chopped
- 1 cauliflower head, roughly chopped
- 1 small bunch (4 to 6) carrots, cut into coins

Directions:
1. Preheat the oven to 400°F.
2. Line a baking sheet with parchment paper.
3. Place the salmon on the prepared sheet.
4. Sprinkle the salmon with ½ teaspoon of salt. Drape each fillet with a few lemon slices.
5. Place the sheet in the preheated oven and bake for 15 to 20 minutes, or until the salmon is opaque and flakes easily with a fork.
6. Fill a pot with 3 inches of water and insert a steamer basket while the salmon cooks. Bring to a boil over high heat.
7. Add the broccoli, cauliflower, and carrots to the pot. Cover and cook for 8 to 10 minutes.
8. Sprinkle with the remaining ½ teaspoon of salt.
9. Top each salmon fillet with a heaping pile of vegetables, and serve.

Nutrition Info:
- Per Serving: Calories: 330 ;Fat: 13g ;Protein: 35g ;Carbs: 20g.

Halibut Al Ajillo

Servings: 2
Cooking Time: 20 Minutes
Ingredients:
- 4 lemon wedges
- 2 halibut fillets
- Black pepper to taste
- 2 garlic cloves, pressed
- 2 tbsp olive oil
- 1 tbsp dill, chopped

Directions:
1. Preheat your oven to 400ºF. Place the fish in a foil-lined baking dish. Sprinkle with black pepper and garlic. Drizzle with oil. Bake for 15 minutes until the fish is firm and well cooked. Top with dill. Serve with lemon wedges.

Nutrition Info:
- Per Serving: Calories: 490;Fat: 19g;Protein: 55g;Carbs: 3g.

Tropical-style Cod

Servings: 4
Cooking Time: 25 Minutes
Ingredients:

- ½ pineapple, diced
- ½ avocado, diced
- 1 cup mango, diced
- 1 lime, juiced
- ¼ tsp chili powder
- 2 tbsp avocado oil
- 1 cup shredded coconut
- 1 egg, beaten
- 4 cod fillets
- Sea salt to taste

Directions:

1. Combine the pineapple, avocado, mango, lime juice, salt, and chili powder in a bowl. Dip each cod fillet in the beaten egg first, then in the shredded coconut. Warm the avocado oil in a skillet over medium heat. Place a fillet and cook for 4-5 minutes on both sides. Repeat the process until all the fillets are cook. Top with the salsa.

Nutrition Info:

- Per Serving: Calories: 370;Fat: 25g;Protein: 5g;Carbs: 20g.

Dense Oven Roasted Cod And Shiitake Mushrooms

Servings: 4 To 6
Cooking Time: 20 Minutes
Ingredients:

- 1½ pounds cod fillets
- ½ teaspoon salt, plus additional for seasoning
- Freshly ground black pepper
- 1 tablespoon extra-virgin olive oil
- 1 leek, white part only, sliced thin
- 8 ounces shiitake mushrooms, stemmed, sliced
- 1 tablespoon coconut aminos
- 1 teaspoon sweet paprika
- ½ cup vegetable broth, or chicken broth

Directions:

1. Preheat the oven to 375°F.
2. Season the cod with salt and pepper. Set aside.
3. Combine in a shallow baking dish the olive oil, leek, mushrooms, coconut aminos, paprika, and ½ teaspoon of salt. Season with pepper, and give everything a gentle toss to coat with the oil and spices.
4. For 10 minutes, place the dish in the preheated oven and bake the vegetables.
5. Stir the vegetables and place the cod fillets on top in a single layer.
6. Pour in the vegetable broth. Return the dish to the oven and bake for 10 to 15 minutes more, or until the cod is firm but cooked through.

Nutrition Info:

- Per Serving: Calories: 221 ;Fat: 6g ;Protein: 32g ;Carbs: 12g.

Sheet Pan Baked Salmon With Asparagus

Servings: 4
Cooking Time: 20 Minutes
Ingredients:

- 1 red bell pepper, sliced
- 1 lb asparagus, trimmed
- 2 tbsp olive oil
- Sea salt and pepper to taste
- 4 salmon fillets
- 1 lemon, zested and sliced

Directions:

1. Preheat your oven to 425°F. Season the asparagus and red pepper slices with salt and drizzle with olive oil. Arrange them on a sheet pan. Sprinkle salmon fillets with pepper and salt and put them skin-side down on top of the vegetables. Garnish with lemon zest and lemon slices. Place in the oven and roast for 12-15 minutes until the salmon is cooked through. Serve warm.

Nutrition Info:

- Per Serving: Calories: 310;Fat: 19g;Protein: 3g;Carbs: 6g.

Mustardy Salmon Patties

Servings: 4
Cooking Time: 25 Minutes
Ingredients:

- ½ tsp garlic powder
- 1 egg, beaten
- 1 lb ground salmon
- ¼ tsp onion powder
- ½ cup almond flour
- 1 tsp Dijon mustard
- 1 tbsp lemon juice
- ¼ tsp chili pepper, chopped
- Sea salt and pepper to taste
- 1 tbsp avocado oil

Directions:

1. Mix the garlic powder, minced salmon, onion powder, almond flour, eggs, mustard, lemon juice, chili pepper, salt, and pepper in a bowl and stir until well incorporated. Shape the mixture into four ½-inch-thick patties.
2. Heat the avocado oil in a large skillet over medium heat. Add the patties to the hot skillet and cook each side for 4-5 minutes until lightly browned and cooked through.

Nutrition Info:

- Per Serving: Calories: 250;Fat: 12g;Protein: 27g;Carbs: 4g.

Beautifully Glazed Salmon With Honey Mustard

Servings: 4
Cooking Time: 8 Minutes
Ingredients:
- 4 tablespoons honey, 90g
- 2 tablespoons Dijon mustard
- Four 4 ounces skin-on salmon fillets, 1 inch thick, pin bones removed
- Olive oil
- Kosher salt
- Freshly ground black pepper

Directions:
1. Whisk together the honey and mustard in a small bowl. Set aside.
2. Use a paper towel to rinse the salmon and pat dry. Brush all sides of each fillet with olive oil and season with a pinch each of salt and pepper.
3. Prepare a grill for direct cooking over medium-high heat to grill the salmon. Fold a 24-by-12-inch piece of aluminum foil to form a square. Crimp the edges upward to form a rim. Prick the foil several times with a fork then brush with olive oil.
4. Place the foil on the grill grate then set the salmon, skin-side down, on the foil, leaving 1 inch between each piece. For 4 minutes, close the lid and grill. Lift the lid and generously brush the fish with the honey mustard. Close the lid and grill for 2 to 3 minutes more for medium, or until the salmon is cooked to the desired doneness. Remove the salmon from the grill.
5. Place a rack in the top third of the oven and preheat the oven to broil to cook the salmon in the oven. Line a baking sheet with aluminum foil and brush with olive oil. Place the salmon, skin-side down, on the foil, leaving 1 inch between each piece. Broil for 2 minutes, then brush each fillet with the honey mustard. Continue broiling for 3 to 4 minutes more, or until the salmon is cooked to the desired doneness. Remove the salmon from the oven.
6. Brush the salmon with more honey mustard and let rest for 3 to 5 minutes before serving.

Nutrition Info:
- Per Serving: Calories: 131 ;Fat: 4g ;Protein: 8g ;Carbs: 18g .

Childhood Favourite Salmon Zoodle Casserole

Servings: 9
Cooking Time: 45 Minutes
Ingredients:
- 2 medium zucchinis
- ¼ teaspoon Himalayan salt, fine
- Béchamel:
- 1 recipe Cauliflower Alfredo
- 3 large eggs
- 1 tablespoon Dijon mustard
- 1 tablespoon red wine vinegar
- 1 teaspoon dill weed, dried
- ½ teaspoon Himalayan salt, fine
- ½ teaspoon nutmeg, ground
- ¼ teaspoon celery salt
- 1 package kelp noodles, 12 ounces
- 1 red onion, thinly sliced
- Three 6 ounces cans wild-caught or smoked salmon, boneless and skinless
- 4 slices bacon, cut into 1-inch pieces

Directions:
1. Preheat the oven to 375°F.
2. Use a spiral slicer or a vegetable peeler to slice the zucchini into noodles. Spread them out on a clean kitchen towel and sprinkle with the salt then let them sit for 10 minutes.
3. Make the béchamel. Place all of the sauce ingredients in a blender. Blend until thick and smooth on high for 30 seconds. Set aside.
4. Assemble the casserole. Drain and rinse the kelp noodles and spread them out in a 9 by 13-inch casserole dish. Add the onion slices. Wrap the zoodles up in the towel and squeeze out the excess liquid over the kitchen sink. Add the zoodles to the casserole dish with the kelp noodles and onions and toss to combine.
5. Drain the canned salmon and flake it over the noodle mixture. Pour the béchamel over the salmon and use a spatula to spread it out evenly. Note that it must get to the bottom noodles. Sprinkle the bacon pieces evenly over the casserole.
6. For 40 minutes, bake the casserole then turn on the broiler. Move the casserole dish to just under it and broil for 2 minutes to toast the top. Remove from the oven and cut into nine rectangles. Serve warm.
7. Cover the casserole dish with plastic wrap or aluminum foil and refrigerate for up to 4 days to store leftovers. Uncover and bake in a preheated 325°F oven for 15 minutes to reheat.

Nutrition Info:
- Per Serving: Calories: 218 ;Fat: 13g ;Carbs: 9g ;Fiber: 4g ;Protein: 17g

Lime-avocado Ahi Poke

Servings: 4
Cooking Time: 10 Minutes + Marinating Time
Ingredients:
- 1 lb sushi-grade ahi tuna, cubed
- 1 cucumber, sliced
- 1 large avocado, diced
- 3 tbsp coconut aminos
- 3 scallions, thinly sliced
- 1 serrano chile, minced
- 1 tsp olive oil
- 1 tsp lime juice
- 1 tsp toasted sesame seeds
- ¼ tsp ground ginger

Directions:

1. Mix the ahi tuna cubes with the coconut aminos, scallions, serrano chile, olive oil, lime juice, sesame seeds, and ginger in a large bowl. Cover the bowl with plastic wrap and marinate in the fridge for 15 minutes. Add the diced avocado to the bowl of ahi poke and stir to incorporate. Arrange the cucumber rounds on a serving plate. Spoon the ahi poke over the cucumber and serve.

Nutrition Info:

- Per Serving: Calories: 210;Fat: 15g;Protein: 9g;Carbs: 10g.

Baked Cod Fillets With Mushroom

Servings: 4
Cooking Time: 30 Minutes
Ingredients:

- 8 oz shiitake mushrooms, sliced
- 1 ½ lb cod fillets
- 1 leek, sliced thin
- Sea salt and pepper to taste
- 1 lemon, zested
- 2 tbsp extra-virgin olive oil
- 1 tbsp coconut aminos
- 1 tsp sweet paprika
- ½ cup vegetable broth

Directions:

1. Preheat your oven to 375°F. In a baking dish, combine the olive oil, leek, mushrooms, coconut aminos, lemon zest, paprika, and salt. Place the cod fillets over and sprinkle it with salt and pepper. Pour in the vegetable broth. Bake for 15-20 minutes, or until the cod is firm but cooked through. Serve and enjoy!

Nutrition Info:

- Per Serving: Calories: 220;Fat: 5g;Protein: 32g;Carbs: 12g.

Battered Bite Size Shrimp With Gluten-free Coconut

Servings: 2
Cooking Time: 15 Minutes
Ingredients:

- 2 cups shrimp, peeled and deveined
- ¼ cup coconut flour
- ½ teaspoon cayenne pepper
- 1 teaspoon garlic powder
- 2 free range eggs, beaten
- ½ cup coconut, shredded
- ¼ cup almond flour
- a pinch of black pepper
- 1 cup arugula or watercress

Directions:

1. Preheat oven to 400°F.
2. Line a baking sheet with parchment paper.
3. In a bowl, mix the coconut flour, cayenne pepper, and garlic powder.
4. Whisk the eggs in another bowl.

5. Add the shredded coconut, almond flour and pepper in a separate bowl.
6. Dip the shrimp into each dish in consecutive order then place on the baking sheet. Bake for 10 to 15 minutes or until cooked through.
7. Serve piping hot and straight from the oven with a side salad of arugula or watercress.

Nutrition Info:

- Per Serving: Calories: 166 ;Fat: 10g ;Protein: 11g ;Carbs: 8g.

Simple Tacos With Fish And Pineapple Salsa

Servings: 6
Cooking Time: 12 Minutes
Ingredients:

- Salsa:
- 1½ cups fresh, or canned, pineapple chunks, cut into small dice
- 1 small red onion, minced
- Juice of 1 lime
- Zest of 1 lime
- Tacos:
- 1 head romaine lettuce
- 3 tablespoons coconut oil
- 14 ounces white fish, skinless and firm, such as cod or halibut
- Juice of 1 lime
- Zest of 1 lime
- ½ teaspoon salt

Directions:

1. Stir together the pineapple and onion in a medium bowl. Add the lime juice and lime zest. Stir well and set aside.
2. Separate the lettuce leaves, choosing the 6 to 12 largest and most suitable to hold the filling. Wash the leaves and pat them dry.
3. Heat the coconut oil in a large pan set over medium-low heat.
4. Brush the fish with lime juice and lime zest. Sprinkle with salt.
5. Place the fish in the pan. Cook for 8 minutes.
6. Flip the fish over and break it up into small pieces. Cook for 3 to 4 minutes more. The flesh should be opaque and flake easily with a fork.
7. Fill the lettuce leaves with the cooked fish and spoon the salsa over the top.

Nutrition Info:

- Per Serving: Calories: 198 ;Fat: 9g ;Protein: 19g ;Carbs: 12g.

Shrimp With Spiralized Veggies

Servings: 4
Cooking Time: 25 Minutes
Ingredients:
- 2 tbsp olive oil
- 1 lb shrimp, deveined
- 1 yellow squash, spiralized
- 1 large zucchini, spiralized
- ¼ cup coconut milk
- ½ cup fresh basil leaves
- 1 lemon, juiced and zested
- 1 garlic clove, minced
- Sea salt and pepper to taste

Directions:
1. Warm the olive oil in a skillet over medium heat. Stir-fry the shrimp for 2-3 minutes. Add the spiralized vegetables and sauté for another 3-4 minutes. Set aside.
2. Blitz the basil leaves, lemon juice, garlic, salt, and pepper in your food processor until chopped thoroughly. Slowly pour in coconut milk while the processor is still running. Pulse until smooth. Pour the sauce over the veggies and shrimp and toss to coat. Scatter lemon zest on top. Serve.

Nutrition Info:
- Per Serving: Calories: 245;Fat: 12g;Protein: 27g;Carbs: 5g.

Tarragon Scallops

Servings: 1
Cooking Time: 10 Minutes
Ingredients:
- 2 garlic cloves, minced
- 1 red chili, minced
- 8 king scallops
- 1 tbsp olive oil
- Juice of ½ lime
- 2 tbsp chopped tarragon

Directions:
1. Warm the olive oil in a skillet over medium heat and fry scallops for about 1 minute per side until lightly golden. Add the chopped chili and garlic cloves to the pan and squeeze the lime juice over the scallops. Saute for 2-3 minutes. Sprinkle the tarragon over the top and serve.

Nutrition Info:
- Per Serving: Calories: 235;Fat: 15g;Protein: 15g;Carbs: 13g.

Famous Herbaceous Sardines With Citrus

Servings: 2
Cooking Time: 15 Minutes
Ingredients:
- 10 sardines, scaled and cleaned
- 2 whole lemons, zest
- handful flat-leaf parsley, chopped
- 2 garlic cloves, finely chopped
- ½ cup black olives, pitted and halved
- 3 tablespoons olive oil
- 1 can tomatoes, chopped
- ½ can chickpeas or butter beans, drained and rinsed
- 8 cherry tomatoes, halved
- a pinch of black pepper

Directions:
1. Add the lemon zest to the chopped parsley and half of the chopped garlic in a bowl. Remember to save a pinch of chopped parsley for garnishing.
2. Put a very large skillet on the hob and heat on high.
3. Now add the oil and once very hot, lay the sardines flat on the pan.
4. Sauté for 3 minutes until golden at the bottom then turn over to fry for another 3 minutes. Place onto a plate to rest.
5. Sauté the remaining garlic for a minute until soft. Pour in the tin of chopped tomatoes, mix and let simmer for 4 to 5 minutes.
6. Go straight to chickpeas if you're avoiding using tomatoes.
7. Tip in the chickpeas or butter beans and fresh tomatoes and stir until heated through.
8. Add the sardines into the lemon and parsley dressing prepared earlier and add to the pan then cook for 3 to 4 minutes more.
9. Serve with a pinch of parsley and remaining lemon zest to garnish once heated through.

Nutrition Info:
- Per Serving: Calories: 473 ;Fat: 32g ;Protein: 22g ;Carbs: 27g .

Sardine & Butter Bean Meal

Servings: 2
Cooking Time: 20 Minutes
Ingredients:
- ½ cup cooked butter beans
- 1 red chili, sliced
- 10 sardines, scaled and cleaned
- 2 lemons, zested
- 2 tbsp parsley, chopped
- 2 garlic cloves, chopped
- ½ cup black olives
- 3 tbsp olive oil
- 2 diced tomatoes

Directions:
1. Mix the lemon zest, red chili, and parsley in a bowl; reserve. Warm the olive oil in a skillet over medium heat and lay the sardines flat on the pan. Saute for 3 minutes until golden underneath and turn over to fry for another 3 minutes. Remove to a plate. Sauté the garlic in the same skillet for 1 minute until softened. Pour in the diced tomatoes and olives and simmer for 4-5 minutes. Tip in the butter beans and tomatoes and stir until heated through. Add the sardines and continue cooking for a further 3-4 minutes. Top with chili dressing and serve.

Nutrition Info:

- Per Serving: Calories: 455;Fat: 31g;Protein: 22g;Carbs: 23g.

Spicy Aromatic Bowl Of Cod

Servings: 2
Cooking Time: 4 Minutes
Ingredients:
- 2 black cod fillets
- a pinch of black pepper
- 1 teaspoon reduced sodium soy sauce
- 2 cups homemade chicken broth
- 1 teaspoon coconut oil
- 1 teaspoon five-spice powder
- 1 tablespoon olive oil
- 3 heads of bok choy
- 1 carrot, sliced
- 1 tablespoon ginger, minced
- 2 cups of udon noodles
- 1 green onion, thinly sliced
- 2 teaspoons cilantro, finely chopped
- 1 teaspoon sesame seeds

Directions:
1. Use pepper to rub the fish.
2. Combine pepper, soy sauce, 1 cup chicken broth, coconut oil and spice blend in a bowl. Mix together and place on one side.
3. Heat the oil in a large saucepan on a medium heat and cook the boy choy, ginger and carrot for 2 minutes until the bok choy appears green.
4. Add the rest of the reserved chicken stock and heat through.
5. Add the udon noodles and stir, bringing to a simmer.
6. Add the green onion and the fish and cook for 10 to 15 minutes until it is tender.
7. Into serving bowls, Add the fish, noodles and vegetables and pour the broth over the top.
8. Garnish with the cilantro and sesame seeds and serve with chopsticks if preferred.

Nutrition Info:
- Per Serving: Calories: 801 ;Fat: 28g ;Protein: 78g ;Carbs: 55g.

Pan-seared Salmon Au Pistou

Servings: 3
Cooking Time: 30 Minutes
Ingredients:
- 2 garlic cloves
- 1 cup fresh oregano leaves
- ¼ cup almonds
- 1 lime, juiced and zested
- Zest of 1 lime
- 2 tbsp extra-virgin olive oil
- 1 tsp turmeric
- 4 salmon fillets
- Sea salt and pepper to taste

Directions:
1. Spritz oregano, almonds, garlic, lime juice, lime zest, 1 tbsp of oil, salt, and pepper in your blender until finely chopped. Transfer the pistou to a bowl and set it aside.
2. Preheat your oven to 400ºF. Lightly season the salmon with salt and pepper. Warm the remaining olive oil in a skillet over medium heat and add the salmon. Sear for 4 minutes per side. Place the skillet in the oven and bake the fish for about 10 minutes, or until it is just cooked through. Serve the salmon topped with pistou.

Nutrition Info:
- Per Serving: Calories: 460;Fat: 25g;Protein: 48g;Carbs: 8g.

Creamy Crabmeat

Servings: 4
Cooking Time: 15 Minutes
Ingredients:
- ¼ cup olive oil
- 1 small red onion, chopped
- 1 lb lump crabmeat
- ½ celery stalk, chopped
- ½ cup plain yogurt
- ¼ cup chicken broth

Directions:
1. Season the crabmeat with some salt and pepper. Heat the oil in your Instant Pot on "Sauté". Add celery and onion and cook for 3 minutes, or until soft. Add the crabmeat and stir in the broth. Seal and lock the lid and set to "Steam" for 5 minutes on high pressure. Once the cooking is complete, do a quick release and carefully open the lid. Stir in the yogurt and serve.

Nutrition Info:
- Per Serving: Calories: 450;Fat: 10g;Protein: 40g;Carbs: 12g.

Mediterranean Salmon

Servings: 4
Cooking Time: 15 Minutes
Ingredients:
- 4 salmon fillets
- 2 tbsp olive oil
- 1 rosemary sprig
- 1 cup cherry tomatoes
- 15 oz asparagus

Directions:
1. Pour 1 cup of water into the Instant Pot and insert the steamer rack. Place the salmon on the steamer rack skin side down, rub with rosemary, and arrange the asparagus on top. Seal the lid and cook on "Manual" for 4 minutes. Perform a quick pressure release and carefully open the lid. Add in the cherry tomatoes on top and cook for another 2 minutes. Perform a quick pressure release. Serve drizzled with olive oil.

Nutrition Info:
- Per Serving: Calories: 475;Fat: 32g;Protein: 43g;Carbs: 6g.

Scallops With Capers

Servings: 4
Cooking Time: 35 Minutes
Ingredients:
- 2 garlic cloves, thinly sliced
- 1 ½ lb sea scallops, cleaned
- 2 tbsp olive oil
- 1 tbsp capers
- 10 oz fresh spinach
- Sea salt and pepper to taste

Directions:
1. Warm 1 tbsp of olive oil in a skillet over medium heat. Lightly season the scallops with salt and pepper. Pan-sear the scallops for about 2 minutes per side, or until opaque and just cooked through. Transfer to a plate and cover loosely with aluminum foil to keep them warm.
2. Wipe the skillet with a paper towel and place it back on the heat. Warm the remaining olive oil and sauté the garlic for about 4 minutes or until caramelized. Stir in spinach and cook for about 3-4 minutes or until tender and wilted. Top with capers and scallops. Serve warm.

Nutrition Info:
- Per Serving: Calories: 230;Fat: 9g;Protein: 29g;Carbs: 9g.

Scallops & Mussels Cauliflower Paella

Servings: 4
Cooking Time: 20 Minutes
Ingredients:
- 1 red bell pepper, diced
- 1 tbsp coconut oil
- 1 cup scallops
- 2 cups mussels
- 1 onion, diced
- 2 cups ground cauliflower
- 2 cups fish stock
- A pinch of turmeric

Directions:
1. Press the Sauté button on the Instant Pot and melt the coconut oil. Add the onion and bell pepper and cook for about 4 minutes. Stir in scallops and turmeric and cook for 2 minutes. Stir in the remaining ingredients and close the lid. Cook for 6 minutes on "Manual" on high pressure. Once cooked, release a quick pressure. Serve.

Nutrition Info:
- Per Serving: Calories: 155;Fat: 5g;Protein: 7g;Carbs: 12g.

Unforgettable Tasty Calamari

Servings: 4
Cooking Time: 20 Minutes
Ingredients:
- 1 cup coconut oil, or more if needed
- ½ cup coconut flour
- 1 teaspoon Himalayan salt, fine
- 1 teaspoon black pepper, ground
- 3 large eggs
- 1 tablespoon red wine vinegar
- 1 cup shredded coconut, unsweetened
- 1 pound cleaned calamari tubes, sliced into ½-inch rings
- Serving:
- 2 limes, cut into wedges
- ½ cup Ginger Sauce
- ½ cup Roasted Beet Marinara

Directions:
1. Set a cooling rack on a sheet pan or line a plate with paper towels.
2. Heat an 8-inch heavy-bottomed pot or skillet over medium heat. Add the coconut oil, it should be 1 inch deep, Heat the oil until it sizzles around the end of a wooden spoon handle when it's inserted in the oil.
3. Bread the calamari while the oil heats. Combine the coconut flour, salt, and pepper in a large bowl. Whisk the eggs with the vinegar in a separate bowl. Place the shredded coconut in another bowl.
4. Add the calamari to the bowl with the flour mixture and toss to coat. Remove half of the calamari and place in a colander then shake to remove the excess flour.
5. Dredge the calamari from the colander by working with three or four rings at a time in the egg mixture and in the shredded coconut. Place it in the skillet with the hot oil. Fry until golden all over, turning once, for 4 minutes. To remove the crispy rings from the oil, use tongs then place on the cooling rack or paper towel–lined plate.
6. Repeat until the breaded calamari are all done. The eggs and shredded coconut should be done by no. Remove the rest of the calamari from the coconut flour and shake to remove the excess flour.
7. Fry all the coconut flour–coated rings together for 5 to 6 minutes, turning and stirring occasionally until they're golden around the edges and all of it are rounded. Remove from the oil and set to drain next to the twice-breaded batch.
8. Serve right away with lime wedges and dipping sauces.
9. Place the calamari on a cooling rack over a sheet pan and store in the oven for up to an hour. Gently heat right before serving at 300°F for 8 to 10 minutes.

Nutrition Info:
- Per Serving: Calories: 422 ;Fat: 19g ;Protein: 36g ;Carbs: 12g .

Trout Fillets With Almond Crust

Servings: 4
Cooking Time: 20 Minutes
Ingredients:
- ½ cup whole-wheat breadcrumbs
- 2 trout fillets
- 1 tbsp extra-virgin olive oil
- 1 tsp Italian seasoning
- 1 lemon, juiced and zested
- ½ cup chopped almonds

Directions:

1. Preheat your oven to 375ºF. Mix breadcrumbs, Italian seasoning, lemon zest, lemon juice, and half of the almonds in a shallow dish. Lay the fillets skin side down onto the oiled baking tray and then flip over so that both sides of your fish are coated in the oil. Roll the fillets into the nut mixture on both sides to coat. Return to the baking tray. Bake for 6-7 minutes on each side and serve.

Nutrition Info:

- Per Serving: Calories: 870;Fat: 50g;Protein: 51g;Carbs: 56g.

Fried Haddock With Roasted Beets

Servings: 4
Cooking Time: 50 Minutes
Ingredients:

- 4 peeled beets, cut into wedges
- 4 haddock fillets
- 2 shallots, thinly sliced
- 2 tbsp apple cider vinegar
- 2 tbsp olive oil, divided
- 1 tsp minced garlic
- 1 tsp chopped mint
- Sea salt to taste

Directions:

1. Preheat your oven to 400ºF. Place the beets, shallots, vinegar, 1 tablespoon of olive oil, garlic, thyme, and sea salt in a medium bowl and toss to coat well. Spread out the beet mixture on a baking dish. Roast in the preheated oven for about 30 minutes, turning once or twice with a spatula, or until the beets are tender.

2. Warm the remaining olive oil in a skillet over medium heat. Add the haddock and sear each side for 4-5 minutes, or until the flesh is opaque and it flakes apart easily. Top with roasted beets.

Nutrition Info:

- Per Serving: Calories: 340;Fat: 9g;Protein: 37g;Carbs: 20g.

Shrimp & Egg Risotto

Servings: 6
Cooking Time: 40 Minutes
Ingredients:

- 4 cups water
- 4 garlic cloves, minced
- 2 eggs, beaten
- ½ tsp grated ginger
- 3 tbsp olive oil
- ¼ tsp cayenne pepper
- 1 ½ cups frozen peas
- 2 cups brown rice
- ¼ cup soy sauce
- 1 cup chopped onion
- 12 oz peeled shrimp, thawed

Directions:

1. Heat the olive oil in your Instant Pot on "Sauté". Add the onion and garlic and cook for 2 minutes. Stir in the remaining ingredients except for the shrimp and eggs.

2. Close the lid and cook on "Manual" for 20 minutes. Wait about 10 minutes before doing a quick release. Stir in the shrimp and eggs. And let them heat for a couple of seconds with the lid off. Serve and enjoy!

Nutrition Info:

- Per Serving: Calories: 220;Fat: 10g;Protein: 13g;Carbs: 20g.

Crispy Coconut Prawns

Servings: 2
Cooking Time: 25 Minutes
Ingredients:

- 1 lb prawns, peeled and deveined
- ¼ cup coconut flour
- ½ tsp cayenne pepper
- 1 tsp garlic powder
- 2 beaten eggs
- ½ cup shredded coconut
- ¼ cup almond flour
- Black pepper to taste

Directions:

1. Preheat your oven to 400ºF. Blend the coconut flour, cayenne pepper, and garlic powder in a bowl. In a separate bowl, whisk the eggs. In a third bowl, add the shredded coconut, almond flour and black pepper. Dip the prawns into each dish in consecutive order, and then place a parchment-lined baking sheet. Bake for 10-15 minutes or until cooked through. Serve and enjoy!

Nutrition Info:

- Per Serving: Calories: 475;Fat: 15g;Protein: 54g;Carbs: 30g.

Extraordinary Scallops With Lime And Cilantro

Servings: 1
Cooking Time: 5 Minutes
Ingredients:

- 8 queen or king scallops
- 1 tablespoon extra sesame oil
- 2 large garlic cloves, finely chopped
- 1 red chili, finely chopped
- ½ lime juice
- 2 tablespoons cilantro, chopped
- a pinch of black pepper

Directions:

1. Heat oil in a skillet on a medium to high heat and fry scallops for a minute on each side until lightly golden.

2. Add the chopped chili and garlic cloves to the pan and squeeze the lime juice over the scallops. Sauté for 2-3 minutes.

3. Remove the scallops and sprinkle the cilantro over the top to serve.

Nutrition Info:

- Per Serving: Calories: 153 ;Fat: 14g ;Protein: 1g ;Carbs: 8g .

Almond-crusted Tilapia

Servings: 4
Cooking Time: 20 Minutes
Ingredients:
- 4 tilapia fillets
- 2 tbsp sliced almonds
- 2 tbsp Dijon mustard
- 1 tsp olive oil
- ¼ tsp black pepper

Directions:
1. Pour 1 cup of water in your Instant Pot. Mix the olive oil, pepper, and mustard in a small bowl. Brush the fish fillets with the mustardy mixture on all sides. Coat the fish in almonds slices. Place the rack in your pot and arrange the fish fillets on it. Close the lid and cook for 5 minutes on "Manual" setting on High pressure. Do a quick pressure release and serve immediately.

Nutrition Info:
- Per Serving: Calories: 330;Fat: 15g;Protein: 46g;Carbs: 4g.

Rosemary Salmon With Orange Glaze

Servings: 4
Cooking Time: 30 Minutes
Ingredients:
- 2 tsp chopped rosemary
- 2 oranges, juiced
- 1 orange, zested
- ¼ cup pure maple syrup
- 2 tsp low-sodium soy sauce
- 1 tsp garlic powder
- 4 salmon fillets

Directions:
1. Preheat your oven to 400°F. Mix the orange juice, orange zest, maple syrup, soy sauce, and garlic powder in a bowl. Add in salmon pieces, flesh-side down, and let marinate for 10 minutes. Transfer each piece skin-side up to a lined baking sheet and bake for 15 minutes until the salmon is lightly browned. Garnish with rosemary and serve.

Nutrition Info:
- Per Serving: Calories: 300;Fat: 12g;Protein: 1g;Carbs: 19g.

Fancy Cod Stew With Cauliflower

Servings: 4
Cooking Time: 30 Minutes
Ingredients:
- 3 cups water
- 1 large cauliflower head, broken into large florets (about 4 cups)
- 1 cup cashews, soaked in water for at least 4 hours
- 1 teaspoon salt
- 1 pound cod, cut into chunks

- 2 cups kale, thoroughly washed and sliced

Directions:
1. Bring the water to a boil in a large pot set over high heat. Reduce the heat to medium.
2. Add the cauliflower. For 12 minutes, cook until tender.
3. Drain and rinse the cashews and place them in a blender.
4. Add the cooked cauliflower and its cooking water to the blender.
5. Add the salt.
6. Blend until smooth. Add more water if you prefer a thinner consistency.
7. Return the blended cauliflower-cashew mixture to the pot. Place the pot over medium heat.
8. Add the cod. Cook for about 15 minutes, or until cooked through.
9. Add the kale. Let it wilt for 3 minutes.

Nutrition Info:
- Per Serving: Calories: 385 ;Fat: 17g ;Protein: 36g ;Carbs: 26g.

Japanese Salmon Cakes

Servings: 2
Cooking Time: 15 Minutes
Ingredients:
- 1 beaten egg
- 1 cup canned wild salmon,
- 2 spring onions, chopped
- ½ tsp honey
- 1 lime, zested
- 2 tsp reduced-salt soy sauce
- 1 tsp wasabi powder
- 2 tbsp coconut oil
- 1 tbsp ginger, minced

Directions:
1. Combine the salmon, egg, ginger, and lime zest, spring onions in a bowl and mix with your hands. Shape the mixture into 4 patties. In a separate bowl, add wasabi powder, soy sauce, and honey and whisk until blended.
2. Warm the coconut oil over medium heat in a skillet and cook the patties for 4 minutes until firm and browned on each side. Glaze the top of each patty with the wasabi mixture and cook for another 15 seconds. Serve.

Nutrition Info:
- Per Serving: Calories: 550;Fat: 30g;Protein: 67g;Carbs: 4g.

Greek-style Sea Bass

Servings: 4
Cooking Time: 25 Minutes
Ingredients:
- 4 sea bass fillets
- 1 small onion, diced
- ½ cup vegetable broth
- 1 cup canned diced tomatoes
- ½ cup chopped black olives
- 2 tbsp capers, drained

- 2 cups packed spinach
- 2 tbsp extra-virgin olive oil
- Sea salt and pepper to taste
- 1 tsp Greek oregano

Directions:

1. Preheat your oven to 375ºF. Coat the fish with olive oil in a baking dish Season with Greek oregano, salt, and pepper. Top the fish with the onion, broth, tomatoes, olives, capers, spinach, salt, and pepper. Cover the baking dish with aluminum foil and place it in the oven. Bake for 15 minutes, or until the fish is cooked through. Serve.

Nutrition Info:

- Per Serving: Calories: 275;Fat: 12g;Protein: 34g;Carbs: 5g.

Gingery Sea Bass

Servings: 2
Cooking Time: 15 Minutes
Ingredients:

- 2 spring onions, sliced
- 2 sea bass fillets
- 1 tsp black pepper
- 1 tbsp extra-virgin olive oil
- 1 tsp grated ginger
- 1 garlic clove, thinly sliced
- 1 red chili, thinly sliced
- 1 lime, zested

Directions:

1. Warm the olive oil in a skillet over medium heat. Sprinkle black pepper over the fish and score the skin of the fish a few times with a sharp knife. Add the sea bass fillet to the skillet with the skin side down. Cook for 5 minutes and turn over. Cook for a further 2 minutes; reserve.

2. Add the chili, garlic, and ginger to the same skillet and cook for 2 minutes or until golden. Remove from the heat and add the spring onions. Scatter the vegetables and lime zest over your sea bass and serve.

Nutrition Info:

- Per Serving: Calories: 205;Fat: 10g;Protein: 24g;Carbs: 5g.

Baked Tilapia With Chili Kale

Servings: 2
Cooking Time: 20 Minutes
Ingredients:

- ½ cup whole-grain breadcrumbs
- ½ cup ground hazelnuts
- 2 tilapia fillets, skinless
- 2 tsp extra-virgin olive oil
- 2 tsp whole-grain mustard
- 5 oz kale, chopped
- 1 red chili, sliced
- 1 clove garlic, mashed

Directions:

1. Preheat your oven to 350ºF. Combine the hazelnuts and breadcrumbs in a bowl. Spread a thin layer of mustard over

the fish and then dip into the breadcrumb mixture. Transfer to a greased baking dish. Bake for 12 minutes or until cooked through. Warm the olive oil in a skillet over medium heat and sauté the garlic for 30 seconds. Add the kale and red chili and cook for 5 more minutes. Serve fish with the kale on the side.

Nutrition Info:

- Per Serving: Calories: 540;Fat: 32g;Protein: 35g;Carbs: 29g.

Aromatic Curried Whitefish

Servings: 4 To 6
Cooking Time: 15 Minutes
Ingredients:

- 2 tablespoons coconut oil
- 1 onion, chopped
- 2 garlic cloves, minced
- 1 tablespoon fresh ginger, minced
- 2 teaspoons curry powder
- 1 teaspoon salt
- ¼ teaspoon black pepper, freshly ground
- 1 piece lemongrass, bruised, 4 inch, and white part only
- 2 cups butternut squash, cubed
- 2 cups broccoli, chopped
- 1 can coconut milk, 13 ½ ounces
- 1 cup vegetable broth, or chicken broth
- 1 pound whitefish fillets, firm
- ¼ cup fresh cilantro, chopped
- 1 scallion, sliced thin
- Lemon wedges

Directions:

1. Melt the coconut oil in a large pot over medium-high heat. Add the onion, garlic, ginger, curry powder, salt, and pepper. Sauté for 5 minutes.

2. Add the lemongrass, butternut squash, and broccoli. Sauté for 2 minutes more.

3. Stir in the coconut milk and vegetable broth and bring to a boil. Reduce the heat to simmer and add the fish. Cover the pot and simmer for 5 minutes, or until the fish is cooked through. Remove the lemongrass.

4. Into a serving bowl, ladle the curry. Garnish with the cilantro and scallion and serve with the lemon wedges.

Nutrition Info:

- Per Serving: Calories: 553 ;Fat: 39g ;Protein: 34g ;Carbs: 22g .

Mango Halibut Curry

Servings: 4
Cooking Time: 20 Minutes
Ingredients:

- 1 tbsp olive oil
- 2 tbsp mango chutney
- 2 tsp ground turmeric
- 2 tsp curry powder
- 1 ½ lb halibut, cubed
- 4 cups chicken broth

- 1 can coconut milk
- Sea salt and pepper to taste
- 2 tbsp cilantro, chopped
- 1 red chili pepper, sliced

Directions:

1. Warm the olive oil in a skillet over medium heat and place in the turmeric and curry powder and cook for 2 minutes. Stir in halibut, chicken broth, coconut milk, mango chutney, salt, and pepper. Bring to a simmer, then cook for 6-7 minutes over low heat until the halibut is opaque and cooked through. Spoon into bowls and top with finely chopped cilantro and chili slices. Enjoy!

Nutrition Info:

- Per Serving: Calories: 430;Fat: 48g;Protein: 1g;Carbs: 6g.

Baked Garlicky Halibut With Lemon

Servings: 2
Cooking Time: 15 Minutes
Ingredients:

- 2 halibut fillets
- a pinch of black pepper
- 2 garlic cloves, pressed
- 2 tablespoons olive oil
- 2 tablespoons low fat Greek yogurt
- 4 lemon wedges

Directions:

1. Preheat the oven to 400°F.
2. Season with pepper and add to a parchment paper-lined baking dish.
3. Scatter the garlic cloves around the fish and drizzle with the oil.
4. Squeeze the lemon juice over the fish.
5. Bake for 15 minutes until the fish is firm and well cooked.
6. Serve and pour over the juices for a delicious garlic feast.

Nutrition Info:

- Per Serving: Calories: 410 ;Fat: 29g ;Protein: 21g ;Carbs: 18g ;.

Sea Scallops In Citrus Dressing

Servings: 4
Cooking Time: 20 Minutes
Ingredients:

- 4 tbsp olive oil
- 1½ lb sea scallops
- Sea salt and pepper to taste
- 1 lemon, zested and juiced
- 1 pink grapefruit, juiced
- 1 tbsp raw honey

Directions:

1. Warm 2 tbsp of the olive oil in a skillet over medium heat. Sprinkle scallops with salt and pepper. Place the scallops in the skillet and cook for 6 minutes on both sides until opaque. Combine the lemon juice and zest, honey,

remaining olive oil, grapefruit juice, and salt in a jar. Close with a lid and shake well to combine. Drizzle the dressing over the scallops and serve.

Nutrition Info:

- Per Serving: Calories: 290;Fat: 17g;Protein: 0g;Carbs: 6g.

Persian Saucy Sole

Servings: 4
Cooking Time: 40 Minutes
Ingredients:

- 1 red onion, chopped
- 2 tsp minced garlic
- 1 tsp grated fresh ginger
- ¼ tsp turmeric
- 2 lb sole fillets
- Sea salt to taste
- 2 tbsp lemon juice
- 1 tbsp coconut oil
- 1 cup canned coconut milk
- 2 tbsp chopped cilantro

Directions:

1. Preheat your oven to 350°F. Place the fillets in a baking dish. Sprinkle it with salt and lemon juice. Roast the fish for 10 minutes. Warm the coconut oil in a pan over medium heat. Add the red onion, garlic, and ginger and sauté for about 3 minutes, or until softened.
2. Stir in coconut milk and turmeric. Bring to a boil. Reduce the heat to low and simmer the sauce for 5 minutes. Remove the skillet from the heat. Pour the sauce over the fish. Cover and bake for about 10 minutes, or until the fish flakes easily with a fork. Top with cilantro and serve.

Nutrition Info:

- Per Serving: Calories: 350;Fat: 20g;Protein: 29g;Carbs: 6g.

Hawaiian Tuna

Servings: 4
Cooking Time: 35 Minutes
Ingredients:

- 2 lb tuna, cubed
- 1 cup pineapple chunks
- ¼ cup chopped cilantro
- 2 tbsp chopped parsley
- 2 garlic cloves, minced
- 1 tbsp coconut oil
- 1 tbsp coconut aminos
- Sea salt and pepper to taste

Directions:

1. Preheat your oven to 400°F. Add the tuna, pineapple, cilantro, parsley, garlic, coconut aminos, salt, and pepper to a baking dish and stir to coat. Bake for 15-20 minutes, or until the fish feels firm to the touch. Serve warm.

Nutrition Info:

- Per Serving: Calories: 410;Fat: 15g;Protein: 59g;Carbs: 7g.

Baked Swordfish With Cilantro And Pineapple

Servings: 4
Cooking Time: 20 Minutes
Ingredients:
- 1 tablespoon coconut oil
- 2 pounds swordfish, or other firm white fish, cut into 2-inch pieces
- 1 cup pineapple chunks, fresh
- ¼ cup fresh cilantro, chopped
- 2 tablespoons fresh parsley, chopped
- 2 garlic cloves, minced
- 1 tablespoon coconut aminos
- 1 teaspoon salt
- ¼ teaspoon black pepper, freshly ground

Directions:
1. Preheat the oven to 400°F.
2. Grease a baking dish with the coconut oil.
3. Add the swordfish, pineapple, cilantro, parsley, garlic, coconut aminos, salt, and pepper to the dish and mix gently the ingredients together.
4. In the preheated oven, place the dish and bake for 15 to 20 minutes, or until the fish feels firm to the touch. Serve warm.

Nutrition Info:
- Per Serving: Calories: 408 ;Fat: 16g ;Protein: 60g ;Carbs: 7g.

Cute Mini Lobster Mac Skillet

Servings: 4
Cooking Time: 20 Minutes
Ingredients:
- Sauce:
- 1½ tablespoons cooking fat
- ½ red onion, diced
- 2 medium carrots, diced
- 5 cloves garlic, minced
- 1 cup bone broth
- 2 tablespoons nutritional yeast
- 1 tablespoon red wine vinegar
- 1 large egg
- 1½ tablespoons cooking fat
- 1 pound broccoli, cut into florets about 3 cups
- 2 tablespoons coconut butter, divided
- 1-pound langostino tails, precooked
- 1 teaspoon Dijon mustard
- 1 teaspoon Himalayan salt, fine
- 1 teaspoon black pepper, ground
- ¼ teaspoon nutmeg, ground
- 3 slices bacon, chopped
- ¼ cup Pickled Red Onions

Directions:
1. Preheat the oven to 400°F.
2. Make the sauce. Heat a large oven-safe skillet over medium heat. Place the cooking fat in it when it's hot then add the onions, carrots, and garlic. Sauté until translucent for 5 minutes. Add the broth, cover, and simmer for 5 minutes or until the carrots are very tender. Mash it with a spoon.
3. Transfer everything from the skillet to a blender or food processor. Add the nutritional yeast and vinegar and blend until smooth. Add the egg and blend until completely smooth with the blender running on low. Set aside.
4. Put the skillet back on the stove over medium heat and add the 1½ tablespoons of fat. Add the broccoli florets and 1 tablespoon of the coconut butter and stir to fully combine and sauté for 2 minutes. Add the langostino tails, mustard, salt, pepper, and nutmeg. Sauté while stirring frequently for 2 minutes.
5. Mix in the sauce. Top with the remaining tablespoon of coconut butter, the bacon, and the pickled onions. Set the skillet on the middle rack of the oven and bake for 8 to 10 minutes, until the bacon is crispy then serve.
6. Store them in an airtight container in the fridge for up to 5 days. Sauté over high heat for 5 minutes to reheat.

Nutrition Info:
- Per Serving: Calories: 348 ;Fat: 23g ;Protein: 27g ;Carbs: 7g .

Seared Salmon With Gremolata

Servings: 4
Cooking Time: 30 Minutes
Ingredients:
- 1 bag mixed greens
- 1 cucumber, sliced thin
- 1 cup watercress
- 4 salmon fillets
- 3 tsp extra-virgin olive oil
- 1 lemon, juiced and zested
- Sea salt and pepper to taste
- 1 bunch basil
- 1 garlic clove

Directions:
1. Preheat your oven to 375°F. Brush the salmon fillets with some olive oil and season with salt and pepper. Place in a baking dish. Add the lemon juice. Bake the fillets for about 20 minutes, or until firm and cooked through.
2. Blend the basil, garlic, and lemon zest in your food processor until everything is coarsely chopped. Arrange the greens, cucumber, and watercress on a serving platter. Drizzle them with the remaining olive oil and season with salt and pepper. Place the salmon fillets on top of the greens and spread the gremolata over the salmon.

Nutrition Info:
- Per Serving: Calories: 275;Fat: 12g;Protein: 33g;Carbs: 10g.

Mediterranean Trout

Servings: 2
Cooking Time: 30 Minutes
Ingredients:
- 2 trout fillets
- ¼ cup juice
- 2 tsp olive oil
- 3 tbsp capers
- Sea salt and pepper to taste
- 1 lemon, juiced and zested

Directions:
1. Warm the olive oil in a skillet over medium heat. Add the trout fillets and cook for 3 minutes per side, or until the center is flaky. Set aside. Add the lemon juice, zest, capers, salt, and pepper to the skillet and cook for 2-3 more minutes. Spoon the sauce over the fish. Serve.

Nutrition Info:
- Per Serving: Calories: 300;Fat: 21g;Protein: 22g;Carbs: 9g.

Parsnip & Tilapia Bake

Servings: 4
Cooking Time: 55 Minutes
Ingredients:
- 2 cups diced parsnip
- 4 onion wedges
- 2 cups diced carrot
- 1 cup asparagus pieces
- 2 tsp cayenne pepper
- 1 tsp minced garlic
- ¼ tsp sea salt
- 2 tbsp olive oil
- 4 skinless tilapia fillets
- Juice of 1 lemon

Directions:
1. Preheat your oven to 350ºF. Take 4 pieces of aluminum foil and fold each piece in half to make four pieces. In a mixing bowl, toss together the sweet potato wedges, carrot, parsnip, onion, asparagus, cayenne pepper, garlic, salt, and olive oil. Place one-fourth of the vegetables in the center of each foil piece. Top each vegetable mound with one tilapia fillet. Sprinkle the fish with lemon juice.
2. Fold the foil to create sealed packages with a bit of space at the top, and arrange the packets on a baking sheet. Bake for about 30 minutes, or until the fish begins to flake and the vegetables are tender. Serve and enjoy!

Nutrition Info:
- Per Serving: Calories: 350;Fat: 5g;Protein: 35g;Carbs: 45g.

Saucy And Natural Flavoured Golden Seared Scallops With Wilted Bacon Spinach

Servings: 2
Cooking Time: 30 Minutes

Ingredients:
- Spinach:
- 4 slices bacon, diced
- 1 small onion, diced
- 1 sprig rosemary, fresh
- ¼ teaspoon nutmeg, ground
- ½ pound baby spinach
- 2 tablespoons bone broth
- 1 tablespoon nutritional yeast
- 2 teaspoons garlic, granulated
- ¼ teaspoon Himalayan salt, fine
- Scallops:
- 1 tablespoon lard
- 8 jumbo scallops
- 1 teaspoon Himalayan salt, fine
- ½ teaspoon turmeric powder
- 2 tablespoons coconut aminos
- 2 tablespoons bone broth

Directions:
1. Cook the spinach by placing the bacon in a large skillet over medium heat. Let it cook undisturbed until it begins to sizzle for 3 minutes. Add the onions, rosemary, and nutmeg. Cook while stirring occasionally for 15 minutes until the bacon is crispy and the onions are translucent. Remove the rosemary sprig. Transfer half of the bacon-and-onion mixture to a dish and set for garnishing.
2. Add the spinach to the skillet a fistful at a time and let each fistful wilt before adding more. Mix in the broth, nutritional yeast, granulated garlic, and salt. Bring to a simmer and cook then stir continuously for 2 minutes.
3. In a large bowl, transfer the spinach mixture cover and set aside but keep it close to the stove to stay warm.
4. Cook the scallops. Wipe the skillet with a paper towel and set it back on the burner over medium heat. Let it heat for 1 to 2 minutes then add the lard. Lay the scallops on a cutting board and pat them dry with a paper towel or clean kitchen towel while the lard heats. Rub the salt and turmeric all over the scallops.
5. Once the lard is hot, add the scallops to the skillet. Be sure not to crowd them. Let them sear undisturbed for 2 minutes then use a very thin spatula to scrape carefully and flip them over, revealing a beautiful golden crust. Sear undisturbed for another 2 minutes, then add the coconut aminos to the skillet. Swirl the pan to get the coconut aminos all over the scallops, then use the spatula to remove the scallops from the skillet and set them on two serving plates.
6. Add the broth to the skillet and bring it to a quick simmer. Use a spatula to deglaze the pan. It will lift up any flavor left behind and any aminos that have caramelized on the bottom. Pour this pan sauce over the scallops.
7. Serve right away with the spinach on the side. Garnish with the reserved bacon and onions then serve.
8. Reheating scallops can make them rubbery. Store leftover spinach and bacon in the fridge for up to 3 days.

Nutrition Info:

- Per Serving: Calories: 279 ;Fat: 12g ;Protein: 28g;Carbs: 13g.

Seared Trout With Greek Yogurt Sauce

Servings: 4
Cooking Time: 30 Minutes
Ingredients:
- 1 garlic clove, minced
- 2 dill pickles, cubed
- ¼ cup Greek yogurt
- 3 tbsp olive oil
- 4 trout fillets, patted dry
- 1 tbsp olive oil
- Sea salt and pepper to taste

Directions:
1. Whisk yogurt, pickles, garlic, 1 tbsp of olive oil, and salt in a small bowl. Set the sauce aside. Season the trout fillets lightly with salt and pepper.
2. Heat the remaining olive oil in a skillet over medium heat. Add the trout fillets to the hot skillet and panfry for about 10 minutes, flipping the fish halfway through or until the fish is cooked to your liking. Spread the salsa on top of the fish and serve.

Nutrition Info:
- Per Serving: Calories: 325;Fat: 15g;Protein: 38g;Carbs: 5g.

Fennel & Shallot Salmon Casserole

Servings: 4
Cooking Time: 30 Minutes
Ingredients:
- 2 shallots, sliced thin
- 1 fennel bulb, sliced
- 4 salmon fillets
- Sea salt and pepper to taste
- 1 tbsp extra-virgin olive oil
- ½ cup vegetable broth
- 1 fresh rosemary sprig

Directions:
1. Preheat your oven to 375ºF. Brush the shallots and fennel with olive oil in a shallow roasting pan. Place the salmon fillets over the vegetables and sprinkle with salt and pepper. Pour in the vegetable broth and add the rosemary sprig to the pan. Cover tightly with aluminum foil. Bake for 20 minutes, or until the salmon is cooked through. Remove and discard the rosemary sprig. Serve.

Nutrition Info:
- Per Serving: Calories: 290;Fat: 15g;Protein: 32g;Carbs: 8g.

Hazelnut Crusted Trout Fillets

Servings: 4
Cooking Time: 30 Minutes
Ingredients:
- 4 boneless trout fillets
- 1 cup hazelnuts, ground

- 1 tbsp coconut oil, melted
- 2 tbsp chopped thyme
- Sea salt and pepper to taste
- Lemon wedges, for garnish

Directions:
1. Preheat your oven to 375ºF. Place the trout fillets on a greased baking sheet skin-side down. Season with salt and pepper. Gently press ¼ cup of ground hazelnuts into the flesh of each fillet. Drizzle the melted coconut oil over the nuts and then sprinkle with thyme. Bake for 15 minutes, or until the fish is cooked through. Serve.

Nutrition Info:
- Per Serving: Calories: 670;Fat: 59g;Protein: 29g;Carbs: 15g.

Salmon & Asparagus Parcels

Servings: 4
Cooking Time: 30 Minutes
Ingredients:
- 16 asparagus spears, sliced
- 4 salmon fillets
- 2 lemons, sliced
- 1 cup cherry tomatoes
- Sea salt and pepper to taste
- 2 tsp extra-virgin olive oil
- ½ cup hollandaise sauce

Directions:
1. Preheat your oven to 400ºF. Cut 4 squares of nonstick baking paper. Divide the fish fillets between the sheets. Season with salt and pepper, then drizzle with olive oil. Place three lemon slices on each fillet, overlapping them slightly to cover the fish. Sprinkle one-fourth each of the asparagus and tomatoes evenly around the fish and season again with salt and pepper. Drizzle with a little olive oil and wrap up the paper around the fish and asparagus to create parcels. Place on a baking sheet and bake for 15-20 minutes or until the salmon is cooked through and the asparagus are tender. Drizzle with hollandaise sauce and serve immediately.

Nutrition Info:
- Per Serving: Calories: 165;Fat: 5g;Protein: 23g;Carbs: 12g.

Yummy Fish Curry

Servings: 4
Cooking Time: 30 Minutes
Ingredients:
- 2 shallots, chopped
- 2 garlic cloves, minced
- 2 tbsp coconut oil
- 1 tbsp minced fresh ginger
- 2 tsp curry powder
- Sea salt and pepper to taste
- 2 cups cubed butternut squash
- 2 cups chopped broccoli
- 1 can coconut milk
- 1 cup vegetable broth
- 1 lb firm white fish fillets
- ¼ cup chopped cilantro
- 1 scallion, sliced thin
- Lemon wedges, for garnish

Directions:
1. Melt the coconut oil in a large pot over medium heat. Add the shallots, garlic, ginger, curry powder, salt, and pepper. Sauté for 5 minutes. Add the butternut squash and broccoli. Sauté for 2 minutes more. Stir in the coconut milk and vegetable broth and bring to a boil. Reduce the heat to simmer and add the fish. Cover the pot and simmer for 5 minutes, or until the fish is cooked through. Remove and discard the lemongrass. Ladle the curry into a serving bowl. Garnish with the cilantro and scallion and serve with lemon wedges.

Nutrition Info:
- Per Serving: Calories: 550;Fat: 39g;Protein: 33g;Carbs: 22g.

Nostalgic Tuna And Avocado Salad Sandwiches

Servings: 4
Cooking Time: 0 Minutes
Ingredients:
- Three 6 ounces cans wild tuna, drained
- 1 large avocado, halved and pitted
- 1 celery stalk, finely chopped
- ½ cup fresh parsley, minced
- 8 slices gluten-free bread, or Quinoa Flatbread

Directions:

1. Roughly mash the tuna in a medium bowl.
2. Into the bowl with the tuna, scoop the avocado flesh and mash together.
3. Stir in the celery and parsley.
4. Divide the tuna salad among 4 bread slices. Top each with a second bread slice and serve.

Nutrition Info:
- Per Serving: Calories: 503 ;Fat: 25g ;Protein: 7g ;Carbs: 31g .

Lemony Spanish Shrimp With Parsley

Servings: 2
Cooking Time: 20 Minutes
Ingredients:
- 2 cups wild or basmati rice
- 4 cups of water
- 12 whole shrimp, peeled, deveined and the tails still intact
- 2 garlic cloves, crushed
- 1 white onion, diced
- 2 tablespoons extra virgin olive oil
- ½ teaspoon red pepper flakes
- 1 tablespoon parsley, crushed
- 1 lemon, juice and zest
- 1 lemon, cut into quarters

Directions:
1. Add the rice and 4 cups of water to a saucepan and boil on a high heat.
2. Lower the heat, cover and simmer for 15 minutes once boiling.
3. Heat the oil in a skillet on a medium heat and then sauté the onion, garlic and red pepper flakes for 5 minutes until soft and add the shrimp.
4. Sauté for 5 to 8 minutes or until shrimp is opaque.
5. Drain the rice and return to the heat for 3 minutes more with the lid on.
6. Add the rice to the shrimps.
7. Add in the parsley, zest and juice of 1 lemon and mix well.
8. Serve in a wide paella dish or a large serving dish. Scatter the lemon wedges around the edge and sprinkle with a little fresher parsley.
9. Season with black pepper to taste.

Nutrition Info:
- Per Serving: Calories: 668 ;Fat: 8g ;Protein: 25g ;Carbs: 130g .

Chapter 7. Soups & Stews

Fennel & Parsnip Bisque

Servings: 6
Cooking Time: 30 Minutes
Ingredients:

- 1 tbsp extra-virgin olive oil
- 2 green onions, chopped
- ½ fennel bulb, sliced
- 2 large carrots, shredded
- 2 parsnips, shredded
- 1 turnip, chopped
- 2 garlic cloves, minced
- ½ tsp dried thyme
- ¼ tsp dried marjoram
- 6 cups vegetable broth
- 1 cup plain soy milk
- 1 tbsp minced fresh parsley

Directions:
1. Heat the oil in a pot over medium heat. Place in green onions, fennel, carrots, parsnips, turnip, and garlic. Sauté for 5 minutes until softened. Add in thyme, marjoram, and broth. Bring to a boil, lower the heat, and simmer for 20 minutes. Transfer to a blender and pulse the soup until smooth. Mix in soy milk. Top with parsley to serve.

Nutrition Info:

- Per Serving: Calories: 115;Fat: 3g;Protein: 2g;Carbs: 20g.

Meatball Soup With Vegetables

Servings: 6
Cooking Time: 40 Minutes
Ingredients:

- 1 tbsp Dijon mustard
- 1 lb ground turkey
- 1 tsp dried basil
- 1 tsp garlic powder
- ½ tsp dried oregano
- Sea salt and pepper to taste
- ¼ tsp red pepper flakes
- 3 tbsp extra-virgin olive oil
- 2 carrots, diced
- 2 garlic cloves, minced
- 1 white onion, diced
- ½ tsp dried thyme
- 6 cups vegetable broth
- 2 cups shredded kale

Directions:
1. Put the mustard, ground turkey, basil, garlic powder, oregano, salt, pepper, and red pepper flakes in a mixing bowl. With your hands, mix the ingredients until they are well combined. Roll the meat mixture into 1-inch balls.
2. Warm the olive oil in a pot over medium heat and sauté the onion, carrots, garlic, and thyme for about 5 minutes,

gently stirring. Add the broth and kale and bring to a boil. Add the meatballs. Simmer for 15-20 minutes until the meatballs are cooked and the kale has softened. Serve.

Nutrition Info:

- Per Serving: Calories: 260;Fat: 15g;Protein: 25g;Carbs: 9g.

Easy To Make Egg Drop Soup

Servings: 4
Cooking Time: 25 Minutes
Ingredients:

- 2 tablespoons sesame oil, toasted
- 2-inch piece fresh ginger, peeled
- 4 cloves garlic, peeled
- 4 cups bone broth
- 1 tablespoon coconut aminos
- 1 tablespoon fish sauce
- Pinch of fine Himalayan salt
- 4 large eggs, whisked
- 2 green onions, sliced,
- 4 sprigs fresh cilantro, minced,

Directions:
1. Heat the sesame oil in a 6- or 8-quart pot over medium heat. Add the ginger and garlic and stir until lightly browned.
2. Add the broth, coconut aminos, fish sauce, and salt. Bring to a low simmer, reduce the heat to low, cover, and cook for 20 minutes.
3. Slowly drizzle in the eggs while stirring the soup so the eggs cook instantly in ribbons as they hit the broth.
4. Garnish with green onions and cilantro and serve hot. Store leftovers in an airtight container in the fridge for up to 5 days.

Nutrition Info:

- Per Serving: Calories: 185 ;Fat: 12g ;Protein: 16g;Carbs: 4g .

Garlic Veggie Bisque

Servings: 6
Cooking Time: 25 Minutes
Ingredients:

- 1 red onion, chopped
- 2 carrots, chopped
- 1 zucchini, sliced
- 1 ripe tomato, quartered
- 2 garlic cloves, crushed
- 3 tbsp extra-virgin olive oil
- ½ tsp dried rosemary
- Sea salt and pepper to taste
- 6 cups vegetable broth
- 1 tbsp minced fresh parsley

Directions:
1. Preheat your oven to 400°F. Arrange the onion, carrots, zucchini, tomato, and garlic on a greased baking dish.

Sprinkle with oil, rosemary, salt, and pepper. Cover with foil and roast for 30 minutes. Uncover and turn them. Roast for another 10 minutes. Transfer the veggies into a pot and pour in the broth. Bring to a boil, lower the heat and simmer for 5 minutes. Transfer to a food processor and blend the soup until smooth. Return to the pot and cook until hot. Serve topped with parsley.

Nutrition Info:
- Per Serving: Calories: 95;Fat: 7g;Protein: 1g;Carbs: 8g.

Chipotle Pumpkin Soup

Servings: 4
Cooking Time: 25 Minutes
Ingredients:
- 2 tbsp sage leaves, minced
- 2 garlic cloves, sliced
- 1 onion, chopped
- 1 can pumpkin purée
- 4 cups vegetable broth
- 2 tbsp extra-virgin olive oil
- 2 tsp chipotle powder
- Sea salt and pepper to taste

Directions:
1. Warm the olive oil in a pot over medium heat. Add the onion and garlic and stir-fry for 3 minutes or until the onion browns. Pour in the pumpkin pur e e and vegetable broth, then sprinkle with chipotle powder, salt, and ground black pepper. Stir. Bring to a boil and simmer for 5 minutes. Serve garnished with chopped sage leaves.

Nutrition Info:
- Per Serving: Calories: 385;Fat: 20g;Protein: 11g;Carbs: 45g.

Coconut Artichoke Soup With Almonds

Servings: 4
Cooking Time: 30 Minutes
Ingredients:
- 1 tbsp extra-virgin olive oil
- 2 medium shallots, chopped
- 10 oz artichoke hearts
- 3 cups vegetable broth
- 1 tsp fresh lemon juice
- Sea salt to taste
- 2 tbsp olive oil
- ⅛ tsp cayenne pepper
- 1 cup plain coconut cream
- 1 tbsp snipped fresh chives
- 2 tbsp toasted almond slices

Directions:
1. Heat the oil in a pot over medium heat. Place in shallots and sauté until softened, about 3 minutes. Add in artichokes, broth, lemon juice, and salt. Bring to a boil, lower the heat, and simmer for 10 minutes. Stir in cayenne pepper. Transfer to a food processor and blend until purée. Return to the pot. Mix in coconut cream and simmer for 5 minutes. Top with chives and almonds.

Nutrition Info:
- Per Serving: Calories: 450;Fat: 43g;Protein: 5g;Carbs: 17g.

Soothing Broth With Mushrooms

Servings: 4
Cooking Time: 10 Minutes
Ingredients:
- 1 tablespoon extra-virgin olive oil
- 1 onion, halved and sliced thin
- 3 garlic cloves, sliced thin
- 1 celery stalk, finely chopped
- 1 pound mushrooms, sliced thin
- 1 teaspoon salt
- ½ teaspoon black pepper, freshly ground
- Pinch nutmeg
- 4 cups vegetable broth
- 2 tablespoon fresh tarragon, chopped

Directions:
1. Heat the olive oil in a large pot over high heat.
2. Add the onion, garlic, and celery. Sauté for 3 minutes.
3. Add the mushrooms, salt, pepper, and nutmeg. Sauté for 5 to 10 minutes more.
4. Add the vegetable broth and bring the soup to a boil. Reduce the heat to simmer. Cook for 5 minutes more.
5. Stir in the tarragon and serve.

Nutrition Info:
- Per Serving: Calories: 111 ;Fat: 5g ;Protein: 9g ;Carbs: 9g .

Comforting Soup With Riced Cauliflower, Cremini Mushrooms, And Baby Spinach

Servings: 2
Cooking Time: 20 Minutes
Ingredients:
- 1 tablespoon ghee or coconut oil
- 2 cups cremini mushrooms, sliced
- 6 cloves garlic, sliced
- 3 sprigs thyme, fresh
- 1 teaspoon fine Himalayan salt
- 1 teaspoon black pepper, ground
- Pinch of ground nutmeg
- 2 tablespoons coconut vinegar
- 1 cup bone broth
- ¼ cup coconut cream
- 1 cup rice cauliflower
- 3 cups baby spinach
- 3 tablespoons collagen peptides
- 2 tablespoons nutritional yeast

Directions:
1. Heat the ghee in a medium-sized pot over medium heat. Add the mushrooms, garlic, thyme sprigs, salt, pepper, and

nutmeg when it begins to brown. Sauté while stirring until aromatic and tender for 8 minutes.

2. Add the vinegar and deglaze the pot, scraping up any goodness that's stuck to the bottom. Add the broth and coconut cream and bring to a simmer.

3. Stir in the riced cauliflower and spinach and cook for 5 minutes, or until the cauliflower is tender. Stir in the collagen peptides and nutritional yeast until dissolved.

4. Serve, sip, and enjoy. Store leftovers in an airtight container in the fridge for up to 5 days or in the freezer for up to 30 days.

Nutrition Info:

- Per Serving: Calories: 305 ;Fat: 16g ;Protein: 25g;Carbs: 17g .

Italian Minestrone Soup

Servings: 4 To 6
Cooking Time: 6 To 8 Hours
Ingredients:

- 1 can diced tomatoes with the juice, 14 ounces
- 1 can kidney beans, 14 ounces, drained and rinsed well
- 2 celery stalks, diced
- 2 carrots, diced
- 1 zucchini, diced
- 1 small onion, diced
- 1 tablespoon lemon juice, freshly squeezed
- 1 teaspoon sea salt
- ½ teaspoon garlic powder
- ½ teaspoon oregano, dried
- ½ teaspoon basil leaves, dried
- ½ teaspoon rosemary, dried
- 2 bay leaves
- 6 cups vegetable broth
- 1 cup packed spinach, fresh

Directions:

1. Combine the tomatoes, kidney beans, celery, carrots, zucchini, onion, lemon juice, salt, garlic powder, oregano, basil, rosemary, bay leaves, and broth in your slow cooker.

2. Cover the cooker and set it to low. Cook for 6 to 8 hours.

3. Remove and discard the bay leaves. Stir in the spinach and let wilt for 5 minutes before serving.

Nutrition Info:

- Per Serving: Calories: 155 ;Protein: 7g ;Carbs: 31g .

Original Vegetable Miso Soup

Servings: 4
Cooking Time: 15 Minutes
Ingredients:

- 1 cup fresh baby spinach
- 4 cups vegetable broth
- 1 cup sliced mushrooms
- ½ tsp fish sauce
- 3 tbsp miso paste
- 4 scallions, sliced

Directions:

1. Add the spinach, broth, mushrooms, and fish sauce in a large pot over medium heat and bring to a boil. Remove from the heat. In a small bowl, mix the miso paste with ½ cup of heated broth mixture to dissolve the miso. Stir the miso mixture into the soup. Sprinkle with scallions.

Nutrition Info:

- Per Serving: Calories: 45;Fat: 0g;Protein: 2g;Carbs: 8g.

Creamy Cauliflower Soup

Servings: 6
Cooking Time: 30 Minutes
Ingredients:

- 1 small white onion, diced
- 3 garlic cloves, minced
- 1 small celery root, peeled, and cut into 1-inch pieces
- 1 head cauliflower, chopped
- 2 tbsp avocado oil
- 4 cups vegetable broth
- 2 scallions, sliced

Directions:

1. Warm the avocado oil in a large pot over medium heat and sauté the onion and garlic for 3 minutes. Add the celery root and cauliflower. Increase the heat to medium and continue to sauté for 5 minutes, or until the cauliflower begins to brown and caramelize on the edges. Stir in the broth and bring to a boil. Reduce the heat to medium-low and simmer for 10 minutes. Remove the pot from the heat. With an immersion blender, or in batches in a standard blender, purée the soup until creamy. Serve immediately sprinkled with the scallions.

Nutrition Info:

- Per Serving: Calories: 185;Fat: 9g;Protein: 8g;Carbs: 10g.

Pressure Cooker Beef Chili

Servings: 4
Cooking Time: 45 Minutes
Ingredients:

- 1 lb ground beef
- ½ cup beef broth
- 1 onion, diced
- 1 tbsp extra-virgin olive oil
- 28 oz canned tomatoes
- 1 ½ tbsp chili powder
- 1 tsp garlic powder
- 2 tbs tomato paste

Directions:

1. Heat the olive oil in your Instant Pot on "Sauté". Add the beef and cook the beef crumbling with a wooden spoon until it browns, about 4 minutes. Add in the onion and cook for 2 more minutes. Add chili powder, garlic powder, tomato paste, and cook for an additional minute. Stir in the tomatoes and beef broth. Seal the lid and cook for 25 minutes on "Manual" on High pressure. Once it goes off, do a quick pressure release. Serve and enjoy!

Nutrition Info:

- Per Serving: Calories: 390;Fat: 28g;Protein: 22g;Carbs: 15g.

Easy Sweet Potato Soup

Servings: 4
Cooking Time: 25 Minutes
Ingredients:
- 8 cups no-salt-added vegetable broth
- 2 tbsp avocado oil
- 1 carrot, chopped
- 1 onion, chopped
- 1 garlic clove, minced
- 4 cups cubed sweet potatoes
- 1 tsp curry powder
- 1 tsp ground turmeric
- Sea salt and pepper to taste

Directions:
1. Warm the avocado oil in a pot over medium heat. Sauté the onion and garlic for 5 minutes until tender and translucent. Mix in sweet potatoes, carrot, vegetable broth, curry powder, turmeric, salt, and pepper and bring to a boil. Simmer for 10 minutes. Puree your soup using an immersion blender until smooth. Serve warm.

Nutrition Info:
- Per Serving: Calories: 260;Fat: 8g;Protein: 4g;Carbs: 46g.

Parsley Tomato Soup

Servings: 4
Cooking Time: 25 Minutes
Ingredients:
- 4 cups no-salt-added vegetable broth
- 2 tbsp parsley, chopped
- 2 tbsp extra-virgin olive oil
- 1 onion, finely chopped
- 2 garlic cloves, minced
- 2 cans diced tomatoes
- Sea salt and pepper to taste

Directions:
1. Warm the olive oil in a pot over medium heat and place the onion. Cook for 7 minutes until browned. Add in garlic and cook for another 30 seconds. Stir in tomatoes, vegetable broth, salt, and pepper and simmer for 5 minutes. Puree the mixture with an immersion blender until smooth. Serve warm topped with parsley.

Nutrition Info:
- Per Serving: Calories: 240;Fat: 8g;Protein: 11g;Carbs: 36g.

Roasted-pumpkin Soup

Servings: 4
Cooking Time: 55 Minutes
Ingredients:
- 2 red onions, cut into wedges
- 2 garlic cloves, skinned
- 10 oz pumpkin, cubed

- 4 tbsp extra-virgin olive oil
- Juice of 1 lime
- 1 tbsp toasted pumpkin seeds

Directions:
1. Preheat your oven to 400ºF. Place onions, garlic, and pumpkin on a baking sheet and drizzle with some olive oil. Season with salt and pepper. Roast for 30 minutes or until the vegetables are golden brown and fragrant. Remove the vegetables from the oven and transfer to a pot. Add 2 cups of water, bring the ingredients to boil over medium heat for 15 minutes. Turn the heat off. Add the remaining olive oil and puree until smooth. Stir in lime juice. Spoon into serving bowls. Garnish with pumpkin seeds. Serve and enjoy!

Nutrition Info:
- Per Serving: Calories: 210;Fat: 16g;Protein: 22g;Carbs: 17g.

Daikon & Sweet Potato Soup

Servings: 6
Cooking Time: 40 Minutes
Ingredients:
- 6 cups water
- 2 tsp olive oil
- 1 chopped onion
- 3 garlic cloves, minced
- 1 tbsp thyme
- 2 tsp paprika
- 2 cups chopped daikon
- 2 cups diced sweet potatoes
- 2 cups chopped parsnips
- ½ tsp sea salt
- 1 cup fresh mint, chopped
- ½ avocado
- 2 tbsp balsamic vinegar
- 2 tbsp pumpkin seeds

Directions:
1. Heat the oil in a pot and place onion and garlic. Sauté for 3 minutes. Add in thyme, paprika, daikon, sweet potato, parsnips, water, and salt. Bring to a boil and cook for 30 minutes. Remove the soup to a food processor and add in balsamic vinegar; purée until smooth. Top with mint and pumpkin seeds to serve.

Nutrition Info:
- Per Serving: Calories: 150;Fat: 6g;Protein: 22g;Carbs: 24g.

Beef-farro Stew

Servings: 4
Cooking Time: 50 Minutes
Ingredients:
- 1 can diced tomatoes
- 1 lb ground beef
- 1 medium onion, chopped
- 2 cups beef broth
- 2/3 cup farro

- 2 tbsp extra-virgin olive oil
- Sea salt and pepper to taste
- 1 cup chopped carrots
- 2 cups broccoli florets
- ½ tsp dried oregano leaves

Directions:

1. Warm the olive oil in a saucepan over medium heat. Add the beef and onion and stir-fry for 7-8 minutes until the beef is brown. Add the remaining ingredients except for the broccoli. Cover and cook for 20 minutes. Stir in broccoli and continue cooking for another 10-15 minutes or until barley is tender. Serve and enjoy!

Nutrition Info:

- Per Serving: Calories: 300;Fat: 13g;Protein: 3g;Carbs: 13g.

Spinach & Mushroom Soup

Servings: 4
Cooking Time: 15 Minutes
Ingredients:

- ½ tsp fish sauce
- 1 cup baby spinach
- 4 scallions, sliced
- 4 cups vegetable broth
- 1 cup mushrooms, sliced
- 3 tbsp miso paste

Directions:

1. Place the fish sauce, 3 cups of water, vegetable broth, and mushrooms in a saucepan over high heat and bring to a boil. Turn the heat off. In a bowl, whisk miso paste and 1/2 cup of vegetable broth until the miso dissolved. Pour it into the pan and combine. Mix in scallions and spinach before serving.

Nutrition Info:

- Per Serving: Calories: 45;Fat: 0g;Protein: 2g;Carbs: 9g.

Shiitake Mushroom Soup

Servings: 4
Cooking Time: 25 Minutes
Ingredients:

- 8 oz shiitake mushrooms, sliced
- 2 tbsp extra-virgin olive oil
- 4 green onions, chopped
- 1 carrot, chopped
- 3 tbsp rice wine
- 2 tsp low-sodium soy sauce
- 4 cups vegetable broth
- Sea salt and pepper to taste
- 2 tbsp parsley, chopped

Directions:

1. Heat the oil in a pot over medium heat. Place the green onions and carrot and cook for 5 minutes. Stir in mushrooms, rice wine, soy sauce, broth, salt, and pepper. Bring to a boil, then lower the heat and simmer for 15 minutes. Top with parsley and serve warm.

Nutrition Info:

- Per Serving: Calories: 150;Fat: 7g;Protein: 2g;Carbs: 21g.

Vegetable Soup With Vermicelli

Servings: 6
Cooking Time: 20 Minutes
Ingredients:

- 1 tbsp extra-virgin olive oil
- 1 onion, chopped
- 4 garlic cloves, minced
- 1 can diced tomatoes
- 6 cups vegetable broth
- 8 oz vermicelli
- 5 oz baby spinach

Directions:

1. Warm the oil in a pot over medium heat. Place in onion and garlic and cook for 3 minutes. Stir in tomatoes, broth, salt, and pepper. Bring to a boil, then lower the heat and simmer for 5 minutes. Pour in vermicelli and spinach and cook for another 5 minutes. Serve warm.

Nutrition Info:

- Per Serving: Calories: 180;Fat: 3g;Protein: 1g;Carbs: 39g.

Wine-braised Beef Stew With Veggies

Servings: 4
Cooking Time: 4 Hours 20 Minutes
Ingredients:

- 12 ounces cremini and button mushrooms, sliced
- 1 ½ lb flank steak, cubed
- Sea salt and pepper to taste
- ½ cup whole-wheat flour
- 1 onion, finely diced
- 2 garlic cloves, minced
- 2 medium carrots, diced
- 2 celery stalks, finely diced
- 1 tbsp tomato paste
- 2 cups dry red wine
- 1 cup beef broth
- 2 bay leaves
- 2 tbsp extra-virgin olive oil
- 2 tbsp chopped parsley
- ½ tsp chili flakes

Directions:

1. Heat the olive oil in a skillet over medium heat. Mix the flour with salt and pepper and dredge in the beef pieces. Place them in the skillet and sear the meat, stirring occasionally, until it is browned on all sides, about 10 minutes total. Transfer the meat to your slow cooker.

2. Add the onion, garlic, carrots, and celery to the skillet and continue cooking for 5 minutes, stirring occasionally, until the onion is softened. Stir in the mushrooms and tomato paste and cook for another 5 minutes. Pour in the red wine to scrape up the browned bits that stick to the bottom of the skillet. Pour the mixture to the slow cooker and add the broth, bay leaves, salt, and pepper. Cover and cook for 4

hours on "Low" until the meat is fork tender. Serve garnished with parsley and chili flakes.

Nutrition Info:
- Per Serving: Calories: 610;Fat: 22g;Protein: 53.6g;Carbs: 25g.

Tomato Lentil Dahl

Servings: 6
Cooking Time: 30 Minutes
Ingredients:
- 1 cup red lentils
- 1 bay leaf
- 1 white onion, diced
- 2 garlic cloves, minced
- 3 cups vegetable broth
- 1 tbsp coconut oil
- 1 medium tomato, diced
- 1 tsp sesame seeds
- 1 tsp ground ginger
- 1 tsp ground cumin
- 1 tsp ground turmeric
- 1 tsp mustard seeds
- Sea salt to taste
- ½ tsp ground cinnamon
- 1 can coconut milk
- 2 tbsp chopped cilantro

Directions:
1. Pour the broth, lentils, and bay leaf in a large pot over medium heat and bring to a boil. Reduce the heat to medium-low and simmer for 20 minutes.
2. Meanwhile, in a medium saucepan over medium heat, sauté the onion and garlic in the coconut oil for 2 minutes. Add the tomato, sesame seeds, ginger, cumin, turmeric, mustard seeds, salt, and cinnamon. Cook, stirring frequently, for 5 minutes. Stir in the coconut milk and bring to a simmer. Remove and discard the bay leaf. Add the coconut milk mixture to the lentils along with the cilantro and stir to combine. Serve and enjoy!

Nutrition Info:
- Per Serving: Calories: 285;Fat: 5g;Protein: 15g;Carbs: 32g.

Moroccan Inspired Lentil Soup

Servings: 2
Cooking Time: 40 Minutes
Ingredients:
- 2 tablespoon extra-virgin olive oil
- 1 yellow onion, diced
- 1 carrot, diced
- 1 clove of minced garlic, diced
- 1 teaspoon cumin, ground
- ½ teaspoon ginger, ground
- 2 tablespoon low-fat Greek yogurt
- ½ teaspoon turmeric, ground
- ½ teaspoon red chili flakes

- 1 can tomatoes, chopped
- 1 cup dried yellow lentils, soaked
- 5 cups of low salt vegetable stock or homemade chicken stock
- 1 lemon

Directions:
1. Heat the oil in a large pan on medium-high heat.
2. Sauté the onion and carrot for 5 to 6 minutes until softened and starting to brown.
3. Add the garlic, ginger, chili flakes, cumin, and turmeric, cook for 2 minutes.
4. Add the tomatoes, scraping any brown bits from the bottom of the pan, and cooking until the liquid is reduced for 15 to 20 minutes).
5. Add the lentils and stock and turn the heat up to reach a boil before lowering the heat, covering, and for 10 minutes, simmer.
6. Serve with a wedge of lemon on the side and a dollop of Greek yogurt.

Nutrition Info:
- Per Serving: Calories: 1048 ;Fat: 53g ;Protein: 19g Carbs: 128g .

Lime Lentil Soup

Servings: 2
Cooking Time: 35 Minutes
Ingredients:
- 1 tsp olive oil
- 1 onion, chopped
- 6 garlic cloves, minced
- 1 tsp chili powder
- ½ tsp ground cinnamon
- Sea salt to taste
- 1 cup yellow lentils
- 1 cup canned diced tomatoes
- 1 celery stalk, chopped
- 10 oz chopped collard greens

Directions:
1. Heat oil in a pot over medium heat. Place onion and garlic and cook for 5 minutes. Stir in chili powder, celery, cinnamon, and salt. Pour in lentils, tomatoes and juices, and 2 cups of water. Bring to a boil, then lower the heat and simmer for 15 minutes. Stir in collard greens. Cook for an additional 5 minutes. Serve in bowls and enjoy!

Nutrition Info:
- Per Serving: Calories: 155;Fat: 3g;Protein: 7g;Carbs: 29g.

Rosemary White Bean Soup

Servings: 4
Cooking Time: 30 Minutes
Ingredients:
- 2 tsp olive oil
- 1 carrot, chopped
- 1 onion, chopped
- 2 garlic cloves, minced

- 1 tbsp rosemary, chopped
- 2 tbsp apple cider vinegar
- 1 cup dried white beans
- ¼ tsp sea salt
- 2 tbsp nutritional yeast

Directions:

1. Heat the oil in a pot over medium heat. Place carrots, onion, and garlic and cook for 5 minutes. Pour in vinegar to deglaze the pot. Stir in 5 cups water and beans and bring to a boil. Lower the heat and simmer for 45 minutes until the beans are soft. Add in salt and nutritional yeast and stir. Serve topped with chopped rosemary.

Nutrition Info:

- Per Serving: Calories: 225;Fat: 3g;Protein: 14g;Carbs: 37g.

Indian Curried Stew With Lentil And Spinach

Servings: 2
Cooking Time: 30 Minutes
Ingredients:

- 1 tablespoon extra-virgin olive oil
- 1 tablespoon curry powder
- 1 cup homemade chicken or vegetable stock
- 1 cup red lentils, soaked
- 1 onion, chopped
- 2 cups butternut squash, cooked peeled, and chopped
- 1 cup spinach
- 2 garlic cloves, minced
- 1 tablespoon cilantro, finely chopped

Directions:

1. Add the oil, chopped onion, and minced garlic, sauté for 5 minutes on low heat in a large pot.
2. Add the curry powder and ginger to the onions and cook for 5 minutes.
3. Add the broth and bring to a boil on high heat.
4. Stir in the lentils, squash, and spinach, reduce heat and simmer for 20 minutes more.
5. Season with pepper to taste and serve with fresh cilantro.

Nutrition Info:

- Per Serving: Calories: 1022 ;Fat: 19g ;Protein: 123g ;Carbs: 91g.

Coconut Butternut Squash Soup

Servings: 4
Cooking Time: 30 Minutes
Ingredients:

- 2 tbsp extra-virgin olive oil
- 2 garlic cloves, minced
- 1 onion, chopped
- 1 tbsp grated ginger
- 1 tbsp green curry paste
- 4 cups vegetable broth
- 1 lb butternut squash, cubed
- Sea salt and pepper to taste

- ¼ cup coconut milk
- 2 tbsp cilantro, minced

Directions:

1. Warm the olive oil in a pot over medium heat. Place the onion, garlic, and ginger and soften for 5 minutes. Add vegetable broth, butternut squash, green curry paste, salt, and pepper and simmer for 10-15 minutes until the squash is soft. Add coconut milk and purée with a stick blender. Garnish with cilantro. Serve warm.

Nutrition Info:

- Per Serving: Calories: 100;Fat: 8g;Protein: 1g;Carbs: 10g.

Pasta & Tomato Soup

Servings: 4
Cooking Time: 30 Minutes
Ingredients:

- 4 cups cubed bread
- ¼ cup olive oil
- 2 garlic cloves, minced
- 8 oz whole-wheat pasta
- 1 can diced tomatoes
- 4 cups vegetable broth
- 2 tbsp minced parsley
- Sea salt and pepper to taste

Directions:

1. Preheat your oven to 400°F. Arrange the bread cubes on a baking tray and toast for 10 minutes, shaking them once. Heat olive oil in a pot over medium heat. Place the garlic, cook for 1 minute. Add in pasta, tomatoes, broth, parsley, salt, and pepper. Bring to a boil, then lower the heat and simmer for 10 minutes. Share the toasted bread into soup bowls and spoon in the soup all over. Serve.

Nutrition Info:

- Per Serving: Calories: 460;Fat: 16g;Protein: 10g;Carbs: 71g.

Chicken & Vegetable Stew With Barley

Servings: 6
Cooking Time: 30 Minutes
Ingredients:

- 1 lb chicken breasts, cubed
- 3 tbsp extra-virgin olive oil
- 1 onion, chopped
- 2 garlic cloves, minced
- 2 turnips, chopped
- 1 cup pearl barley
- 1 can diced tomatoes
- 3 tsp dried mixed herbs
- Sea salt and pepper to taste

Directions:

1. Warm the olive oil in a pot over medium heat. Add the chicken, onion, and garlic and sauté for 6-8 minutes. Stir in the turnips, barley, tomatoes, 3 cups of water, and herbs. Cook for 20 minutes. Adjust the seasoning. Serve.

Nutrition Info:

Minestrone Soup With Quinoa

Servings: 6
Cooking Time: 30 Minutes
Ingredients:

- 14 oz canned cannellini beans, drained
- 3 tbsp extra-virgin olive oil
- 2 garlic cloves, minced
- 1 white onion, diced
- 2 carrots, chopped
- 2 celery stalks, diced
- 1 small zucchini, diced
- ½ red bell pepper, diced
- 5 cups vegetable broth
- 14 oz canned diced tomatoes
- 1 cup kale
- ½ cup quinoa, rinsed well
- 1 tbsp lemon juice
- 2 tsp dried rosemary
- 2 tsp dried thyme
- 1 bay leaf
- Sea salt and pepper to taste

Directions:

1. Warm the olive oil in a large pot over medium heat and sauté the garlic, onion, carrots, and celery for 3 minutes. Add the zucchini and red bell pepper, and sauté for 2 minutes. Stir in the broth, tomatoes, beans, kale, quinoa, lemon juice, rosemary, thyme, bay leaf, and salt, and season with black pepper. Bring to a simmer, reduce the heat to low, cover, and cook for 15 minutes, or until the quinoa is cooked. Remove the bay leaf. Serve hot.

Nutrition Info:

- Per Serving: Calories: 320;Fat: 5g;Protein: 17g;Carbs: 43g.

Black-eyed Pea Soup

Servings: 6
Cooking Time: 45 Minutes
Ingredients:

- 2 carrots, chopped
- 1 onion, chopped
- 15 oz canned black-eyed peas
- 1 tsp low-sodium soy sauce
- 1 tsp onion powder
- ½ tsp garlic powder
- Sea salt and pepper to taste
- ¼ cup chopped black olives

Directions:

1. Place carrots, onion, black-eyed peas, 6 cups of water, soy sauce, onion powder, garlic powder, and pepper in a pot. Simmer slowly for 20 minutes. Allow cooling for a few minutes. Transfer to a food processor and blend until smooth. Stir in black olives. Serve and enjoy!

Spinach, Rice & Bean Soup

Servings: 6
Cooking Time: 45 Minutes
Ingredients:

- 6 cups baby spinach
- 2 tbsp extra-virgin olive oil
- 1 onion, chopped
- 2 garlic cloves, minced
- 15 oz canned black-eyed peas
- 6 cups vegetable broth
- Sea salt and pepper to taste
- ½ cup brown rice

Directions:

1. Heat oil in a pot over medium heat. Place the onion and garlic and sauté for 3 minutes. Pour in broth and season with salt and pepper. Bring to a boil, then lower the heat and stir in rice. Simmer for 15 minutes. Stir in peas and spinach and cook for another 5 minutes. Serve warm.

Nutrition Info:

- Per Serving: Calories: 200;Fat: 5g;Protein: 1g;Carbs: 32g.

Lovage Fish Soup

Servings: 4
Cooking Time: 25 Minutes
Ingredients:

- 1 tsp dried lovage leaves, crushed
- 2 tbsp extra-virgin olive oil
- 1 leek, sliced
- 1 tsp ground turmeric
- 1 tsp minced ginger root
- 2 sweet potatoes, diced
- 4 cups vegetable broth
- 1 lb white fish fillets, cubed
- Sea salt and pepper to taste

Directions:

1. Warm the olive oil in a pot over high heat. Sweet the leek for 3 minutes. Add turmeric, ginger root, and sweet potatoes and cook for 1 more minute. Pour in vegetable broth and bring it to a boil. Lower the heat and simmer for 10 minutes until the potatoes are tender. Put in fish cubes and cook for another 5 minutes. Adjust the seasonings. Sprinkle with dried lovage and serve.

Nutrition Info:

- Per Serving: Calories: 230;Fat: 6g;Protein: 31g;Carbs: 22g.

Powerful Zuppa Toscana

Servings: 4 To 6
Cooking Time: 5 To 6 Hours
Ingredients:

- 4 cups vegetable broth
- 2 cups de-ribbed kale, chopped
- 2 small sweet potatoes, peeled and diced
- 1 medium zucchini, diced
- 15 ounces can cannellini beans, rinsed and drained well
- 1 celery stalk, diced
- 1 carrot, diced
- 1 small onion, diced
- ½ teaspoon garlic powder
- ½ teaspoon sea salt
- ¼ teaspoon red pepper flakes
- Freshly ground black pepper

Directions:
1. Combine the broth, kale, sweet potatoes, zucchini, beans, celery, carrot, onion, garlic powder, salt, and red pepper flakes in your slow cooker, and season with black pepper.
2. Cover the cooker and set it to low. Cook for 5 to 6 hours and serve.

Nutrition Info:

- Per Serving: Calories: 209 ;Fat: 1g ;Protein: 8g ;Carbs: 43g .

Brown Rice & Bean Chili

Servings: 6
Cooking Time: 30 Minutes
Ingredients:

- 30 oz roasted tomatoes and peppers
- 3 tbsp extra-virgin olive oil
- 1 onion, chopped
- 4 garlic cloves, minced
- 1 can kidney beans
- ½ cup brown rice
- 2 cups vegetable stock
- 3 tbsp chili powder
- 1 tsp sea salt

Directions:
1. Heat the olive oil in a pot over medium heat. Add the onion and garlic and cook for 3 minutes until fragrant. Stir in kidney beans, rice, tomatoes and peppers, stock, chili powder, and salt. Cook for 20 minutes. Serve warm.

Nutrition Info:

- Per Serving: Calories: 255;Fat: 9g;Protein: 5g;Carbs: 39g.

Beef & Mushroom Rice Soup

Servings: 6
Cooking Time: 40 Minutes
Ingredients:

- 1 lb stew beef meat, cubed
- 3 tbsp extra-virgin olive oil
- 1 onion, chopped
- 1 carrot, chopped
- 1 celery stalk, chopped
- 1 cup wild mushrooms, sliced
- ½ cup brown rice
- 7 cups vegetable broth
- 1 tsp dried dill weed
- Sea salt and pepper to taste

Directions:
1. Heat the oil in a pot over medium heat. Add the beef, onion, carrot, and celery and sauté for 6-8 minutes. Add in mushrooms, rice, broth, dill weed, salt, and pepper. Bring to a boil, then lower the heat and simmer uncovered for 30 minutes. Serve and enjoy!

Nutrition Info:

- Per Serving: Calories: 330;Fat: 11g;Protein: 21g;Carbs: 39g.

Mushroom & Bean Stew

Servings: 4
Cooking Time: 35 Minutes
Ingredients:

- 8 oz porcini mushrooms, sliced
- 1 can cannellini beans, drained
- 2 tbsp extra-virgin olive oil
- 1 onion, chopped
- 1 carrot, chopped
- 2 garlic cloves, minced
- 1 red bell pepper, chopped
- ½ cup capers
- 1 zucchini, chopped
- 1 can diced tomatoes
- 1 cup vegetable broth
- Sea salt and pepper to taste
- 3 cups fresh baby spinach
- ½ tsp dried basil

Directions:
1. Heat oil in a pot and sauté onion, carrot, garlic, mushrooms, and bell pepper for 5 minutes. Stir in capers, zucchini, tomatoes, broth, salt, and pepper. Bring to a boil, then lower the heat and simmer for 20 minutes. Add in beans and basil. Simmer for 2-3 minutes. Serve.

Nutrition Info:

- Per Serving: Calories: 300;Fat: 8g;Protein: 9g;Carbs: 58g.

Cayenne Pumpkin Soup

Servings: 6
Cooking Time: 55 Minutes
Ingredients:

- 1 pumpkin, sliced
- 3 tbsp extra-virgin olive oil
- 1 tsp sea salt
- 2 red bell peppers
- 1 onion, halved
- 1 head garlic

- ¼ tsp cayenne pepper
- ½ tsp ground coriander
- ½ tsp ground cumin
- Toasted pumpkin seeds

Directions:

1. Preheat your oven to 350°F. Brush the pumpkin slices with oil and sprinkle with salt. Arrange them skin-side-down and on a greased baking dish; bake for 20 minutes. Brush the onion with oil. Cut the top of the garlic head and brush with oil. Add the bell peppers, onion, and garlic to the pumpkin. Bake for 10 minutes. Cool.

2. Take out the flesh from the pumpkin skin and transfer to a food processor. Cut the pepper roughly, peel and cut the onion, and remove the cloves from the garlic head. Transfer to the food processor and pour in 6 cups of water. Blend the soup until smooth. If it's very thick, add a bit of water to reach your desired consistency. Sprinkle with salt, cayenne pepper, coriander, and cumin. Serve.

Nutrition Info:

- Per Serving: Calories: 130;Fat: 8g;Protein: 1g;Carbs: 16g.

Southwest Shrimp Soup

Servings: 6
Cooking Time: 25 Minutes
Ingredients:

- 1 tablespoon olive oil
- 1 sweet onion, chopped, or about 1 cup precut packaged onion
- 2 stalks celery, chopped, or about ¾ to 1 cup precut packaged celery
- 2 teaspoons minced garlic, bottled
- 6 cups Herbed Chicken Bone Broth
- 2 cups cubed sweet potato
- 2 carrots, diced, or about 1½ cups precut packaged carrots
- ½ teaspoon cumin, ground
- ½ teaspoon coriander, ground
- 1 pound haddock, cut into 1-inch pieces
- ½ pound peeled and deveined shrimp, chopped
- 1 cup spinach, fresh
- 2 tablespoons fresh cilantro, chopped

Directions:

1. Place a large stockpot over medium-high heat and add the olive oil.

2. Add the onion, celery, and garlic. Sauté for about 3 minutes or until softened.

3. Stir in the chicken broth, sweet potato, carrots, cumin, and coriander. Bring the soup to a boil. Reduce the heat to low and simmer for 10 minutes or until the vegetables are tender.

4. Stir in the haddock and shrimp. Simmer for 10 minutes more.

5. For 2 minutes, stir in the spinach and simmer.

6. Serve the soup topped with cilantro.

Nutrition Info:

- Per Serving: Calories: 255 ;Fat: 8g ;Protein:26g ;Carbs: 20g .

Easy Garbanzo Soup

Servings: 4
Cooking Time: 25 Minutes
Ingredients:

- 2 tbsp extra-virgin olive oil
- 1 onion, chopped
- 1 green bell pepper, diced
- 1 carrot, peeled and diced
- 4 garlic cloves, minced
- 1 can garbanzo beans
- 1 cup spinach, chopped
- 4 cups vegetable stock
- ¼ tsp ground cumin
- Sea salt to taste

Directions:

1. Heat the oil in a pot over medium heat. Place in onion, garlic, bell pepper, and carrot and sauté for 5 minutes until tender. Stir in garbanzo beans, spinach, stock, cumin, and salt. Cook for 10 minutes. Mash the garbanzo using a potato masher, leaving some chunks. Serve.

Nutrition Info:

- Per Serving: Calories: 120;Fat: 7g;Protein: 2g;Carbs: 13g.

Homemade Succotash Stew

Servings: 4
Cooking Time: 30 Minutes
Ingredients:

- 1 cup canned chickpeas
- 2 tbsp extra-virgin olive oil
- 1 onion, chopped
- 2 carrots, sliced
- 1 can diced tomatoes
- 16 oz frozen succotash
- 2 cups vegetable broth
- 2 tsp low-sodium soy sauce
- 1 tsp dry mustard
- ½ tsp dried thyme
- ½ tsp ground allspice
- ¼ tsp cayenne pepper
- Sea salt and pepper to taste

Directions:

1. Heat oil in a saucepan. Place in onion and sauté for 3 minutes. Stir in chickpeas, carrots, tomatoes, succotash, broth, soy sauce, mustard, sugar, thyme, allspice, and cayenne pepper. Sprinkle with salt and pepper. Bring to a boil and simmer for 20 minutes. Serve hot and enjoy!

Nutrition Info:

- Per Serving: Calories: 390;Fat: 12g;Protein: 16g;Carbs: 59g.

Scrumptious Sweet Potato Soup

Servings: 6
Cooking Time: 35 Minutes
Ingredients:

- 1 tablespoon olive oil
- 1 sweet onion, chopped, or about 1 cup precut packaged onion
- 2 teaspoons fresh ginger, grated
- 8 cups Herbed Chicken Bone Broth
- 2 pounds sweet potatoes about 4, peeled and diced, or 6 cups precut packaged sweet potatoes
- 1 carrot, diced, or ¾ cup precut packaged carrots
- ¼ cup maple syrup, pure
- 1 teaspoon cinnamon, ground
- ¼ teaspoon nutmeg, ground
- 1 cup coconut cream, plus 1 tablespoon
- Sea salt

Directions:

1. Place a large stockpot over medium-high heat and add the olive oil.
2. Add the onion and ginger. Sauté for about 3 minutes or until softened.
3. Stir in the chicken broth, sweet potatoes, carrot, maple syrup, cinnamon, and nutmeg. Bring the soup to a boil. Reduce the heat to low and simmer for about 30 minutes, or until the vegetables are tender.
4. Purée the soup in a food processor until very smooth and work in batches. Transfer the soup back to the pot.
5. Stir in the coconut cream and reheat the soup.
6. Season with sea salt, drizzle with coconut cream, garnish with a fresh herb of your choice, and serve.

Nutrition Info:

- Per Serving: Calories: 353 ;Fat: 13g ;Protein: 5g;Carbs: 58g .

Extraordinary Creamy Green Soup

Servings: 4 To 6
Cooking Time: 15 Minutes
Ingredients:

- 3 cups water
- 2 cups coconut milk, unsweetened
- 1½ teaspoons sea salt, plus additional as needed
- 4 cups tightly packed kale, washed thoroughly, stemmed, and roughly chopped
- 4 cups tightly packed spinach, stemmed and roughly chopped
- 4 cups tightly packed collard greens, stemmed and roughly chopped
- 1 bunch fresh parsley, stemmed and roughly chopped

Directions:

1. Bring the water, coconut milk, and salt to a boil in a large pot set over high heat. Reduce the heat to low.
2. Add the kale, spinach, and collard greens 1 cup at a time then let them wilt before adding the next cup. Continue until all the greens have been added to the pot.

3. For 8 to 10 minutes, simmer.
4. blend the soup in a blender until smooth, working in batches if necessary and taking care of the hot liquid.
5. Taste, and adjust the seasoning before serving.

Nutrition Info:

- Per Serving: Calories: 334 ;Fat: 29g ;Protein: 7g ;Carbs: 18g .

French Peasant Turkey Stew

Servings: 4
Cooking Time: 40 Minutes
Ingredients:

- 2 cups leftover roast turkey, shredded
- 2 sweet potatoes, cut into quarters
- 2 cups baby carrots
- 1 cup sliced mushrooms
- 1 jar chicken gravy
- 2 cups chicken broth
- 1 tsp dried rosemary
- ½ cup frozen green peas

Directions:

1. Add the sweet potatoes, baby carrots, mushrooms, chicken gravy, broth, and rosemary to a medium pot over medium heat. Bring to a boil, reduce the heat and simmer covered 20 minutes, stirring occasionally, or until vegetables are tender. Stir in turkey and peas. Simmer for another 5 minutes until heated through. Serve and enjoy!

Nutrition Info:

- Per Serving: Calories: 285;Fat: 10g;Protein: 28g;Carbs: 21.8g.

Hot Lentil Soup With Zucchini

Servings: 4
Cooking Time: 30 Minutes
Ingredients:

- 2 tbsp extra-virgin olive oil
- 1 onion, chopped
- 1 zucchini, chopped
- 1 garlic clove, minced
- 1 tbsp hot paprika
- 1 can diced tomatoes
- 1 cup red lentils, rinsed
- 4 cups vegetable broth
- 3 cups chopped Swiss chard

Directions:

1. Heat the oil in a pot over medium heat. Place in onion, zucchini, and garlic and sauté for 5 minutes until tender. Add in paprika, tomatoes, lentils, broth, salt, and pepper. Bring to a boil, then lower the heat and simmer for 15 minutes, stirring often. Add in the Swiss chard and cook for another 3-5 minutes. Serve immediately.

Nutrition Info:

- Per Serving: Calories: 300;Fat: 8g;Protein: 13g;Carbs: 46g.

Peppery Soup With Tomato

Servings: 2
Cooking Time: 35 Minutes
Ingredients:

- 2 red bell peppers
- 4 beef tomatoes
- 1 sweet onion, chopped
- 1 garlic clove, chopped
- 3 cups homemade chicken broth
- 2 habanero chilis, stems removed and chopped
- 2 tablespoon extra-virgin olive oil

Directions:

1. Preheat the broiler to medium-high heat and grill the bell peppers, turning halfway for 10 minutes until the skins are blackened.
2. Heat water in a pan on medium to high heat and cut a small x at the bottom of each tomato using a sharp knife.
3. Transfer to separate dish pepper once cooked and cover.
4. For 20 seconds, blanch the tomatoes in simmering water.
5. Remove and plunge into ice-cold water.
6. Peel and chop tomatoes, reserving the juices.
7. Sauté the onion, garlic, chili, and 2 tablespoons of oil in a saucepan on medium-high heat, stirring for 8-10 minutes until golden.
8. Add the tomatoes with the juices, the peppers, and broth to the onions and cover and simmer for 10-15 minutes or until heated through.
9. Purée in a blender and serve.

Nutrition Info:

- Per Serving: Calories: 741| Fat: 32g ;Protein: 82g ;Carbs: 30g .

Easy To Make Bone Broth Of Chicken

Servings: 6 To 8
Cooking Time: 8 To 24 Hours
Ingredients:

- 2 pounds organic chicken bones, or 1 leftover organic chicken carcass
- 1 small onion, quartered, skin on
- 1-inch piece fresh ginger, roughly chopped
- 1 small bunch fresh fennel, roughly chopped
- 1 small bunch fresh parsley, roughly chopped
- 10 to 12 cups cold water

Directions:

1. Combine the chicken bones, onion, ginger, fennel, parsley, and water in a slow cooker. The amount of water needed will depend on the size of your cooker. Cover everything by 1 to 2 inches.
2. For a minimum of 8 hours, cover and cook on low.
3. Strain the broth by discarding the vegetables and bones. Cover and refrigerate until needed.

Nutrition Info:

- Per Serving: Calories: 86 ;Fat: 2g ;Protein: 6g ;Carbs: 8g .

Bell Pepper & Mushroom Soup

Servings: 6
Cooking Time: 45 Minutes
Ingredients:

- 3 tbsp extra-virgin olive oil
- 1 onion, chopped
- 1 large carrot, chopped
- 2 red bell peppers, diced
- 1 lb mushrooms, quartered
- 6 cups vegetable broth
- ¼ cup chopped parsley
- 1 tsp minced fresh thyme
- Sea salt and pepper to taste

Directions:

1. Heat the oil in a pot over medium heat. Place onion, carrot, and celery and cook for 5 minutes. Add in bell peppers and broth and stir. Bring to a boil, lower the heat, and simmer for 20 minutes. Adjust the seasonings. Serve topped with parsley and thyme.

Nutrition Info:

- Per Serving: Calories: 115;Fat: 7g;Protein: 3g;Carbs: 12g.

Mediterranean Vegetable Stew

Servings: 4
Cooking Time: 30 Minutes
Ingredients:

- 2 tbsp extra-virgin olive oil
- 1 onion, chopped
- 2 carrots, chopped
- ½ tsp ground cumin
- ½ tsp ground ginger
- ½ tsp paprika
- ½ tsp saffron
- 1 can diced tomatoes
- 5 oz broccoli florets
- 2 cups winter squash, diced
- 1 ½ cups vegetable broth
- 1 can chickpeas
- 1 tsp lemon zest
- Sea salt and pepper to taste
- ½ cup pitted green olives
- ½ cup slivered almonds

Directions:

1. Heat the oil in a pot over medium heat. Place onions and carrots and sauté for 5 minutes. Add in cumin, ginger, paprika, salt, pepper, and saffron and cook for 30 seconds. Stir in tomatoes, broccoli, squash, chickpeas, and broth. Bring to a boil, then lower the heat and simmer for 20 minutes. Add in olives and lemon zest and simmer for 2-3 minutes. Garnish with almonds to serve.

Nutrition Info:

- Per Serving: Calories: 295;Fat: 1g;Protein: 7g;Carbs: 36g.

Chili Cannellini Bean Stew

Servings: 4
Cooking Time: 40 Minutes
Ingredients:

- 2 cans cannellini beans
- 1 can mild chopped green chilies
- 2 tbsp extra-virgin olive oil
- 1 onion, chopped
- 1 can diced tomatoes
- 2 tbsp tamarind paste
- 1 cup vegetable broth
- 2 tbsp chili powder
- 1 tsp ground coriander
- ½ tsp ground cumin
- Sea salt and pepper to taste
- 1 cup green peas

Directions:

1. Heat the oil in a pot over medium heat. Place in the onion and sauté for 3 minutes until translucent. Stir in beans, tomatoes, and chilies. Cook for 5 minutes more. In a bowl, whisk the tamarind paste with broth. Pour the mixture into the pot. Stir in chili powder, coriander, cumin, salt, and pepper. Bring to a boil, then lower the heat and simmer for 20 minutes. Add in peas and cook for another 5 minutes. Serve warm and enjoy!

Nutrition Info:

- Per Serving: Calories: 400;Fat: 10g;Protein: 7g;Carbs: 69g.

Brussels Sprouts & Tofu Soup

Servings: 4
Cooking Time: 40 Minutes
Ingredients:

- 7 oz firm tofu, cubed
- 2 tsp olive oil
- 1 cup sliced mushrooms
- 1 lb Brussels sprouts, halved
- 1 garlic clove, minced
- ½-inch piece minced ginger
- Sea salt to taste
- 2 tbsp apple cider vinegar
- 2 tsp low-sodium soy sauce
- 1 tsp pure date sugar
- ¼ tsp red pepper flakes
- 1 scallion, chopped

Directions:

1. Heat the oil in a skillet over medium heat. Place mushrooms, Brussels sprouts, garlic, ginger, and salt. Sauté for 7-8 minutes until the veggies are soft. Pour in 4 cups of water, vinegar, soy sauce, sugar, pepper flakes, and tofu. Bring to a boil, then lower the heat and simmer for 5-10 minutes. Top with scallions and serve.

Nutrition Info:

- Per Serving: Calories: 135;Fat: 8g;Protein: 9g;Carbs: 8g.

Spicy Thai Soup

Servings: 6
Cooking Time: 30 Minutes
Ingredients:

- ¾ cup toasted cashews
- 2 red chili peppers, diced
- 3 garlic cloves, minced
- 1 white onion, diced
- 2 tbsp coconut oil
- 1 ½ tbsp minced ginger
- 2 carrots, chopped
- 1 butternut squash, diced
- 1 small cabbage, shredded
- 1 lb trimmed green beans
- 3 cups vegetable broth
- 1 can coconut milk
- Sea salt and pepper to taste
- 1 cup mung bean sprouts
- 4 tbsp coconut shavings

Directions:

1. Warm the coconut oil in a large pot over medium heat and sauté the cashews and sauté for 2 minutes. Remove them from the pan and set aside. Add the peppers, garlic, and onion, and sauté for 6 minutes. Then add the ginger and carrots, and sauté for about 3 minutes, or until the carrots and squash begin to soften. Stir in the cabbage, green beans, broth, coconut milk, and salt. Season with pepper. Simmer for 15 minutes. Turn off the heat and stir in the bean sprouts and coconut shavings. Pour into soup bowls and serve immediately.

Nutrition Info:

- Per Serving: Calories: 340;Fat: 26g;Protein: 6g;Carbs: 24g.

Spinach & Sweet Potato Lentil Soup

Servings: 4
Cooking Time: 55 Minutes
Ingredients:

- 2 tbsp extra-virgin olive oil
- 1 onion, chopped
- 2 garlic cloves, minced
- 4 cups vegetable broth
- 2 sweet potatoes, cubed
- ½ tsp dried oregano
- ¼ tsp crushed red pepper
- Sea salt to taste
- 4 cups chopped spinach
- 1 cup green lentils, rinsed

Directions:

1. Warm the oil in a pot over medium heat. Place the onion and garlic and cook covered for 5 minutes. Stir in broth, sweet potatoes, oregano, red pepper, lentils, and salt. Bring to a boil, then lower the heat and simmer uncovered for 30 minutes. Add in spinach and cook for another 5 minutes. Serve immediately.

Mushroom Curry Soup

Servings: 4
Cooking Time: 15 Minutes
Ingredients:
- ½ cup sliced shiitake mushrooms
- 1 tbsp coconut oil
- 1 red onion, sliced
- 1 carrot, chopped
- 2 garlic cloves, minced
- 1 can coconut milk
- 4 cups vegetable stock
- 1 can tomato sauce
- 2 tbsp cilantro, chopped
- Juice from 1 lime
- Sea salt to taste
- 2 tbsp red curry paste

Directions:
1. Melt coconut oil in a pot over medium heat. Place in onion, garlic, carrot, and mushrooms and sauté for 5 minutes. Pour in coconut milk, vegetable stock, tomato sauce, cilantro, lime juice, salt, and curry paste. Cook until heated through. Serve and enjoy!

Nutrition Info:
- Per Serving: Calories: 310;Fat: 28g;Protein: 2g;Carbs: 16g.

Cannellini Bean Soup

Servings: 4
Cooking Time: 8 Hours 15 Minutes
Ingredients:
- 2 cans cannellini beans, rinsed and drained
- 4 cups vegetable broth
- 2 onions, thinly sliced
- ¼ cup extra-virgin olive oil
- Sea salt and pepper to taste
- ½ tsp garlic powder
- 1 bay leaf

Directions:
1. Add onions, oil, beans, broth, garlic powder, bay leaf, salt and pepper to your slow cooker. Cover and cook for 8 hours on "Low". Remove and discard the bay leaf. Serve.

Nutrition Info:
- Per Serving: Calories: 330;Fat: 15g;Protein: 10g;Carbs: 39g.

Green Bean & Zucchini Velouté

Servings: 6
Cooking Time: 30 Minutes
Ingredients:
- 2 tbsp minced jarred pimiento
- 3 tbsp extra-virgin olive oil
- 1 onion, chopped
- 1 garlic clove, minced
- 2 cups green beans
- 4 cups vegetable broth
- 3 medium zucchini, sliced
- ½ tsp dried marjoram
- ½ cup plain almond milk

Directions:
1. Heat oil in a pot and sauté onion and garlic for 5 minutes. Add in green beans and broth. Cook for 10 minutes. Stir in zucchini and cook for 10 minutes. Transfer to a food processor and pulse until smooth. Return to the pot and mix in almond milk; cook until hot. Top with pimiento.

Nutrition Info:
- Per Serving: Calories: 95;Fat: 7g;Protein: 2g;Carbs: 8g.

Warm Chili Pumpkin Soup

Servings: 4
Cooking Time: 40 Minutes
Ingredients:
- 1 tablespoon unsalted butter, ghee, or avocado oil
- 1 medium onion, diced
- 3 radishes, diced
- 2 cloves garlic, minced
- 4 ribs celery, diced
- 1 teaspoon mustard, dry
- 1 teaspoon fine Himalayan salt
- 1 teaspoon garam masala
- 1 teaspoon black pepper, ground
- 1 pound 85% lean ground beef
- ½ cup canned pumpkin purée, unsweetened
- 2 cups bone broth
- ¼ cup Homemade Mayo
- 2 tablespoons coconut cream
- ¼ cup fresh cilantro, minced

Directions:
1. Heat a large pot over medium-high heat. In the pot, melt the butter then add the onions, radishes, garlic, and celery. Sauté while stirring until the onions are translucent and aromatic for 8 minutes.
2. Add the seasonings, mix well, and cook until they become fragrant for 2 minutes.
3. Add the ground beef, crumbling it up as you go. To make sure it breaks apart well use a whisk.
4. Cook and stir often until all of the ground beef is browned and crumbly for 8 minutes.
5. Add the pumpkin purée and the broth and bring to a simmer. For 10 to 15 minutes, reduce the heat to low and simmer.
6. Stir in the mayo until well dissolved and remove from the heat. Swirl in the coconut cream and sprinkle with the cilantro.
7. Store in an airtight container in the fridge for up to 5 days or in the freezer for up to 30 days. Bring to a simmer on the stovetop to reheat.

Nutrition Info:
- Per Serving: Calories: 502 ;Fat: 35g ;Protein: 41g ;Carbs: 8g .

Dairy-free Rice Soup With Mushrooms

Servings: 4 To 6
Cooking Time: 6 To 8 Hours
Ingredients:

- 1½ cups uncooked wild rice
- 6 cups vegetable broth
- 2 carrots, diced
- 1 celery stalk, diced
- ½ medium onion, diced
- ¼ cup porcini mushrooms, dried
- 1 tablespoon extra-virgin olive oil
- 1 teaspoon sea salt
- ½ teaspoon garlic powder
- ½ teaspoon thyme leaves, dried
- 1 bay leaf
- Freshly ground black pepper

Directions:
1. Combine the rice, broth, carrots, celery, onion, mushrooms, olive oil, salt, garlic powder, thyme, and bay leaf in your slow cooker and season with pepper.
2. Cover the cooker and set it to low. Cook for 6 to 8 hours.
3. Remove and discard the bay leaf before serving.

Nutrition Info:
- Per Serving: Calories: 425 ;Fat: 4g ;Protein: 16g ;Carbs: 78g.

Italian Bean Soup

Servings: 6
Cooking Time: 1 Hour 25 Minutes
Ingredients:

- 3 tbsp extra-virgin olive oil
- 2 celery stalks, chopped
- 2 carrots, chopped
- 3 shallots, chopped
- 3 garlic cloves, minced
- ½ cup brown rice
- 6 cups vegetable broth
- 1 can diced tomatoes
- 2 bay leaves
- Sea salt and pepper to taste
- 2 cans white beans
- ¼ cup chopped basil

Directions:
1. Heat oil in a pot over medium heat. Place celery, carrots, shallots, and garlic and cook for 5 minutes. Add in brown rice, broth, tomatoes, bay leaves, salt, and pepper. Bring to a boil, then lower the heat and simmer uncovered for 20 minutes. Stir in beans and basil and cook for 5 minutes. Discard bay leaves. Sprinkle with basil and serve.

Nutrition Info:
- Per Serving: Calories: 180;Fat: 8g;Protein: 2g;Carbs: 25g.

Rice Noodle Soup With Beans

Servings: 6
Cooking Time: 10 Minutes
Ingredients:

- 2 carrots, chopped
- 2 celery stalks, chopped
- 6 cups vegetable broth
- 8 oz brown rice noodles
- 1 can pinto beans
- 1 tsp dried thyme

Directions:
1. Place a pot over medium heat and add in the carrots, celery, and vegetable broth. Bring to a boil. Add in noodles, beans, dried thyme, salt, and pepper. Reduce the heat and simmer for 5 minutes. Serve and enjoy!

Nutrition Info:
- Per Serving: Calories: 210;Fat: 1g;Protein: 6g;Carbs: 45g.

Chapter 8. Vegetarian Mains

Baked Mustard Beans

Servings: 4
Cooking Time: 25 Minutes
Ingredients:
- 2 cans Great Northern beans
- 2 tbsp olive oil
- 1 onion, minced
- 2 garlic cloves, minced
- 1 can diced tomatoes
- ½ cup pure date syrup
- 1 ½ tsp dry mustard
- ¼ tsp cayenne pepper
- Sea salt and pepper to taste

Directions:
1. Preheat your oven to 350ºF. Heat the oil in a pot over medium heat. Place in onion and garlic and sauté for 3 minutes. Add in tomatoes, date syrup, mustard, cayenne pepper, salt, and pepper. Cook for 5 minutes. Pour the beans into a baking dish and stir in the sauce to coat. Bake for 10 minutes. Serve warm.

Nutrition Info:
- Per Serving: Calories: 815;Fat: 9g;Protein: 40g;Carbs: 148.6g.

Baked Tempeh & Brussels Sprouts

Servings: 4
Cooking Time: 30 Minutes
Ingredients:
- 3 tbsp olive oil
- 1 cup tempeh, cubed
- 1 lb halved Brussels sprouts
- 5 garlic cloves, minced
- 1 ¼ cups coconut cream
- 2 tbsp grated Parmesan
- Sea salt and pepper to taste

Directions:
1. Preheat your oven to 400ºF. Warm the olive oil in a large skillet over medium heat and fry the tempeh cubes until browned on both sides, about 6 minutes. Remove onto a plate and set aside. Pour the Brussels sprouts and garlic into the skillet and sauté until fragrant. Mix in coconut cream and simmer for 4 minutes. Add tempeh cubes and combine well. Pour the sauté into a baking dish and sprinkle with Parmesan cheese. Bake for 10 minutes or until golden brown on top. Serve with tomato salad.

Nutrition Info:
- Per Serving: Calories: 510;Fat: 42g;Protein: 17g;Carbs: 26g.

Challenging Grain-free Fritters

Servings: 12
Cooking Time: 20 Minutes
Ingredients:

- 2 cups chickpea flour
- 1½ cups water
- 2 tablespoons chia seeds, ground
- ½ teaspoon salt
- 3 cups lightly packed spinach leaves, finely chopped
- 1 tablespoon coconut oil, or extra-virgin olive oil

Directions:
1. Whisk together the chickpea flour, water, chia seeds, and salt in a medium bowl. Ensure that there are no lumps by mixing it well.
2. Fold in the spinach.
3. Melt the coconut oil in a nonstick skillet set over medium-low heat.
4. Working in batches, use a ¼-cup measure to drop the batter into the pan. Flatten the fritters to about ½ inch thick. Don't crowd the pan.
5. Cook for 5 to 6 minutes. Flip the fritters and cook for 5 minutes more.
6. Transfer to a serving plate.

Nutrition Info:
- Per Serving: Calories: 318 ;Fat: 10g ;Protein: 15g ;Carbs: 45g .

Pasta Primavera With Cherry Tomatoes

Servings: 4
Cooking Time: 25 Minutes
Ingredients:
- 8 oz whole-wheat fidelini
- 2 tbsp olive oil
- ½ tsp paprika
- 1 small red onion, sliced
- 2 garlic cloves, minced
- 1 cup dry white wine
- Sea salt and pepper to taste
- 18 cherry tomatoes, halved
- 1 lemon, zested and juiced
- 1 cup basil leaves

Directions:
1. Heat the olive oil in a pot. Add the paprika, onion, garlic, and stir-fry for 2-3 minutes. Mix in white wine, pasta, salt, and pepper. Cover with water. Cook until the water absorbs and the fidelini al dente, 5 minutes. Mix in cherry tomatoes, lemon zest, lemon juice, and basil. Serve.

Nutrition Info:
- Per Serving: Calories: 365;Fat: 14g;Protein: 11g;Carbs: 49g.

Tomato & Alfredo Penne

Servings: 4
Cooking Time: 20 Minutes
Ingredients:
- 2 cups almond milk
- 1 ½ cups vegetable broth
- 3 tbsp olive oil
- 1 large garlic clove, minced
- 16 oz whole-wheat penne
- ½ cup coconut cream
- 18 halved cherry tomatoes
- ¾ cup grated Parmesan
- 2 tbsp chopped parsley

Directions:
1. Bring almond milk, vegetable broth, olive oil, and garlic to a boil in a large pot, 5 minutes. Mix in the fettuccine and cook until tender while frequently tossing for about 10 minutes. Mix in coconut cream, tomatoes, Parmesan cheese, salt, and pepper. Cook for 3 minutes or until the cheese melts. Garnish with some parsley and serve warm.

Nutrition Info:
- Per Serving: Calories: 720;Fat: 27g;Protein: 22g;Carbs: 100g.

Feels Like Autumn Loaf With Root Vegetable

Servings: 6 To 8
Cooking Time: 55 Minutes To 1 Hour
Ingredients:
- 1 onion, finely chopped
- 2 tablespoons water
- 2 cups carrots, grated
- 1½ cups sweet potatoes, grated
- 1½ cups rolled oats, gluten-free
- ¾ cup butternut squash, purée
- 1 teaspoon salt

Directions:
1. Preheat the oven to 350°F.
2. Line a loaf pan with parchment paper.
3. Sauté the onion in the water in a large pot set over medium heat for 5 minutes, or until soft.
4. Add the carrots and sweet potatoes. Cook for 2 minutes. Remove the pot from the heat.
5. Stir in the oats, butternut squash purée, and salt. Mix well.
6. Transfer the mixture to the prepared loaf pan, pressing down evenly.
7. Place the pan in the preheated oven and bake for 50 to 55 minutes, uncovered, or until the loaf is firm and golden.
8. Cool for 10 minutes before slicing.

Nutrition Info:
- Per Serving: Calories: 169 ;Fat: 2g ;Protein: 5g ;Carbs: 34g .

Restorative Stew With Lentil And Corn

Servings: 4 To 6
Cooking Time: 15 Minutes
Ingredients:
- 1 tablespoon extra-virgin olive oil
- 1 onion, chopped
- 3 carrots, peeled and sliced
- 8 Brussels sprouts, halved
- 1 large turnip, peeled, quartered, and sliced
- 1 garlic clove, sliced
- 6 cups vegetable broth
- One 15 ounces can lentils, drained and rinsed
- 1 cup corn, frozen
- 1 teaspoon salt
- ¼ teaspoon black pepper, freshly ground
- 1 tablespoon fresh parsley, chopped

Directions:
1. Heat the oil over high heat in a Dutch oven.
2. Add the onion and sauté until softened for 3 minutes.
3. Add the carrots, Brussels sprouts, turnip, and garlic and sauté for 3 minutes more.
4. Add the broth and bring to a boil. Reduce to a simmer and cook until the vegetables are tender for 5 minutes.
5. Add the lentils, corn, salt, pepper, and parsley, and cook for a minute to heat the lentils and corn. Serve hot.

Nutrition Info:
- Per Serving: Calories: 240 ;Fat: 4g ;Protein: 10g ;Carbs: 42g.

Versatile Zucchini Patties

Servings: 2
Cooking Time: 5 Minutes
Ingredients:
- 2 medium zucchinis, shredded
- 1 teaspoon salt, divided
- 2 eggs
- 2 tablespoons chickpea flour
- 1 scallion, chopped
- 1 tablespoon fresh mint, chopped
- ½ teaspoon salt
- 2 tablespoons extra-virgin olive oil

Directions:
1. In a fine-mesh strainer, place the shredded zucchini and sprinkle it with ½ teaspoon of salt. Set aside to drain while assembling the other ingredients.
2. Beat together the eggs, chickpea flour, scallion, mint, and the remaining ½ teaspoon of salt in a medium bowl.
3. Gently squeeze the zucchini to drain as much liquid as possible before adding it to the egg mixture. Stir to mix well.
4. Place a large skillet over medium-high heat.
5. Add the olive oil when the pan is hot. Drop the zucchini mixture by spoonful into the pan. Gently flatten the zucchini with the back of a spatula.
6. Cook for 2 to 3 minutes, or until golden brown. Flip and cook for about 2 minutes more on the other side.

7. Serve warm or at room temperature.

Nutrition Info:

- Per Serving: Calories: 263 ;Fat: 20g ;Protein: 10g ;Carbs: 16g .

Mushroom & Green Bean Biryani

Servings: 4

Cooking Time: 50 Minutes

Ingredients:

- 1 cup chopped mushrooms
- 1 cup brown rice
- 3 tbsp olive oil
- 3 white onions, chopped
- 6 garlic cloves, minced
- 1 tsp ginger puree
- 1 tbsp turmeric powder
- ¼ tsp cinnamon powder
- 2 tsp garam masala
- ½ tsp cardamom powder
- ½ tsp cayenne powder
- ½ tsp cumin powder
- 1 tsp smoked paprika
- 3 large tomatoes, diced
- 2 green chilies, minced
- 1 tbsp tomato puree
- 1 cup chopped mustard greens
- 1 cup Greek yogurt

Directions:

1. Warm the olive oil in a large pot over medium heat. Sauté the onions until softened, 3 minutes. Mix in the garlic, ginger, turmeric, cardamom, garam masala, cayenne pepper, cumin, paprika, and salt. Stir-fry for 1-2 minutes. Pour in the tomatoes, green chili, tomato puree, and mushrooms. Once boiling, mix in the rice and cover it with water. Cover the pot and cook until the liquid absorbs and the rice is tender, 15-20 minutes. Open the lid and fluff in the mustard greens and parsley. Top with coconut yogurt and serve.

Nutrition Info:

- Per Serving: Calories: 395;Fat: 13g;Protein: 6g;Carbs: 59g.

Grilled Tempeh With Green Beans

Servings: 4

Cooking Time: 15 Minutes

Ingredients:

- 1 lb tempeh, sliced
- 1 lb green beans, trimmed
- Sea salt and pepper to taste
- 3 tbsp olive oil
- 1 tbsp maple syrup
- 1 lemon, juiced

Directions:

1. Preheat a grill pan over medium heat. Season the tempeh and green beans with salt and black pepper and brush them with some olive oil. Grill the tempeh and green beans on both sides until golden brown and tender, 10 minutes. Transfer to serving plates. In a small bowl, whisk the remaining olive oil, maple syrup, lemon juice, and drizzle all over the food. Serve warm.

Nutrition Info:

- Per Serving: Calories: 360;Fat: 23g;Protein: 23g;Carbs: 23g.

White Salad With Walnut Pesto

Servings: 4

Cooking Time: 25 Minutes

Ingredients:

- 1 lb sweet potato chunks
- 3 cups cauliflower florets
- 1 can cannellini beans
- 10 Kalamata olives, halved
- ½ cup walnuts
- 2 garlic cloves, minced
- ½ cup chopped parsley
- ¼ cup walnut oil
- ¼ cup olive oil
- ¼ cup white wine vinegar
- Sea salt to taste
- ¼ tsp crushed red pepper

Directions:

1. Cook the sweet potatoes for 15 minutes in salted water. Add in the cauliflower and cook for another 5 minutes until the veggies are tender. Drain and remove to a bowl. Stir in beans, olives, and half of the walnuts. In a food processor, mix the remaining walnuts, garlic, parsley, walnut oil, olive oil, vinegar, salt, sugar, and red pepper. Blitz until well blended. Pour the dressing over the salad and toss to combine. Serve and enjoy!

Nutrition Info:

- Per Serving: Calories: 355;Fat: 24g;Protein: 7g;Carbs: 30g.

Zucchini & Pepper Hash With Fried Eggs

Servings: 4

Cooking Time: 25 Minutes

Ingredients:

- 4 tbsp olive oil
- 1 onion, chopped
- 1 red bell pepper, chopped
- 4 zucchinis, cubed
- Sea salt and pepper to taste
- 4 eggs

Directions:

1. Warm 2 tbsp of olive oil in a skillet over medium heat. Place in onion, red bell pepper, zucchini, salt, and pepper and cook for 10-15 minutes until the zucchini are tender and browned. Divide the veggies between 4 plates.

2. Warm the remaining olive oil in a skillet. Break the eggs, sprinkle with salt and cook for 3-4 minutes until the whites

set. Flip the eggs and turn the heat off. Let cook for 1 minute. Serve each sweet potato plate with a fried egg.

Nutrition Info:

- Per Serving: Calories: 390;Fat: 20g;Protein: 9g;Carbs: 48g.

Health Supportive Vegetable Curry

Servings: 4 To 6
Cooking Time: 15 Minutes

Ingredients:

- 1 tablespoon coconut oil
- 1 onion, chopped
- 2 cups (½-inch) butternut squash cubes
- 1 large sweet potato, peeled and cut into ½-inch cubes
- 2 garlic cloves, sliced
- One 13 ½ ounces can coconut milk
- 2 cups vegetable broth
- 2 teaspoons curry powder
- 1 teaspoon salt
- 2 tablespoons fresh cilantro, chopped

Directions:

1. Heat the oil over high heat in a Dutch oven.
2. Add the onion and sauté until softened for 3 minutes.
3. Add the butternut squash, sweet potato, and garlic and sauté for 3 minutes more.
4. Add the coconut milk, broth, curry powder, and salt and bring to a boil. Reduce to a simmer and cook until the vegetables are tender for 5 minutes.
5. Top with cilantro and serve.

Nutrition Info:

- Per Serving: Calories: 120 ;Fat: 5g ;Protein: 2g ;Carbs: 20g .

Mushroom Lettuce Wraps

Servings: 4
Cooking Time: 25 Minutes

Ingredients:

- 4 oz baby Bella mushrooms, sliced
- 2 tbsp olive oil
- 1 ½ lb tofu, crumbled
- 1 lettuce, leaves extracted
- 1 cup grated Parmesan
- 1 large tomato, sliced

Directions:

1. Warm the olive oil in a skillet, add mushrooms, and sauté until browned and tender, about 6 minutes. Transfer to a plate. Add the tofu to the skillet and cook until brown, about 10 minutes. Spoon the tofu and mushrooms into the lettuce leaves, sprinkle with the Parmesan cheese, and share the tomato slices on top. Serve immediately.

Nutrition Info:

- Per Serving: Calories: 530;Fat: 29g;Protein: 39g;Carbs: 40g.

Spicy Moong Beans

Servings: 4

Cooking Time: 40 Minutes

Ingredients:

- 1 tsp paprika
- 2 tsp curry powder
- 2 cups moong beans, soaked
- 1 onion, diced
- 1 tsp turmeric
- Juice of 1 lime
- 1 jalapeno pepper, chopped
- 1 sprig curry leaves
- 4 garlic cloves, minced
- 2 tbsp olive oil
- 1 ½ tsp cumin seeds
- 2 tomatoes, chopped
- 1-inch piece ginger, grated

Directions:

1. Heat the oil in the pressure cooker on "Sauté". Add the cumin seeds and sauté for about a minute and a half. Add the onion and cook until translucent, about 2 minutes. Add the garlic, curry, turmeric, ginger, and salt. Cook for one more minute. Stir in the jalapeño and tomatoes and cook for 5 minutes, or until soft. Add the beans and pour water to cover the ingredients. Cover by at least 2 inches. Add the lime juice and curry leaves and close the lid. Select "Manual" and cook for 15 minutes on high pressure. Do a quick pressure release. Serve.

Nutrition Info:

- Per Serving: Calories: 330;Fat: 5g;Protein: 10g;Carbs: 63g.

Satisfying Mushroom Risotto

Servings: 4
Cooking Time: 20 Minutes

Ingredients:

- 2 tablespoons extra-virgin olive oil
- 1 large shallot, sliced
- 1 garlic clove, minced
- 1 pint sliced mushrooms
- 1½ cups arborio rice
- 3 cups vegetable broth, warmed
- 1 teaspoon salt
- ½ teaspoon black pepper, freshly ground
- Pinch ground nutmeg
- 1 tablespoon fresh thyme leaves, chopped
- Balsamic vinegar

Directions:

1. Heat the olive oil in a large skillet over high heat. Add the shallot and garlic. Sauté for 3 minutes.
2. Add the mushrooms and rice. Sauté for 3 minutes more.
3. Lower the heat to medium-high. Add the vegetable broth one cup at a time while stirring constantly until the rice has absorbed the liquid before adding another cup of broth.

4. Add the salt, pepper, and nutmeg once all the broth is absorbed. Taste the risotto to see if the rice is cooked through. It should be tender but not mushy.

5. Transfer the risotto to a serving dish. Garnish with thyme leaves and drizzle with balsamic vinegar.

Nutrition Info:
- Per Serving: Calories: 359 ;Fat: 9g ;Protein: 10g ;Carbs: 60g .

Savoy Cabbage Rolls With Tofu

Servings: 4
Cooking Time: 30 Minutes
Ingredients:
- 1 head Savoy cabbage, leaves separated (scraps kept)
- 2 tbsp olive oil
- 2 cups tofu, crumbled
- ½ onion, chopped
- 2 garlic cloves, minced
- Sea salt and pepper to taste
- 1 cup buckwheat groats
- 1 ¾ cups vegetable stock
- 1 bay leaf
- 2 tbsp chopped cilantro
- 23 oz canned diced tomatoes

Directions:
1. Warm the olive oil in a large bowl and cook the tofu until golden brown, 8 minutes. Stir in the onion and garlic until softened and fragrant, 3 minutes. Season with salt and black pepper and mix in the buckwheat, bay leaf, and vegetable stock. Close the lid, allow boiling, and then simmer until all the liquid is absorbed. Open the lid, remove the bay leaf, and adjust the taste with salt and pepper. Lay the cabbage leaves on a flat surface and add 3 to 4 tablespoons of the cooked buckwheat onto each leaf. Roll the leaves to secure the filling firmly. Pour the tomatoes with juices into a medium pot, season with a little salt, pepper, and lay the cabbage rolls in the sauce. Cook over medium heat until the cabbage softens, 5-8 minutes. Garnish with more cilantro and serve.

Nutrition Info:
- Per Serving: Calories: 330;Fat: 18g;Protein: 23g;Carbs: 24g.

Tuscan-style Asparagus Frittata

Servings: 4
Cooking Time: 20 Minutes
Ingredients:
- 2 tbsp olive oil
- 10 asparagus, trimmed
- 10 cherry tomatoes
- 6 eggs
- 1 tbsp fresh thyme, chopped
- 1 tsp Italian spice blend

Directions:
1. Preheat your oven to 390°F. Warm the olive oil in a skillet over medium heat and place the asparagus and cook

for 5 minutes. Stir in tomatoes and cook for another 3 minutes. Beat the eggs, thyme, and Italian spice blend in a bowl and pour it over the veggies and move the skillet to spread the egg. Low the heat and cook for 3 minutes until the edges are set. Pull eggs away from the edges of the pan and move them to allow the uncooked egg to spread into the pan. Cook for 2-3 minutes until set. Bake in the oven for 3-5 minutes until browns. Serve warm.

Nutrition Info:
- Per Serving: Calories: 230;Fat: 15g;Protein: 6g;Carbs: 16g.

Hot Quinoa Florentine

Servings: 4
Cooking Time: 30 Minutes
Ingredients:
- ½ tsp crushed red pepper
- 2 tbsp olive oil
- 1 onion, chopped
- 3 cups fresh baby spinach
- 3 garlic cloves, minced
- 2 cups quinoa well
- 4 cups vegetable broth
- Sea salt and pepper to taste

Directions:
1. Warm the olive oil in a pot over medium heat, place the onion and spinach, and cook for 3 minutes. Stir in garlic and crushed red pepper and cook for another 30 seconds. Mix in quinoa, vegetable broth, salt, and pepper, bring to a boil, low the heat, and simmer for 15-20 minutes until the liquid is absorbed. Fluff the quinoa and serve.

Nutrition Info:
- Per Serving: Calories: 410;Fat: 13g;Protein: 8g;Carbs: 63g.

Tempeh & Vegetable Stir-fry

Servings: 4
Cooking Time: 30 Minutes
Ingredients:
- 1 can whole tomatoes
- 1 lb crumbled tempeh
- 1 yellow onion, chopped
- 1 can tomato sauce
- 2 tbsp plain vinegar
- 1 tbsp pure date sugar
- 1 tsp dried mixed herbs
- 1 head cabbage, sliced
- 1 red bell pepper, cut into strips

Directions:
1. Drain the tomatoes and reserve their liquid. Chop the tomatoes and set aside. Add the tempeh to a large skillet and cook until brown, 10 minutes. Mix in the onion, tomato sauce, vinegar, date sugar, mixed herbs, and chopped tomatoes. Close the lid and cook until the liquid reduces, 10 minutes. Stir in the cabbage and bell pepper; cook until softened, 5 minutes. Serve and enjoy!

- Per Serving: Calories: 390;Fat: 16g;Protein: 24g;Carbs: 44g.

Kale Pizza With Grilled Zucchini

Servings: 4
Cooking Time: 30 Minutes
Ingredients:
- ¼ cup capers
- ½ cup grated Parmesan
- 3 ½ cups whole-wheat flour
- 1 tsp yeast
- 1 tsp sea salt
- 1 pinch sugar
- 3 tbsp olive oil
- 1 cup marinara sauce
- 2 large zucchinis, sliced
- ½ cup chopped kale
- 1 tsp oregano

Directions:
1. Preheat your oven the 350ºF and lightly grease a pizza pan with cooking spray. In a bowl, mix flour, nutritional yeast, salt, sugar, olive oil, and 1 cup of warm water until smooth dough forms. Allow rising for an hour or until the dough doubles in size. Spread the dough on the pizza pan and apply marinara sauce and oregano on top.
2. Heat a grill pan, season the zucchinis with salt, black pepper, and cook in the pan until slightly charred on both sides. Sit the zucchini on the pizza crust and top with kale, capers, and Parmesan cheese. Bake for 20 minutes. Cool for 5 minutes, slice, and serve.

Nutrition Info:
- Per Serving: Calories: 530;Fat: 16g;Protein: 19g;Carbs: 83g.

Mediterranean Chickpeas With Vegetables

Servings: 6
Cooking Time: 40 Minutes
Ingredients:
- 3 tbsp olive oil
- 1 red onion, chopped
- 2 carrots, chopped
- 1 celery stalk, chopped
- 2 garlic cloves, minced
- 1 tsp grated fresh ginger
- 1 tsp ground cumin
- ½ tsp turmeric
- 2 parsnips, chopped
- 8 oz green beans, chopped
- 1 can chickpeas
- 1 can diced tomatoes
- 1 ½ cups vegetable broth
- 1 tsp fresh lemon juice

Directions:

1. Heat the oil in a pot over medium heat. Place in onion, carrots, celery, garlic, and ginger. Sauté for 5 minutes. Add cumin, turmeric, parsnips, green beans, chickpeas, tomatoes and juices, and broth. Bring to a boil, then lower the heat and sprinkle with salt and pepper. Simmer for 30 minutes. Sprinkle with lemon juice and cilantro.

Nutrition Info:
- Per Serving: Calories: 205;Fat: 9g;Protein: 5g;Carbs: 29g.

Leafy Green Risotto

Servings: 6
Cooking Time: 20 Minutes
Ingredients:
- 3 ½ cups veggie broth
- 1 cup spinach, packed
- 1 cup kale leaves, packed
- ¼ cup grated Parmesan
- ¼ cup diced onion
- 3 tbsp olive oil
- 2 tsp olive oil
- 1 ½ cups arborio brown rice
- 4 sun-dried tomatoes, minced
- A pinch of nutmeg
- Sea salt and pepper to taste

Directions:
1. Heat the olive oil in your cooker on "Sauté". Add the onions and cook until soft, about 2 minutes. Add rice and cook for 3-4 more minutes. Pour the broth over. Close the lid and cook for 6 minutes on "Manual". Do a quick pressure release and stir in the remaining ingredients. Leave for a minute or two or until the greens become wilted. Serve and enjoy.

Nutrition Info:
- Per Serving: Calories: 270;Fat: 10g;Protein: 6g;Carbs: 40g.

Mushroom Pizza

Servings: 4
Cooking Time: 35 Minutes
Ingredients:
- 1 cup chopped button mushrooms
- ½ cup sliced mixed bell peppers
- 2 tsp olive oil
- Sea salt and pepper to taste
- 1 whole-wheat pizza crust
- 1 cup tomato sauce
- 1 cup grated Parmesan
- 4 basil leaves

Directions:
1. Warm the olive oil in a skillet and sauté mushrooms and bell peppers for 10 minutes until softened. Season with salt and black pepper. Put the pizza crust on a pizza pan, spread the tomato sauce all over, and scatter vegetables evenly on top. Sprinkle with Parmesan. Bake for 20 minutes until the cheese has melted. Garnish with basil.

Nutrition Info:
- Per Serving: Calories: 420;Fat: 24g;Protein: 30g;Carbs: 39g.

Soft Zucchini With White Beans And Olives Stuffing

Servings: 4
Cooking Time: 20 Minutes
Ingredients:
- 4 large zucchinis, halved lengthwise
- 2 tablespoons extra-virgin olive oil, plus additional for brushing
- ½ teaspoon salt, plus additional for seasoning
- Freshly ground black pepper
- Pinch ground rosemary
- One 15 ounces can white beans, drained and rinsed
- ½ cup pitted green olives, chopped
- 2 garlic cloves, minced
- 1 cup arugula, coarsely chopped
- ¼ cup fresh parsley, chopped
- 1 tablespoon apple cider vinegar

Directions:
1. Preheat the oven to 375°F.
2. Brush a rimmed baking sheet with olive oil.
3. Carefully scoop out using a small spoon or melon baller and discard the seeds from the zucchini halves.
4. Brush the scooped-out section of each zucchini boat with olive oil and lightly season the inside of each boat with salt, pepper, and rosemary.
5. Transfer the zucchini to the prepared baking sheet, cut-side up. Place the sheet in the preheated oven and roast for 15 to 20 minutes, or until the zucchini are tender and lightly browned.
6. Lightly mash in a medium bowl the white beans with a fork.
7. Add the olives, garlic, arugula, parsley, cider vinegar, the remaining ½ teaspoon of salt, and the remaining 2 tablespoons of olive oil. Season with pepper and mix well.
8. Spoon the bean mixture into the zucchini boats and serve.

Nutrition Info:
- Per Serving: Calories: 269| Fat: 12g ;Protein: 13g ;Carbs: 38g.

Savoury Pasta With Sun-dried Tomato And Nut

Servings: 2
Cooking Time: 20 Minutes
Ingredients:
- 1 cup 100% whole grain pasta
- 1 clove of garlic, minced
- ¼ cup of walnuts, coarsely chopped
- ½ cup sun-dried tomatoes, drained & chopped
- 2 tablespoons extra virgin olive oil
- 1 bunch fresh basil, chopped

- 100g of low-fat mozzarella cheese
- pinch of black pepper

Directions:
1. Boil a large saucepan of water on high heat.
2. Add the pasta and cook following directions on the package.
3. Prepare the sauce while the pasta is cooking.
4. Put minced garlic in a bowl.
5. Add sun-dried tomatoes, walnuts, basil, mozzarella, and oil.
6. Once the pasta is cooked, drain and add to the sauce.
7. Toss through until the pasta is well coated.
8. Transfer the dish onto a serving plate.

Nutrition Info:
- Per Serving: Calories: 245 ;Fat: 13g ;Protein: 5g ;Carbs: 29g.

Carrot & Black Bean Chili

Servings: 4
Cooking Time: 25 Minutes
Ingredients:
- 2 tbsp olive oil
- 1 onion, chopped
- 2 carrots, chopped
- 1 tsp grated fresh ginger
- 1 green bell pepper, chopped
- 2 tbsp chili powder
- 1 can diced tomatoes
- 1 can black beans
- 3 minced green onions

Directions:
1. Heat the oil in a pot over medium heat. Place in onion, carrot, ginger, bell pepper, and chili powder. Sauté for 5 minutes until tender. Stir in tomatoes, 2 cups of water, beans, salt, and pepper. Bring to a boil, then lower the heat, and simmer for 15 minutes. Top with green onions.

Nutrition Info:
- Per Serving: Calories: 230;Fat: 9g;Protein: 6g;Carbs: 34g.

Roasted Butternut Squash With Chimichurri

Servings: 4
Cooking Time: 15 Minutes
Ingredients:
- Zest and juice of 1 lemon
- ½ red bell pepper, chopped
- 1 jalapeño pepper, chopped
- 1 cup olive oil
- ½ cup chopped parsley
- 2 garlic cloves, minced
- 1 lb butternut squash
- 1 tbsp olive oil
- 3 tbsp toasted pine nuts

Directions:

1. In a bowl, add lemon zest and juice, bell pepper, jalapeno, olive oil, parsley, garlic, salt, and pepper. Use an immersion blender to grind the ingredients until your desired consistency is achieved; set aside the chimichurri.

2. Slice the butternut squash into rounds and remove the seeds. Drizzle with olive oil and season with salt and black pepper. Preheat a grill pan over medium heat.Cook the squash for 2 minutes on each side or until browned. Remove to serving plates, scatter the pine nuts on top, and serve with the chimichurri and red cabbage salad.

Nutrition Info:

- Per Serving: Calories: 615;Fat: 62g;Protein: 2g;Carbs: 17g.

Rice With Green Lentil & Celery

Servings: 4
Cooking Time: 50 Minutes
Ingredients:

- 2 tbsp olive oil
- 1 lb tempeh, cut into cubes
- 1 yellow onion, chopped
- Sea salt and pepper to taste
- 1 tsp chili powder
- 1 tsp cumin powder
- 2 celery stalks, chopped
- 2 carrots diced
- 4 garlic cloves, minced
- 3 cups vegetable broth
- 1 tsp oregano
- 1 cup green lentils
- ¼ cup diced tomatoes
- 1 lime, juiced
- 1 cup brown rice

Directions:

1. Heat the olive oil in a large pot, season the tempeh with salt, pepper, and cook for 10 minutes. Stir in chili powder, cumin powder, onion, celery, carrots, garlic, and cook for 5 minutes. Pour in vegetable broth, oregano, green lentils, tomatoes, brown rice, and green chilies. Cover the pot and cook for 18-20 minutes. Open the lid, adjust the taste with salt and pepper. Mix in the lime juice. Serve.

Nutrition Info:

- Per Serving: Calories: 535;Fat: 23g;Protein: 24g;Carbs: 61g.

Herby Quinoa With Walnuts

Servings: 4
Cooking Time: 20 Minutes
Ingredients:

- 2 minced sundried tomatoes
- 1 cup quinoa
- 2 cups vegetable broth
- 2 garlic cloves, minced
- ¼ cup chopped chives
- 2 tbsp chopped parsley
- 2 tbsp chopped basil

- 2 tbsp chopped mint
- 1 tbsp olive oil
- ½ tsp lemon zest
- 1 tbsp lemon juice
- 2 tbsp minced walnuts

Directions:

1. In a pot, combine quinoa, vegetable broth, and garlic. Boil until the quinoa is tender and the liquid absorbs, 10-15 minutes. Fuff with a fork and stir in chives, parsley, basil, mint, tomatoes, olive oil, zest, lemon juice, and walnuts. Warm for 5 minutes. Serve.

Nutrition Info:

- Per Serving: Calories: 225;Fat: 8g;Protein: 28g;Carbs: 31g.

Ultimate Burger With Hummus

Servings: 4
Cooking Time: 30 Minutes
Ingredients:

- 1 tablespoon extra-virgin olive oil, plus additional for brushing
- Two 15 ounces cans garbanzo beans, drained and rinsed
- ¼ cup tahini
- 1 tablespoon lemon juice, freshly squeezed
- 2 teaspoons lemon zest
- 2 garlic cloves, minced
- 2 tablespoons chickpea flour
- 4 scallions, minced
- 1 teaspoon salt

Directions:

1. Preheat the oven to 375°F.
2. Brush a baking sheet with olive oil.
3. Combine the garbanzo beans, tahini, lemon juice, lemon zest, garlic, and the remaining 1 tablespoon of olive oil in a food processor. Pulse until smooth.
4. Add the chickpea flour, scallions, and salt. Pulse to combine.
5. Form the mixture into four patties and place them on the prepared baking sheet. Place the sheet in the preheated oven and bake for 30 minutes.

Nutrition Info:

- Per Serving: Calories: 408 ;Fat: 18g ;Protein: 19g ;Carbs: 43g .

Scallion & Feta Fried Rice

Servings: 4
Cooking Time: 25 Minutes
Ingredients:

- 2 tbsp olive oil
- 8 oz feta cheese, crumbled
- 6 scallions, thinly sliced
- 2 cups kale, chopped
- 3 cups cooked brown rice
- ¼ cup stir-fry sauce

Directions:

1. Warm the olive oil in a skillet over medium heat and place in the scallions and kale; cook for 5-7 minutes until the veggies are tender. Mix in brown rice and stir-fry sauce and cook for 3-5 minutes until all heat through. Top with feta cheese and serve. Enjoy!

Nutrition Info:
- Per Serving: Calories: 300;Fat: 12g;Protein: 4g;Carbs: 37g.

Acorn Squash Stuffed With Beans & Spinach

Servings: 4
Cooking Time: 60 Minutes
Ingredients:
- 2 lb large acorn squash
- 2 tbsp olive oil
- 3 garlic cloves, minced
- 1 can white beans
- 1 cup chopped spinach
- ½ cup vegetable stock
- Sea salt and pepper to taste
- ½ tsp cumin powder
- ½ tsp chili powder

Directions:
1. Preheat your oven to 350°F. Cut the squash in half and scoop out the seeds. Season with salt and pepper and place face down on a sheet pan. Bake for 45 minutes.
2. Heat olive oil in a pot over medium heat. Sauté garlic until fragrant, 30 seconds and mix in beans and spinach; allow wilting for 2 minutes. Season with salt, black pepper, cumin powder, and chili powder. Cook for 2 minutes and turn the heat off. When the squash is fork-tender, remove from the oven and fill the holes with the bean and spinach mixture. Serve and enjoy!

Nutrition Info:
- Per Serving: Calories: 240;Fat: 8g;Protein: 3g;Carbs: 40g.

Watercress & Mushroom Spaghetti

Servings: 4
Cooking Time: 30 Minutes
Ingredients:
- ½ lb chopped button mushrooms
- 1 lb whole-wheat spaghetti
- 2 tbsp olive oil
- 2 shallots, chopped
- 2 garlic cloves, minced
- 4 tsp low-sodium soy sauce
- 1 tsp hot sauce
- A handful of watercress
- ¼ cup chopped parsley
- Sea salt and pepper to taste

Directions:
1. Cook spaghetti in lightly salted water in a large pot over medium heat until al dente, 10 minutes. Drain and set aside.

Heat the olive oil in a skillet and sauté shallots, garlic, and mushrooms for 5 minutes. Stir in soy sauce, and hot sauce. Cook for 1 minute. Toss spaghetti in the sauce along with watercress and parsley. Season with black pepper. Dish the food and serve warm.

Nutrition Info:
- Per Serving: Calories: 485;Fat: 9g;Protein: 13g;Carbs: 90g.

Frittata With Kale & Seeds

Servings: 4
Cooking Time: 30 Minutes
Ingredients:
- 2 tbsp sour cream
- 2 tbsp olive oil
- 4 cups chopped kale
- 3 garlic cloves, minced
- 8 eggs
- Sea salt and pepper to taste
- 2 tbsp sunflower seeds

Directions:
1. Preheat your oven to 390°F. Warm the olive oil in a skillet over medium heat and place in kale. Cook for 5 minutes until soft. Add in garlic and cook for another 30 seconds. Beat the eggs, sour cream, salt, and pepper in a bowl and pour it over the kale. Cook for 3 minutes over low heat until set. Pull the eggs away from the edges of the pan and move the pan to allow the uncooked egg to spread into the pan. Cook for 3 minutes until set. Top with sunflower seeds and bake in the oven for 3-5 minutes until browns. Slice into wedges. Serve warm.

Nutrition Info:
- Per Serving: Calories: 230;Fat: 18g;Protein: 2g;Carbs: 10g.

Hot Paprika Lentils

Servings: 6
Cooking Time: 20 Minutes
Ingredients:
- 1 onion, chopped
- 3 tbsp olive oil
- 1 tbsp hot paprika
- 2 ¼ cups lentils, drained
- 3 garlic cloves, minced
- ½ tsp dried thyme

Directions:
1. Heat the oil in a pot over medium heat. Place the onion and garlic and sauté for 3 minutes. Add in paprika, salt, pepper, 5 cups water, lentils, and thyme. Bring to a boil, lower the heat and simmer for 15 minutes, stirring often.

Nutrition Info:
- Per Serving: Calories: 105;Fat: 7g;Protein: 3g;Carbs: 9g.

Traditional Buckwheat Noodle Pad Thai

Servings: 4
Cooking Time: 15 Minutes
Ingredients:
- 1 package buckwheat soba noodles, 8 ounces
- 1 tablespoon coconut oil
- 1 red onion, chopped
- 2 garlic cloves, minced
- 2 teaspoons fresh ginger, minced
- 1 zucchini, chopped
- 2 bok choy, sliced thin
- 1 tablespoon coconut aminos
- 1 tablespoon apple cider vinegar
- 3 tablespoons almond butter or cashew butter
- 2 tablespoons sesame oil, toasted
- 1 tablespoon raw honey or coconut sugar
- ¼ cup vegetable broth, or water
- Salt
- 2 scallions, sliced thin
- ¼ cup fresh cilantro, chopped
- 2 tablespoons sesame seeds

Directions:
1. Cook the soba noodles according to the package directions, drain and set aside.
2. Melt the coconut oil in a large pan over high heat. Add the red onion, garlic, ginger, zucchini, and bok choy. Sauté for 5 minutes.
3. Add the coconut aminos, cider vinegar, almond butter, sesame oil, honey, and vegetable broth. Cook for 2 minutes while stirring constantly.
4. Add the soba noodles to the pan and sauté them, using a large spatula to scoop the mixture from the bottom of the pan to the top to combine the vegetables with the noodles. Season with salt, and transfer the Pad Thai to a serving dish. Garnish with scallions, cilantro, and sesame seeds.

Nutrition Info:
- Per Serving: Calories: 486 ;Fat: 21g ;Protein: 19g ;Carbs: 63g .

Dijon Faro & Walnut Salad

Servings: 4
Cooking Time: 50 Minutes
Ingredients:
- 1 cup faro
- 1 red onion, sliced
- 1 garlic clove, minced
- 2 tbsp white wine vinegar
- 1 tbsp Dijon mustard
- ¼ cup olive oil
- ½ tsp dried oregano
- Sea salt and pepper to taste
- ½ diced red bell pepper
- 1/3 cup chopped walnuts
- 2 tbsp minced parsley

Directions:
1. Cook faro in salted water for 25 minutes. Drain and set aside to cool. Put the onion, garlic, vinegar, mustard, oil, oregano, salt, and pepper in a bowl. Mix to combine. To the cooled faro, add bell peppers, walnuts, and parsley; stir. Drizzle with the onion mixture and serve.

Nutrition Info:
- Per Serving: Calories: 365;Fat: 20g;Protein: 2g;Carbs: 39g.

Unique And High In Fiber Portabella Mushroom Cups

Servings: 4
Cooking Time: 10 Minutes
Ingredients:
- 4 portabella mushrooms, large
- ½ cup wild rice/brown rice/quinoa, cooked
- 1 red bell pepper, chopped
- 1 beef tomato, chopped
- 4 cups of water
- ½ cucumber, chopped
- 1 green onion, sliced
- 4 teaspoons extra virgin olive oil
- 1 tablespoon of Dijon mustard
- 1 tablespoon white wine vinegar
- pinch of black pepper

Directions:
1. Preheat the broiler to medium-high heat.
2. In a separate bowl, combine the cooked quinoa, bell pepper, cucumber, green onion, mustard, white wine vinegar.
3. On a baking sheet, place the portabella mushrooms and lightly brush with olive oil.
4. Stack the mushroom caps with the quinoa mixture.
5. Place under the broiler for 10 minutes, then serve immediately.

Nutrition Info:
- Per Serving: Calories: 54 ;Fat: 2g ;Protein: 2g ;Carbs: 7g .

Avocado & Egg Salad Lettuce Cups

Servings: 4
Cooking Time: 10 Minutes
Ingredients:
- 1 avocado, stoned and diced
- 2 tbsp cilantro, chopped
- 8 hard-boiled eggs, chopped
- ¼ cup paleo mayonnaise
- 1 tsp Dijon mustard
- Sea salt and pepper to taste
- 4 large lettuce leaves

Directions:
1. Mix the avocado, eggs, cilantro, mayonnaise, mustard, salt, and pepper in a bowl until well combined. Spoon the salad into each lettuce leaf and serve well-chilled.

Basil & Tofu Stuffed Portobello Mushrooms

Servings: 4
Cooking Time: 25 Minutes
Ingredients:

- 4 large portobello mushrooms, stems removed
- Sea salt and pepper to taste
- ½ tsp olive oil
- 1 small onion, chopped
- 1 cup chopped fresh kale
- ¼ cup crumbled tofu
- 1 tbsp chopped fresh basil

Directions:
1. Preheat your oven to 350ºF. Lightly oil the mushrooms with some cooking spray and season with black pepper and salt. Arrange the mushrooms on a baking sheet and bake in the oven until tender, 10 to 15 minutes. Heat olive oil in a skillet and sauté onion until tender, 3 minutes. Stir in kale until wilted, 3 minutes. Spoon the mixture into the mushrooms and top with the tofu cheese and basil.

Nutrition Info:

- Per Serving: Calories: 45;Fat: 2g;Protein: 1g;Carbs: 4g.

Slightly Crunchy Roasted Broccoli And Cashews

Servings: 4
Cooking Time: 20 Minutes
Ingredients:

- 6 cups broccoli florets
- 2 tablespoons extra-virgin olive oil
- 1 teaspoon salt
- 1 tablespoon coconut aminos
- ½ cup toasted cashews

Directions:
1. Preheat the oven to 375°F.
2. Toss the broccoli with olive oil and salt in a large bowl. Transfer the broccoli to a baking sheet and spread it into a single layer. Place the sheet in the preheated oven and roast for 15 to 20 minutes, or until the broccoli is tender.
3. Toss the roasted broccoli with the coconut aminos and cashews in a large bowl and serve.

Nutrition Info:

- Per Serving: Calories: 209 ;Fat: 15g ;Protein: 6g ;Carbs: 15g .

Gingery Pea & Sweet Potato Skillet

Servings: 4
Cooking Time: 25 Minutes
Ingredients:

- 4 sweet potatoes, diced

Directions:
1. 2 tbsp olive oil

2. 1 medium onion, chopped
3. 1 tsp red chili powder
4. 1 tsp ginger-garlic paste
5. 1 tsp cumin powder
6. ¼ tsp turmeric powder
7. Sea salt and pepper to taste
8. 1 cup fresh green peas
9. Steam the sweet potatoes in a safe microwave bowl in the microwave for 8-10 minutes or until softened. Heat the olive oil in a wok and sauté the onion until softened, 3 minutes. Mix in the chili powder, ginger-garlic paste, cumin powder, turmeric powder, salt, and pepper. Cook until the fragrant release, 1 minute. Stir in the green peas, sweet potatoes, and cook until softened, 2-3 minutes.

Nutrition Info:

- Per Serving: Calories: 220;Fat: 7g;Protein: 3g;Carbs: 35.1g.

Cabbage & Bean Stir-fry

Servings: 2
Cooking Time: 20 Minutes
Ingredients:

- 2 tbsp peanuts, chopped
- 1 cup cooked white beans
- 1 tsp olive oil
- 2 carrots, julienned
- 1 cup sliced red cabbage
- 1 red bell pepper, sliced
- 2 scallions, chopped
- 3 tbsp mint, chopped
- 1 cup bean sprouts
- ¼ cup peanut sauce
- ¼ cup cilantro, chopped
- 2 lime wedges

Directions:
1. Heat oil in a skillet and cook carrots, cabbage, and bell pepper for 10-15 minutes. Stir in scallions, mint, and bean sprouts and cook for 1-2 minutes. Remove to a bowl. Mix in white beans and peanut sauce; toss to combine. Garnish with cilantro and peanuts. Serve with lime wedges on the side.

Nutrition Info:

- Per Serving: Calories: 405;Fat: 14g;Protein: 96g;Carbs: 57g.

Quinoa & Chickpea Pot

Servings: 2
Cooking Time: 15 Minutes
Ingredients:

- 2 tsp extra-virgin olive oil
- 1 cup cooked quinoa
- 1 can chickpeas
- 1 bunch arugula chopped
- 1 tbsp soy
- Sea salt and pepper to taste

Directions:

1. Heat the oil in a skillet over medium heat. Stir in quinoa, chickpeas, and arugula and cook for 3-5 minutes until the arugula wilts. Pour in soy sauce, salt, and pepper. Toss to coat. Serve immediately.

Nutrition Info:

- Per Serving: Calories: 340;Fat: 10g;Protein: 14g;Carbs: 50g.

Awesome Barley Jambalaya

Servings: 4
Cooking Time: 25 Minutes
Ingredients:

- 2 tbsp olive oil
- 1 onion, chopped
- 2 celery stalks, chopped
- 1 green bell pepper, chopped
- 2 garlic cloves, minced
- 1 cup pearl barley
- 2 cans kidney beans
- 1 can diced tomatoes
- 1 tsp dried rosemary
- 2 ½ cups vegetable broth
- 1 tbsp chopped parsley
- Sriracha sauce

Directions:

1. Heat the oil in a pot over medium heat. Place in onion, celery, bell pepper, and garlic. Sauté for 5 minutes. Add in barley, beans, tomatoes, rosemary, salt, and pepper. Stir in broth and simmer for 15 minutes. Top with parsley and drizzle with sriracha sauce to serve.

Nutrition Info:

- Per Serving: Calories: 440;Fat: 9g;Protein: 11g;Carbs: 78g.

Homemade Burgers With Bean And Yam

Servings: 4 To 6
Cooking Time: 35 Minutes
Ingredients:

- 1 cup rolled oats, gluten-free
- 3 cups cooked navy beans, 1½ cups dried
- 2 cups yam/sweet potato purée, about 2 yams/sweet potatoes, steamed and mashed
- ½ cup sunflower seed butter, or tahini
- 1 tablespoon fresh ginger, grated
- ½ teaspoon salt

Directions:

1. Pulse the oats in a food processor a few times until a rough meal form.
2. Add the beans, yam purée, sunflower seed butter, ginger, and salt. Blend until well mixed. You can make this completely smooth, or leave it slightly chunky.
3. For 30 minutes, refrigerate the mixture to be firm.
4. Preheat the oven to 350°F.
5. Line a baking sheet with parchment paper or Silpat.

6. Scoop the mixture onto the prepared sheet using a ◆?cup or ½-cup measure. Gently pat the mixture down so the patties are 1 inch thick. Makes about 12 patties.
7. Place the sheet in the preheated oven and bake for 35 minutes. Flip the burgers halfway through the cooking time.

Nutrition Info:

- Per Serving: Calories: 581 ;Fat: 19g ;Protein: 27g ;Carbs: 81g .

Broccoli Stuffed Cremini Mushrooms

Servings: 4
Cooking Time: 35 Minutes
Ingredients:

- ½ head broccoli, cut into florets
- 1 lb cremini mushroom caps
- 2 tbsp olive oil
- 1 onion, chopped
- 1 tsp garlic, minced
- 1 red bell pepper, chopped
- 1 tsp Cajun seasoning mix
- Sea salt and pepper to taste
- ¼ cup tofu, crumbled

Directions:

1. Preheat your oven to 360ºF. Bake mushroom caps in a greased baking dish for 10-12 minutes. In a food processor, place broccoli and pulse until it becomes like small rice-like granules. In a heavy-bottomed skillet, warm olive oil; stir in bell pepper, garlic, and onion and sauté until fragrant. Place in pepper, salt, and Cajun seasoning mix. Fold in broccoli rice. Divide the filling mixture among mushroom caps. Top with tofu and bake for 17 more minutes. Serve warm.

Nutrition Info:

- Per Serving: Calories: 175;Fat: 9g;Protein: 13g;Carbs: 19g.

Black Bean Burgers

Servings: 4
Cooking Time: 20 Minutes
Ingredients:

- 4 whole-grain hamburger buns, split
- 3 cans black beans
- 2 tbsp whole-wheat flour
- 2 tbsp quick-cooking oats
- ¼ cup chopped fresh basil
- 2 tbsp pure barbecue sauce
- 1 garlic clove, minced
- Sea salt and pepper to taste

Directions:

1. In a bowl, mash the black beans and mix in the flour, oats, basil, barbecue sauce, garlic salt, and black pepper until well combined. Mold patties out of the mixture.
2. Heat a grill pan to medium heat and lightly grease with cooking spray. Cook the bean patties on both sides until light brown and cooked through, 10 minutes. Place the patties between the burger buns and garnish with your favorite topping. Serve warm.

Magical One-pot Tomato Basil Pasta

Servings: 4
Cooking Time: 10 Minutes
Ingredients:
- 2 tablespoons extra-virgin olive oil, plus additional for drizzling
- 1 onion, sliced thin
- 2 garlic cloves, sliced thin
- 1 pound penne pasta, gluten-free
- One 15 ounces can tomatoes, chopped
- 1½ teaspoons salt
- ¼ teaspoon black pepper, freshly ground
- ¼ cup chopped fresh basil, plus 4 whole basil leaves
- 4½ cups water

Directions:
1. Heat 2 tablespoons of olive oil in a large, heavy-bottomed Dutch oven over medium heat. Add the onion and garlic. Stir to coat with the oil.
2. Add the pasta, tomatoes, salt, pepper, the 4 whole basil leaves, and water to the pot. Bring the liquid to a boil and cover the pot. Cook for 8 to 10 minutes. Check the pasta to see if it is cooked and add more water if necessary. Cook until the pasta is tender.
3. Transfer the pasta to a serving bowl and garnish with the remaining ¼ cup of chopped basil and a drizzle of olive oil.

Nutrition Info:
- Per Serving: Calories: 518 ;Fat: 11g ;Protein: 10g ;Carbs: 95g.

Broccoli Gratin

Servings: 4
Cooking Time: 50 Minutes
Ingredients:
- 1 can cream mushroom soup
- ¾ cup whole-wheat bread crumbs
- 1 tbsp olive oil
- 2 cups broccoli florets
- 1 cup paleo mayonnaise
- 3 tbsp coconut cream
- 1 red onion, chopped
- 2 cups grated Parmesan
- 3 tbsp almond butter, melted

Directions:
1. Preheat your oven to 350ºF. Heat the olive oil in a medium skillet and sauté the broccoli florets until softened, 8 minutes. Turn the heat off and mix in the mushroom soup, mayonnaise, salt, black pepper, coconut cream, and onion. Spread the mixture into the baking sheet. In a small bowl, mix the breadcrumbs with the almond butter and distribute the mixture on top. Top with Parmesan cheese. Place the casserole in the oven and bake until golden on top and the cheese melts. Serve warm.

Rice, Lentil & Spinach Pilaf

Servings: 4
Cooking Time: 25 Minutes
Ingredients:
- ½ cup wild rice
- 1 can lentils
- 1 can diced tomatoes
- 1 tsp dried thyme
- Sea salt and pepper to taste
- 3 cups baby spinach

Directions:
1. In a pot over medium heat, bring the rice and 1 ½ cups of salted water to a boil. Reduce the heat, cover, and simmer for 20 minutes. Add in lentils, tomatoes, thyme, salt, and pepper. Stir and cook until heated through. Mix in the spinach, cook for 2 minutes until the spinach wilts.

Nutrition Info:
- Per Serving: Calories: 135;Fat: 1g;Protein: 8g;Carbs: 28g.

Lovely Spring Roll Wraps With Vegetable

Servings: 4 To 6
Cooking Time: 0 Minutes
Ingredients:
- 10 rice paper wrappers
- 2 cups lightly packed baby spinach, divided
- 1 cup grated carrot, divided
- 1 cucumber, halved, seeded, and cut into thin, 4-inch-long strips, divided
- 1 avocado, halved, pitted, and cut into thin strips, divided

Directions:
1. Place a cutting board on a flat surface with the vegetables in front of you.
2. Fill a large, shallow bowl with warm water that is hot enough to cook the wrappers, but warm enough to touch it comfortably.
3. Soak 1 wrapper in the water and then place it on the cutting board.
4. Fill the middle of the wrapper with ¼ cup of spinach, 2 tablespoons of grated carrot, a few cucumber slices, and 1 or 2 slices of avocado.
5. Fold the sides over the middle, and then roll the wrapper tightly from the bottom like a burrito-style.
6. Repeat with the remaining wrappers and vegetables.
7. Serve immediately.

Nutrition Info:
- Per Serving: Calories: 246 ;Fat: 10g ;Protein: 4g ;Carbs: 36g.

Favourite Pizza With Quinoa Flatbread

Servings: 4 To 6
Cooking Time: 40 Minutes
Ingredients:
* 1 Quinoa Flatbread
* 1 cup pearl onions, halved
* 2 tablespoons extra-virgin olive oil
* 2 cups arugula
* 1 can artichoke hearts in water, 14 ounces

Directions:
1. Prepare the flatbread according to the recipe's instructions. Remove it from the oven when the flatbread is done and increase the heat to 375°F.
2. Toss together the pearl onions and olive oil in a small baking dish.
3. Place the dish in the preheated oven and roast for 10 minutes.
4. Scatter the onions over the crust.
5. Top with the arugula and artichoke hearts.
6. Place the pizza back in the oven and bake for 12 minutes.
7. Cool the pizza slightly before slicing and serving.

Nutrition Info:
* Per Serving: Calories: 181 ;Fat: 13g Protein: 4g ;;Carbs: 13g.

Herbaceous Omelette

Servings: 2
Cooking Time: 5 Minutes
Ingredients:
* 3 large eggs
* 1 tablespoon fresh chives, chopped
* 1 tablespoon fresh parsley, chopped
* 1 teaspoon turmeric, ground
* ¼ teaspoon cumin, ground
* ½ teaspoon salt
* 2 tablespoons extra-virgin olive, divided

Directions:
1. Whisk together the eggs, chives, parsley, turmeric, cumin, and salt in a medium bowl.
2. Heat 1 tablespoon of oil in an omelet pan over medium-high heat.
3. Pour half of the egg mixture into the hot pan.
4. Reduce the heat to medium and let the eggs cook until the bottom starts to set.
5. Gently move the eggs around the edges using a heat-proof spatula so the uncooked egg can spill over the sides of the cooked egg and set.
6. Continue to cook the omelet until just set, but still soft. Use the spatula to fold the omelet in half, then slide it out of the pan and onto a serving dish.
7. Repeat with the remaining egg mixture and 1 tablespoon of oil. Serve.

Nutrition Info:
* Per Serving: Calories: 240 ;Fat: 21g ;Protein: 11g ;Carbs: 3g.

Hot And Spicy Scrambled Tofu And Spinach

Servings: 2
Cooking Time: 10 Minutes
Ingredients:
* 1 pack extra firm tofu, pressed and crumbled
* 1 tablespoon of extra virgin olive oil
* 2 stems of spring onion, finely chopped
* 1 cup spinach leaves
* 1 clove of garlic, finely chopped
* 1 teaspoon lemon juice
* 1 teaspoon black pepper

Directions:
1. Heat olive oil in a skillet on medium heat.
2. Add the spring onion, tomatoes, and garlic and sauté for 3-4 minutes.
3. Lower the heat and add the tofu, lemon juice, and pepper.
4. Sauté for 3 to 5 minutes.
5. Turn the heat off and add the spinach then stir until spinach is wilted.
6. Transfer to a serving dish and enjoy.

Nutrition Info:
* Per Serving: Calories: 42 ;Fat: 3g ;Protein: 1g ;Carbs: 3g.

Rich In Nutrients Noodles With Tahini And Kale

Servings: 4
Cooking Time: 8 To 10 Minutes
Ingredients:
* 8 ounces brown rice spaghetti, or buckwheat noodles
* 4 cups kale, lightly packed
* ½ cup tahini
* ¾ cup hot water, plus additional as needed
* ¼ teaspoon salt, plus additional as needed
* ½ cup fresh parsley, chopped

Directions:
1. Cook the noodles according to the package instructions. Toss in the kale during the last 30 seconds of cook time. Drain the noodles and kale in a colander. Transfer to a large bowl.
2. Stir together the tahini, hot water, and salt in a medium bowl. Add more water if prefer a thinner sauce.
3. Add the parsley and sauce to the noodles. Toss to coat. Taste, and adjust the seasoning if necessary.
4. Serve hot or cold.

Nutrition Info:
* Per Serving: Calories: 404 ;Fat: 18g ;Protein: 15g ;Carbs: 54g.

Zoodle Bolognese

Servings: 4
Cooking Time: 45 Minutes
Ingredients:
- 4 tbsp olive oil
- 1 white onion, chopped
- 1 garlic clove, minced
- 3 oz carrots, chopped
- 3 cups crumbled tofu
- 2 tbsp tomato paste
- 1 ½ cups diced tomatoes
- Sea salt and pepper to taste
- 1 tbsp dried basil
- 1 tbsp Worcestershire sauce
- 2 lb zucchini, spiralized

Directions:
1. Pour half of the olive oil into a saucepan and heat over medium heat. Add onion, garlic, and carrots and sauté for 3 minutes or until the onions are soft and the carrots caramelized. Pour in tofu, tomato paste, tomatoes, salt, pepper, basil, and Worcestershire sauce. Stir and cook for 15 minutes. Mix in some water if the mixture is too thick and simmer further for 20 minutes. Warm the remaining olive oil in a skillet and toss in the zoodles quickly, about 1 minute. Season with salt and black pepper. Divide into serving plates and spoon the Bolognese on top. Serve.

Nutrition Info:
- Per Serving: Calories: 415;Fat: 18g;Protein: 15g;Carbs: 53g.

Quinoa A La Puttanesca

Servings: 4
Cooking Time: 30 Minutes
Ingredients:
- 1 cup brown quinoa
- 2 cups water
- Sea salt to taste
- 4 cups tomatoes, diced
- 4 pitted green olives, sliced
- 4 Kalamata olives, sliced
- 1 ½ tbsp capers
- 2 garlic cloves, minced
- 1 tbsp olive oil
- 1 tbsp chopped parsley
- ¼ cup chopped basil
- 1/8 tsp red chili flakes

Directions:
1. Add quinoa, water, and salt to a medium pot and cook for 15 minutes. In a bowl, mix tomatoes, green olives, olives, capers, garlic, olive oil, parsley, basil, and red chili flakes. Allow sitting for 5 minutes. Serve with quinoa.

Nutrition Info:
- Per Serving: Calories: 230;Fat: 7g;Protein: 7g;Carbs: 35g.

Marinated Tempah And Spaghetti Squash

Servings: 2
Cooking Time: 50 Minutes
Ingredients:
- 1 pack of tempeh, drained and cubed
- 1 spaghetti squash or pumpkin, halved and deseeded
- 3 tablespoons tamari or reduced
- sodium soy sauce
- 1 can tomatoes, chopped
- 1 tablespoon extra-virgin olive oil
- 2 cloves of garlic, chopped finely
- 1 cup small broccoli florets
- ½ cup of baby spinach

Directions:
1. Preheat the oven to 375°F. Get a medium-sized bowl and toss together the tamari, tempeh, garlic.
2. Marinate and set aside for 30 minutes and overnight if possible. Grab a large baking dish and arrange the squash halves with the cut side down.
3. Pour half a cup of water into the dish. For 45 minutes, bake or until tender, and remove the dish out of the oven. Turn the squash over and allow it to slightly cool.
4. Get a large skillet and heat oil at medium heat.
5. Add tempeh and cook for 7 to 8 minutes until golden brown while occasionally stirring.
6. Remove the tempeh and keep warm on a plate.
7. Heat chopped tomatoes in a medium-sized pot at medium heat, and then add the broccoli and allow to cook until tender for 5 minutes. Stir the spinach in and remove it from heat.
8. Use a fork to scrape off spaghetti squash strands onto a platter. Spoon broccoli and hot chopped tomatoes over the dish.
9. Top with the tempeh to serve.

Nutrition Info:
- Per Serving: Calories: 193 ;Fat: 13g ;Protein: 9g ;Carbs: 15g.

Vegetarian Sloppy Joes

Servings: 4
Cooking Time: 30 Minutes
Ingredients:
- 2 tbsp avocado oil
- 2 garlic cloves, minced
- 1 yellow onion, chopped
- 1 celery stalk, chopped
- 1 carrot, minced
- ½ red bell pepper, chopped
- 1 lb cooked lentils
- 7 tbsp tomato paste
- 2 tbsp apple cider vinegar
- 1 tbsp maple syrup
- 1 tsp chili powder
- 1 tsp Dijon mustard

- ½ tsp dried oregano

Directions:

1. Warm 1 tbsp of avocado oil in a skillet over medium heat and place the garlic, carrot, onion, and celery and cook for 3 minutes until the onion is translucent. Add lentils and remaining avocado oil and cook for 5 more minutes.

2. Put in bell peppers and cook for 2 more minutes. Stir in tomato paste, apple cider vinegar, maple syrup, chili powder, Dijon mustard, and oregano and cook for another 10 minutes. Serve over rice.

Nutrition Info:

- Per Serving: Calories: 275;Fat: 8g;Protein: 14g;Carbs: 30g.

Special Butternut Squash Chili

Servings: 4
Cooking Time: 60 Minutes
Ingredients:

- 1 butternut squash, cubed
- 2 tbsp olive oil
- 1 onion, chopped
- 3 cups tomato salsa
- 1 can garbanzo beans
- 1 cup frozen green peas
- ½ tsp cayenne pepper
- ½ tsp ground allspice

Directions:

1. Heat the oil in a saucepan over medium heat. Place in onion and squash and cook for 10 minutes until tender. Add in tomato salsa, garbanzo beans, green peas, cayenne pepper, allspice, salt, and pepper. Pour in 2 cups of water. Cook for 15 minutes. Serve and enjoy!

Nutrition Info:

- Per Serving: Calories: 300;Fat: 8g;Protein: 1g;Carbs: 47g.

Hot Lentil Tacos With Guacamole

Servings: 4
Cooking Time: 35 Minutes
Ingredients:

- ½ cup red lentils
- 2 tbsp olive oil
- ½ cup minced onion
- ½ cup roasted cashews
- ¼ cup chickpea flour
- 1 tbsp minced parsley
- 2 tsp hot powder
- Sea salt to taste
- 4 coconut flour tortillas
- Shredded romaine lettuce
- Guacamole

Directions:

1. Place the lentils in a pot and cover them with cold water. Bring to a boil and simmer for 15-20 minutes. Heat the oil in a skillet over medium heat. Add the onion cook for 5 minutes. Set aside. In a blender, mince cashews, add in

cooked lentils and onion mixture. Pulse to blend. Transfer to a bowl and stir in flour, parsley, hot powder, and salt. Mix to combine. Mold patties out of the mixture. Heat the remaining oil in a skillet over medium heat. Brown the patties for 10 minutes on both sides. Put one patty in each tortilla, top with lettuce and guacamole.

Nutrition Info:

- Per Serving: Calories: 500;Fat: 25g;Protein: 15g;Carbs: 55g.

Spicy Black Bean

Servings: 6
Cooking Time: 1 Hour
Ingredients:

- 2 onions, chopped
- 2 tablespoons water
- 4 cups cooked black beans, 2 cups dried, or 2 14 ounces cans
- 28 ounces can crush tomatoes
- 4 teaspoons chili powder
- 1½ teaspoons salt, plus additional as needed

Directions:

1. Sauté the onions in the water in a large pot set over medium heat for 5 minutes, or until soft.

2. Add the black beans, tomatoes, chili powder, and salt. Bring to a boil. Reduce the heat to low. Simmer for 1 hour while stirring occasionally

3. Taste, and adjust the seasoning if necessary.

Nutrition Info:

- Per Serving: Calories: 294| Fat: 1g ;Protein: 18g ;Carbs: 55g ,

Mixed Vegetables With Quinoa

Servings: 4 To 6
Cooking Time: 15 Minutes
Ingredients:

- 3 tablespoons extra-virgin olive oil
- 1½ cups Brussels sprouts, quartered
- 1 large zucchini, chopped
- 1 onion, chopped
- 3 garlic cloves, sliced
- 2½ cups quinoa, cooked
- 1 cup vegetable broth or tomato sauce
- 1 tablespoon lemon juice, fresh
- 1 teaspoon oregano, dried
- 1 teaspoon salt
- ¼ teaspoon black pepper, freshly ground

Directions:

1. Heat the oil over high heat in a large skillet.

2. Add the Brussels sprouts, zucchini, onion, and garlic and sauté until the vegetables are tender for 5 to 7 minutes.

3. Add the quinoa and broth, cover, and cook for 5 minutes more.

4. Add the lemon juice, oregano, salt, and pepper and stir to fluff the quinoa.

5. Serve warm or at room temperature.

Nutrition Info:
- Per Serving: Calories: 270 ;Fat: 13g ;Protein: 8g ;Carbs: 34g .

Chipotle Kidney Bean Chili

Servings: 4
Cooking Time: 30 Minutes
Ingredients:
- 2 tbsp olive oil
- 1 onion, chopped
- 2 garlic cloves, minced
- 1 can tomato sauce
- 1 tbsp chili powder
- 1 chipotle chili, minced
- 1 tsp ground cumin
- ½ tsp dried marjoram
- 1 can kidney beans
- Sea salt and pepper to taste
- ½ tsp cayenne pepper

Directions:
1. Heat the oil in a pot over medium heat. Place in onion and garlic and sauté for 3 minutes. Put in tomato sauce, chipotle chili, chili powder, cumin, cayenne pepper, marjoram, salt, and pepper and cook for 5 minutes. Stir in kidney beans and 2 cups of water. Bring to a boil, then lower the heat and simmer for 15 minutes, stirring often.

Nutrition Info:
- Per Serving: Calories: 260;Fat: 11g;Protein: 6g;Carbs: 37g.

Oozing Homemade Sushi With Avocado

Servings: 4
Cooking Time: 15 Minutes
Ingredients:
- 1½ cups dry quinoa
- 3 cups water, plus additional for rolling
- ½ teaspoon salt
- 6 nori sheets
- 3 avocados, halved, pitted, and sliced thin, divided
- 1 small cucumber, halved, seeded, and cut into matchsticks, divided

Directions:
1. In a fine-mesh sieve, rinse the quinoa.
2. Combine the rinsed quinoa, water, and salt in a medium pot set over high heat. Bring to a boil. Reduce the heat to low. Cover and simmer for 15 minutes. Fluff the quinoa with a fork.
3. Lay out 1 nori sheet on a cutting board. Spread ½ cup of quinoa over the sheet, leaving 2 to 3 inches uncovered at the top.
4. Place 5 or 6 avocado slices across the bottom of the nori sheet in a row. Add 5 or 6 cucumber matchsticks on top.
5. Tightly roll up the nori sheet by starting at the bottom sheet. Dab the uncovered top with water to seal the roll.
6. Slice the sushi roll into 6 pieces.

7. Repeat with the remaining 5 nori sheets, quinoa, and vegetables.
8. Serve.
Nutrition Info:
- Per Serving: Calories: 557 ;Fat: 33g ;Protein: 13g ;Carbs: 57g .

Vegetarian Spaghetti Bolognese

Servings: 6
Cooking Time: 25 Minutes
Ingredients:
- 16 oz cooked whole-wheat spaghetti
- 1 cup cauliflower florets
- 2 cups shredded carrots
- 6 garlic cloves, minced
- 2 tbsp tomato paste
- 1 ½ tbsp dried oregano
- 28 oz canned diced tomatoes
- 2 tbsp balsamic vinegar
- 1 tbsp dried basil
- 10 oz mushrooms
- 2 cups chopped eggplants
- 1 cup water
- 1 ½ tsp dried rosemary
- Sea salt and pepper to taste

Directions:
1. Add the cauliflower, mushrooms, eggplant, and carrots to a food processor and process until finely ground. Add them to your Instant Pot. Stir in the rest of the ingredients. Seal the lid and cook for 8 minutes on "Manual" on high pressure. Once the cooking cycle has finished, release the pressure naturally for 10 minutes. Pour the sauce over the spaghetti. Serve and enjoy!

Nutrition Info:
- Per Serving: Calories: 360;Fat: 2g;Protein: 15g;Carbs: 75g.

Parsley Bean & Olives Salad

Servings: 4
Cooking Time: 15 Minutes
Ingredients:
- 1 cup green olives, sliced
- 2 cans black beans
- 1 chopped red bell pepper
- ¼ cup red onions, sliced
- 2 garlic cloves, crushed
- ¼ cup chopped parsley
- Sea salt and pepper to taste
- 2 tbsp fresh lime juice
- ¼ cup olive oil

Directions:
1. Combine the olives, beans, bell pepper, and onion in a bowl. Set aside. In a food processor, put garlic, lime juice, 2 tbsp water, olive oil, parsley, salt, and pepper. Pulse until blended. Add to the salad and mix to combine.

Nutrition Info:
- Per Serving: Calories: 365;Fat: 19g;Protein: 2g;Carbs: 39g.

Seitan & Lentil Chili

Servings: 4
Cooking Time: 35 Minutes
Ingredients:
- 2 tbsp olive oil
- 1 onion, chopped
- 8 oz seitan, chopped
- 1 cup lentils
- 1 can diced tomatoes
- 1 tsp low-sodium soy sauce
- 1 tbsp chili powder
- 1 tsp ground cumin
- 1 tsp ground allspice
- ½ tsp ground oregano
- ¼ tsp ground cayenne
- Sea salt and pepper to taste

Directions:
1. Heat the oil in a pot over medium heat. Place in onion and seitan and cook for 10 minutes. Add in lentils, diced tomatoes, 2 cups of water, soy sauce, chili powder, cumin, allspice, sugar, oregano, cayenne pepper, salt, and pepper. Simmer for 20 minutes. Serve and enjoy!

Nutrition Info:
- Per Serving: Calories: 230;Fat: 14g;Protein: 18g;Carbs: 18g.

Chapter 9. Salads

All Green Salad With Basil-cherry Dressing

Servings: 4
Cooking Time: 25 Minutes
Ingredients:
- ¼ cup olive oil
- ½ cup pitted cherries
- 2 tbsp lemon juice
- 2 tbsp raw honey
- 1 tsp chopped fresh basil
- Sea salt to taste
- 5 oz blanched broccoli florets
- 2 cups mixed greens
- 1 cup snow peas
- ½ cucumber, sliced
- 2 green onions, thinly sliced

Directions:
1. Combine the cherries, olive oil, lemon juice, honey, salt, and basil in your food processor and pulse until smooth. Add the broccoli, mixed greens, snow peas, cucumber, and green onions to a salad bowl. Coat with dressing.

Nutrition Info:
- Per Serving: Calories: 190;Fat: 15g;Protein: 3g;Carbs: 18g.

Radish & Tomato Salad

Servings: 4
Cooking Time: 15 Minutes
Ingredients:
- 2 tomatoes, sliced
- 6 small red radishes, sliced
- 2 ½ tbsp white wine vinegar
- ½ tsp chopped chervil
- Sea salt and pepper to taste
- ¼ cup olive oil

Directions:
1. Mix the tomatoes and radishes in a bowl. Set aside. In another bowl, whisk the vinegar, chervil, salt, and pepper until mixed. Pour over the salad and toss to coat. Serve.

Nutrition Info:
- Per Serving: Calories: 140;Fat: 14g;Protein: 1g;Carbs: 4g.

Crunchylicious Colourful Asian Salad

Servings: 6
Cooking Time: 0 Minutes
Ingredients:
- ¼ medium head red cabbage
- ¼ medium head green cabbage
- 2 green onions, minced
- Leaves from 2 sprigs fresh basil, minced
- Leaves from 4 sprigs fresh cilantro, minced
- 1 teaspoon fine Himalayan salt
- Dressing:
- Juice of 4 limes
- 3 tablespoons avocado oil
- 2 tablespoons coconut aminos
- 4 cloves garlic, minced
- One 1 inch piece ginger, peeled and minced

Directions:
1. Lay one of the cabbage wedges on the cutting board and to trim off the core on the diagonal use a sharp knife. Then slice the cabbage as thinly as possible. Repeat with the

second wedge. In a large bowl, combine the shredded red and green cabbage.

2. Add the green onions, basil, and cilantro and toss with the cabbage. Sprinkle in the salt and toss to combine.

3. Make the dressing by placing the lime juice, avocado oil, and coconut aminos in a small bowl. Add the garlic and ginger and whisk to combine.

4. Pour the dressing over the cabbage and toss to thoroughly distribute the dressing if you're serving the salad right away.

5. Store the salad in an airtight container in the fridge with a folded paper towel to absorb moisture if you're not serving the salad right away. Store the dressing in a separate airtight container in the fridge. Both the salad and the dressing will keep for up to 5 days.

Nutrition Info:

- Per Serving: Calories: 103 ;Fat: 7g ;Protein: 1g ;Carbs: 7g .

Seitan & Spinach Salad A La Puttanesca

Servings: 4
Cooking Time: 15 Minutes
Ingredients:

- 4 tbsp olive oil
- 8 oz seitan, cut into strips
- 2 garlic cloves, minced
- ½ cup black olives, halved
- ½ cup green olives, halved
- 2 tbsp capers
- 3 cups baby spinach
- 20 cherry tomatoes, halved
- 2 tbsp balsamic vinegar
- 2 tbsp torn fresh basil leaves
- 2 tbsp minced fresh parsley
- 1 cup pomegranate seeds
- Sea salt and pepper to taste

Directions:

1. Heat half of the olive oil in a skillet over medium heat. Place the seitan and brown for 5 minutes on all sides. Add in garlic and cook for 30 seconds. Remove to a bowl and let cool. Stir in olives, capers, spinach, and tomatoes. In another bowl, whisk the remaining oil, balsamic vinegar, salt, and pepper until well mixed. Pour this dressing over the seitan salad and toss to coat. Top with basil, parsley, and pomegranate seeds. Serve and enjoy!

Nutrition Info:

- Per Serving: Calories: 305;Fat: 23g;Protein: 14g;Carbs: 18g.

Nutritious Bowl With Lentil, Vegetable, And Fruit

Servings: 4 To 6
Cooking Time: 0 Minutes
Ingredients:

- 1 cup red lentils

- 2 cups water
- 4 cups cooked brown rice
- One 15 ounces can lentils, drained and rinsed
- Chicken Lettuce Wraps sauce
- 1 head radicchio, cored and torn into pieces, divided
- 1 small jicama, peeled and cut into thin sticks, divided
- 2 red Bartlett ripe pears, cored, quartered, and sliced, divided
- 2 scallions, sliced, divided

Directions:

1. Combine the red lentils and the water in a medium bowl. Cover and refrigerate overnight. Drain the lentils when ready to prepare the salad.

2. Combine the brown rice and canned lentils in a medium bowl. Stir in half of the Chicken Lettuce Wraps sauce. Let the mixture stand for 30 minutes, or overnight.

3. Divide the lentil-rice mixture among serving bowls. Top each bowl with equal amounts of the soaked and drained red lentils. Garnish each serving with the radicchio, jicama, pears, and scallions.

4. Drizzle each with some of the remaining Chicken Lettuce Wraps sauce.

Nutrition Info:

- Per Serving: Calories: 989 ;Fat: 31g ;Protein: 31g ;Carbs: 151g .

Colorful Salad

Servings: 6
Cooking Time: 5 Minutes
Ingredients:

- 1 cup English peas, shelled
- 3 Chioggia beets, sliced
- 6 cups mixed greens
- 1 red onion, sliced
- 1 avocado, sliced
- 5 tsp lemon-mustard dressing

Directions:

1. Combine peas, beets, mixed greens, onion, and avocado in a bowl. Toos in the lemon-mustard dressing. Serve.

Nutrition Info:

- Per Serving: Calories: 110;Fat: 7g;Protein: 12g;Carbs: 16g.

Porky Salad With Spinach

Servings: 2
Cooking Time: 0 Minutes
Ingredients:

- 2 cups baby spinach
- 8 (½-inch-thick) slices leftover Pan-Seared Pork Loin
- 4 leftover Roasted Fingerling Potatoes, cut in half lengthwise
- 1 green apple, cored and thinly sliced
- ½ red bell pepper, thinly sliced
- ¼ cup Ginger-Turmeric Dressing

Directions:

1. Toss together the spinach, pork loin, potatoes, green apple, and red bell pepper in a medium bowl.
2. Pour the dressing over and toss to combine.
3. Divide between two bowls and serve.

Nutrition Info:
- Per Serving: Calories: 590 ;Fat: 39g ;Protein: 42g ;Carbs: 19g .

Bell Pepper & Quinoa Salad

Servings: 4
Cooking Time: 15 Minutes
Ingredients:
- 2 cups cooked quinoa
- ½ red onion, diced
- 1 red bell pepper, diced
- 1 orange bell pepper, diced
- 1 carrot, diced
- ¼ cup olive oil
- 2 tbsp rice vinegar
- 1 tsp low-sodium soy sauce
- 1 garlic clove, minced
- 1 tbsp grated fresh ginger
- Sea salt and pepper to taste

Directions:
1. Combine the quinoa, onion, bell peppers, and carrots in a bowl. In another bowl, mix the olive oil, rice vinegar, soy sauce, garlic, ginger, salt, and pepper. Pour over the quinoa and toss to coat. Serve and enjoy!

Nutrition Info:
- Per Serving: Calories: 270;Fat: 16g;Protein: 6g;Carbs: 28g.

Orange Berry Salad

Servings: 4
Cooking Time: 10 Minutes
Ingredients:
- 1 tbsp honey
- 1 orange, zested and juiced
- 1 cup fresh strawberries
- 1 cup fresh blueberries
- 1 cup fresh raspberries
- 1 tbsp grated fresh ginger

Directions:
1. Mix together the blueberries, raspberries, strawberries, ginger, orange zest, and orange juice in a mixing bowl. Drizzle with honey and serve.

Nutrition Info:
- Per Serving: Calories: 91;Fat: 1g;Protein: 2g;Carbs: 22.4g.

Beet Slaw With Apples

Servings: 4
Cooking Time: 10 Minutes
Ingredients:
- 2 tbsp olive oil
- Juice of 1 lemon

- ½ beet, shredded
- Sea salt to taste
- 2 peeled apples, julienned
- 4 cups shredded red cabbage

Directions:
1. Mix the olive oil, lemon juice, beet, and salt in a bowl. In another bowl, combine the apples and cabbage. Pour over the vinaigrette and toss to coat. Serve right away.

Nutrition Info:
- Per Serving: Calories: 145;Fat: 7g;Protein: 2g;Carbs: 21g.

Lemony Spinach Salad

Servings: 4
Cooking Time: 10 Minutes
Ingredients:
- 2 tbsp pine nuts, toasted
- 6 cups baby spinach
- 2 tbsp lemon juice
- ¼ cup Dijon mustard
- 1 ½ tbsp maple syrup
- 2 tbsp extra-virgin olive oil
- Sea salt to taste

Directions:
1. Combine all the ingredients, except for the spinach and pine nuts, in a small bowl. Mix well. Put the spinach in a large serving bowl, drizzle with the lemon dressing, toss to combine well. Top with pine nuts and serve.

Nutrition Info:
- Per Serving: Calories: 155;Fat: 15g;Protein: 2g;Carbs: 8g.

Coleslaw & Spinach Salad With Grapefruit

Servings: 4
Cooking Time: 10 Minutes
Ingredients:
- 1 large grapefruit
- 2 cups coleslaw mix
- 2 cups green leaf lettuce, torn
- 2 cups baby spinach
- 1 bunch watercress
- 6 radishes, sliced
- Juice of 1 lemon
- 2 tsp date syrup
- 1 tsp white wine vinegar
- Sea salt and black pepper
- ¼ cup extra-virgin olive oil

Directions:
1. Slice the grapefruit by cutting the ends, peeling all the white pith, and making an incise in the membrane to take out each segment. Transfer to a bowl. Stir in coleslaw, lettuce, spinach, watercress, and radishes. In a bowl, mix the lemon juice, date syrup, vinegar, salt, and pepper. Gently

beat the olive oil until emulsified. Pour over the salad and toss to coats. Serve and enjoy!

Nutrition Info:

- Per Serving: Calories: 205;Fat: 14g;Protein: 1g;Carbs: 21g.

Mom´s Caesar Salad

Servings: 4
Cooking Time: 10 Minutes
Ingredients:

- ½ cup cashews
- ½ cup water
- 3 tbsp olive oil
- Juice of ½ lime
- 1 tbsp white miso paste
- 1 tsp low-sodium soy sauce
- 1 tsp Dijon mustard
- 1 tsp garlic powder
- Sea salt and pepper to taste
- 2 heads romaine lettuce, torn
- 2 tsp capers
- 1 cup cherry tomatoes, halved
- 4 oz shaved Parmesan cheese
- Whole-what bread croutons

Directions:

1. In a blender, put cashews, water, olive oil, lime juice, miso paste, soy sauce, mustard, garlic powder, salt, and pepper. Blend until smooth. Mix the lettuce with half of the dressing in a bowl. Add capers, tomatoes, and Parmesan cheese. Serve topped with croutons.

Nutrition Info:

- Per Serving: Calories: 415;Fat: 28g;Protein: 17g;Carbs: 30g.

Pleasant And Tender Salad With Kale

Servings: 4
Cooking Time: 0 Minutes
Ingredients:

- 1 pound dinosaur or curly kale
- 1 teaspoon fine Himalayan salt
- ¼ cup ripe green olives, pitted
- 2 tablespoons Garlic Confit
- 2 tablespoons Toum or Homemade Mayo
- Juice of 1 lemon

Directions:

1. Tear the kale leaves into 1- to 2-inch pieces and place in a bowl with the salt. Massage with your hands the salt into the kale for 2 minutes, or until the kale begins to release some liquid and has become very tender.
2. Add the olives, garlic confit, toum, and lemon juice. Toss to combine and serve, or store in a quart-sized jar in the fridge for up to 4 days.

Nutrition Info:

- Per Serving: Calories: 87 ;Fat: 2g ;Protein: 3g;Carbs: 13g .

Hazelnut & Pear Salad

Servings: 4
Cooking Time: 10 Minutes
Ingredients:

- ¼ cup chopped hazelnuts
- 4 pears, peeled and chopped
- 2 tbsp honey
- 2 tbsp balsamic vinegar
- 2 tbsp extra-virgin olive oil

Directions:

1. Combine the pears and hazelnuts in a salad bowl. Drizzle with honey, balsamic vinegar, and olive oil. Serve.

Nutrition Info:

- Per Serving: Calories: 265;Fat: 12g;Protein: 4g;Carbs: 40g.

Ruby Salad With Avocado Dressing

Servings: 4
Cooking Time: 20 Minutes
Ingredients:

- 1 peeled grapefruit, cut into chunks
- ¼ cup roasted sunflower seeds
- ¼ cup extra-virgin olive oil
- ¼ cup lime juice
- ½ peeled avocado, pitted
- 2 tbsp raw honey
- Sea salt to taste
- ¼ cup dried cranberries
- 4 cups fresh spinach
- ¼ cup sliced radishes

Directions:

1. Combine the olive oil, avocado, lime juice, honey, ¼ cup of water, and sea salt in your food processor and pulse until your desired consistency is reached. In a large bowl, toss the spinach with half of the dressing. Divide the dressed spinach among 4 plates. Top each with grapefruit, radishes, sunflower seeds, and cranberries. Drizzle the remaining dressing over the salads and serve.

Nutrition Info:

- Per Serving: Calories: 125;Fat: 9g;Protein: 3g;Carbs: 15g.

Out Of This World Salad With Basil And Tomato

Servings: 4
Cooking Time: 0 Minutes
Ingredients:

- 4 large heirloom tomatoes, chopped
- ¼ cup fresh basil leaves, torn
- 2 garlic cloves, finely minced
- ¼ cup extra-virgin olive oil
- ½ teaspoon sea salt
- ¼ teaspoon black pepper, freshly ground

Directions:

1. Gently mix together the tomatoes, basil, garlic, olive oil, salt, and pepper in a medium bowl.
2. Serve and enjoy.

Nutrition Info:
- Per Serving: Calories: 140 ;Fat: 14g ;Protein: 1g ;Carbs: 4g .

Superb Salad With Chickpea

Servings: 4
Cooking Time: 20 Minutes
Ingredients:
- 1 large bunch kale, thoroughly washed, stemmed, and cut into thin strips
- 2 teaspoons lemon juice, freshly squeezed
- 2 tablespoons extra-virgin olive oil, divided
- ¾ teaspoon sea salt, divided
- 2 cups cooked chickpeas, 14-oz
- 1 teaspoon sweet paprika

Directions:
1. Combine the kale, lemon juice, 1 tablespoon of olive oil, and ¼ teaspoon of salt in a large bowl.
2. Massage with your hands the kale for 5 minutes, or until it starts to wilt and becomes bright green and shiny.
3. Add the remaining 1 tablespoon of olive oil to a skillet set over medium-low heat.
4. Stir in the chickpeas, paprika, and remaining ½ teaspoon of salt. Cook for about 15 minutes, or until warm. The chickpeas might start to crisp in spots.
5. Pour the chickpeas over the kale. Toss well.
6. Serve immediately.

Nutrition Info:
- Per Serving: Calories: 359 ;Fat: 20g ;Protein: 13g ;Carbs: 35g .

Zucchini & Bell Pepper Salad With Beans

Servings: 2
Cooking Time: 40 Minutes
Ingredients:
- 1 can cannellini beans
- 1 tbsp olive oil
- 2 tbsp balsamic vinegar
- 1 tsp minced fresh chives
- 1 garlic clove, minced
- 1 tbsp rosemary, chopped
- 1 tbsp oregano, chopped
- A pinch of sea salt
- 1 green bell pepper, sliced
- 1 zucchini, diced
- 2 carrots, diced

Directions:
1. In a bowl, mix the olive oil, balsamic vinegar, chives, garlic, rosemary, oregano, and salt. Stir in the beans, bell pepper, zucchini, and carrots. Serve and enjoy!

Nutrition Info:

- Per Serving: Calories: 150;Fat: 8g;Protein: 1g;Carbs: 1g.

High-spirited Salmon Salad

Servings: 2
Cooking Time: 0 Minutes
Ingredients:
- 3 cups baby spinach
- ½ cucumber, thinly sliced
- 1 small fennel bulb, trimmed and thinly sliced
- 2 leftover Basic Baked Salmon fillets, flaked
- 1 small ripe avocado, peeled, pitted, and sliced
- ¼ cup extra-virgin olive oil
- 2 tablespoons lemon juice, fresh
- 1 teaspoon salt
- ¼ teaspoon black pepper, freshly ground
- 1 teaspoon fresh dill, chopped

Directions:
1. Arrange the spinach on a serving platter or in a bowl.
2. Top with the cucumber, fennel, salmon, and avocado.
3. Whisk together the olive oil, lemon juice, salt, pepper, and dill in a small bowl or shake in a small jar with a tight-fitting lid.
4. Pour the dressing over the salad, and serve.

Nutrition Info:
- Per Serving: Calories: 590 ;Fat: 48g ;Protein: 23g ;Carbs: 20g .

Basil-tomato Salad

Servings: 4
Cooking Time: 10 Minutes
Ingredients:
- 3 tsp balsamic vinegar
- 2 garlic cloves, minced
- 4 heirloom tomatoes, diced
- ¼ cup basil leaves, torn
- 2 tbsp extra-virgin olive oil
- Sea salt and pepper to taste

Directions:
1. In a bowl, whisk balsamic vinegar, oil, salt, and pepper. Add the tomatoes, basil, and garlic and mix. Serve.

Nutrition Info:
- Per Serving: Calories: 140;Fat: 15g;Protein: 1g;Carbs: 5g.

Refreshingly Spicy Chicken Salad With Cumin And Mango

Servings: 2
Cooking Time: 15 Minutes
Ingredients:
- 2 free range chicken breasts, skinless
- 1 teaspoon oregano, finely chopped
- 1 garlic clove, minced
- 1 teaspoon chili flakes
- 1 teaspoon cumin
- 1 teaspoon turmeric

- 1 tablespoon extra-virgin olive oil
- 1 lime, juiced
- 1 cup mango, cubed
- ½ iceberg/romaine lettuce or similar, sliced

Directions:

1. Mix oil, garlic, herbs, and spices with the lime juice in a bowl.
2. Add the chicken and marinate for at least 30 minutes up to overnight.
3. Preheat the broiler when ready to serve to medium-high heat.
4. Add the chicken to a lightly greased baking tray and broil for 10-12 minutes or until cooked through.
5. In a serving bowl, combine the lettuce with the mango.
6. Serve immediately once the chicken is cooked on top of the mango and lettuce.

Nutrition Info:

- Per Serving: Calories: 216 ;Fat: 9g ;Protein: 19g ;Carbs: 19g .

Radicchio & Cabbage Coleslaw

Servings: 2
Cooking Time: 10 Minutes
Ingredients:

- ½ head cabbage, shredded
- ¼ head radicchio, shredded
- 1 large carrot, shredded
- ¾ cup paleo mayonnaise
- ¼ cup soy milk
- 1 tbsp cider vinegar
- ½ tsp dry mustard
- ¼ tsp celery seeds
- Sea salt and pepper to taste

Directions:

1. Combine cabbage, radicchio, and carrot in a bowl. In another bowl, whisk mayonnaise, soy milk, mustard, vinegar, celery seeds, salt, and pepper. Pour over the slaw and toss to coat. Serve immediately.

Nutrition Info:

- Per Serving: Calories: 370;Fat: 30g;Protein: 9g;Carbs: 19g.

Irresistible Pear And Walnut Salad

Servings: 4
Cooking Time: 0 Minutes
Ingredients:

- 4 pears, peeled, cored, and chopped
- ¼ cup walnuts, chopped
- 2 tablespoons honey
- 2 tablespoons balsamic vinegar
- 2 tablespoons extra-virgin olive oil

Directions:

1. Combine the pears and walnuts in a medium bowl.
2. Whisk the honey, balsamic vinegar, and olive oil in a small bowl. Toss with the pears and walnuts.

Nutrition Info:

- Per Serving: Calories: 263 ;Fat: 12g ;Protein: 3g ;Carbs: 41g.

Chickpea & Celery Salad

Servings: 4
Cooking Time: 5 Minutes
Ingredients:

- 1 can chickpeas
- 1 head fennel bulb, sliced
- ½ cup sliced red onion
- ½ cup celery leaves, chopped
- ¼ cup paleo mayonnaise
- Sea salt and pepper to taste

Directions:

1. In a bowl, mash the chickpeas until chunky. Stir in fennel bulb, onion, celery, mayonnaise, salt, and pepper. Serve.

Nutrition Info:

- Per Serving: Calories: 165;Fat: 7g;Protein: 7g;Carbs: 21g.

Beetroot Salad With Mackerel

Servings: 2
Cooking Time: 30 Minutes
Ingredients:

- 12 oz smoked mackerel
- 1 lime, zested and juiced
- 1 cup peeled sweet potatoes
- 2 spring onions, sliced
- 4 cooked beetroot wedges
- 2 tbsp chopped dill
- 2 tbsp olive oil
- 1 tsp crushed caraway seeds

Directions:

1. Boil the potatoes in a small saucepan for 15 minutes over medium heat. Drain, cool and slice. Flake the mackerel into a bowl and add the cooled potatoes, green onions, beetroot and dill. Pour in the olive oil, lime juice, caraway seeds, lime zest, and black pepper and toss to coat. Serve.

Nutrition Info:

- Per Serving: Calories: 535;Fat: 38g;Protein: 33g;Carbs: 15g.

Delectable Roasted Cauliflower With Almond Sauce

Servings: 4
Cooking Time: 20 Minutes
Ingredients:

- 1 head cauliflower, cut into florets
- ¼ cup extra-virgin olive oil
- ½ teaspoon turmeric, ground
- 1 ½ teaspoons sea salt, divided
- ½ teaspoon freshly ground black pepper, divided
- 1 cup plain almond yogurt, unsweetened
- ¼ cup almond butter

- 1 scallion, sliced
- 1 garlic clove, minced
- 1 tablespoon fresh parsley, chopped
- 1 tablespoon lemon juice, freshly squeezed
- 1 tablespoon maple syrup

Directions:

1. Preheat the oven to 400°F.

2. Mix together the cauliflower, olive oil, turmeric, 1 teaspoon of salt, and ¼ teaspoon of pepper in a large bowl.

3. Transfer the seasoned cauliflower to a rimmed baking sheet, placing it in a single layer. Place the sheet in the preheated oven and roast for 20 to 30 minutes, or until the cauliflower is lightly browned and tender.

4. Combine the yogurt, almond butter, scallions, garlic, parsley, lemon juice, maple syrup, the remaining ½ teaspoon of salt, and the remaining ¼ teaspoon of pepper in a blender. Purée until smooth.

5. Place the roasted cauliflower in a serving dish and spoon the almond sauce over it.

Nutrition Info:

- Per Serving: Calories: 277 ;Fat: 23g ;Protein: 7g ;Carbs: 15g.

Summer Salad

Servings: 4
Cooking Time: 25 Minutes
Ingredients:

- 1 Lebanese cucumber, cubed
- 4 cups watermelon cubes
- 1 cup snow peasp halved
- 1 scallion, chopped
- 2 cups shredded kale
- 1 tbsp chopped cilantro
- ½ lime, zested and juiced
- ½ cup olive oil
- 2 tbsp honey
- Sea salt to taste

Directions:

1. Whisk the olive oil, lime zest, lime juice, honey, and salt in a bowl. Add the watermelon, cucumber, snow peas, scallion, and toss to coat. Top with the watermelon mixture. Serve garnished with cilantro.

Nutrition Info:

- Per Serving: Calories: 350;Fat: 25g;Protein: 3g;Carbs: 30g.

Daikon Salad With Caramelized Onion

Servings: 4
Cooking Time: 50 Minutes
Ingredients:

- 1 lb daikon, peeled
- 2 cups sliced sweet onions
- 2 tsp olive oil
- Sea salt to taste
- 1 tbsp rice vinegar

Directions:

1. Place the daikon in a pot with salted water and cook 25 minutes, until tender. Drain and let cool. In a skillet over low heat, warm olive oil and add the onion. Sauté for 10-15 minutes until caramelized. Sprinkle with salt. Remove to a bowl. Chop the daikon into wedges and add to the onion bowl. Stir in the vinegar. Serve.

Nutrition Info:

- Per Serving: Calories: 90;Fat: 3g;Protein: 2g;Carbs: 15g.

Avocado Salad With Mango & Almonds

Servings: 2
Cooking Time: 10 Minutes
Ingredients:

- 1 avocado, sliced
- 1 Romaine lettuce, torn
- ¼ cup dressing
- ¼ cup almonds, toasted
- 1 tbsp chives, chopped
- 1 mango, sliced

Directions:

1. Share the avocado and lettuce between bowls and top each with mango and chives. Sprinkle with dressing and almonds. Serve immediately.

Nutrition Info:

- Per Serving: Calories: 505;Fat: 40g;Protein: 8g;Carbs: 42g.

Chinese-style Cabbage Salad

Servings: 6
Cooking Time: 15 Minutes
Ingredients:

- 4 cups shredded red cabbage
- 2 cups sliced white cabbage
- 1 cup red radishes, sliced
- ¼ cup fresh orange juice
- 2 tbsp Chinese black vinegar
- 1 tsp low-sodium soy sauce
- 2 tbsp olive oil
- 1 tsp grated fresh ginger
- 1 tbsp black sesame seeds

Directions:

1. Mix the red cabbage, white cabbage, and radishes in a bowl. In another bowl, whisk the orange juice, vinegar, soy sauce, olive oil, and ginger. Pour over the slaw and toss to coat. Marinate covered in the fridge for 2 hours. Serve topped with sesame seeds.

Nutrition Info:

- Per Serving: Calories: 80;Fat: 6g;Protein: 2g;Carbs: 7g.

Tropical Salad

Servings: 4
Cooking Time: 15 Minutes
Ingredients:

- 2 cups blanched snow peas, sliced
- ½ cup chopped roasted almonds
- ½ tsp minced garlic
- ½ tsp grated fresh ginger
- ¼ cup olive oil
- ¼ tsp crushed red pepper
- 3 tbsp rice vinegar
- 3 tbsp water
- 1 tsp low-sodium soy sauce
- ½ papaya, chopped
- 1 large carrot, shredded
- 1 peeled cucumber, sliced
- 1 shredded romaine lettuce
- Sea salt to taste

Directions:
1. Combine garlic, ginger, olive oil, red pepper, vinegar, water, salt, and soy sauce in a bowl. Add papaya, snow peas, cucumber slices, and carrot and toss to coat. Spread the lettuce on a plate. Top with salad and almonds.

Nutrition Info:

- Per Serving: Calories: 280;Fat: 20g;Protein: 1g;Carbs: 23g.

Effortless Half-sour Pickled Salad

Servings: 2
Cooking Time: 0 Minutes
Ingredients:

- 1 large cucumber, cut into 4-inch spears
- Brine:
- 2 cups water
- 1 cup apple cider vinegar
- ½ teaspoon Himalayan salt, fine
- 1 whole clove
- 1 bay leaf
- ½ medium Hass avocado, peeled, pitted, and sliced
- ¼ cup Pickled Red Onions
- 2 or 3 slices Genoa salami
- 2 or 3 slices soppressata or smoked turkey
- ¼ teaspoon fine Himalayan salt
- 1 tablespoon avocado oil

Directions:
1. Place the cucumber spears in a clean glass container.
2. Bring the water, vinegar, salt, and clove to a light simmer in a saucepan over medium heat. Add the bay leaf to the cucumbers and pour the brine over them.
3. Cover and refrigerate for 3 hours or up to overnight. Arrange the pickled cucumbers on a plate with the avocado slices and pickled onions to serve. Roll up the deli meats and place them around the spears. Sprinkle everything with the salt and drizzle with the avocado oil.

4. Store leftovers in an airtight container in the fridge for up to 2 days.
Nutrition Info:

- Per Serving: Calories: 236 ;Fat: 20g ;Protein: 6g;Carbs: 11g .

Lettuce & Tomato Salad With Quinoa

Servings: 4
Cooking Time: 25 Minutes
Ingredients:

- 1 cup quinoa, rinsed
- ⅓ cup white wine vinegar
- 2 tbsp extra-virgin olive oil
- 1 tbsp chopped fresh dill
- Sea salt and pepper to taste
- 2 cups sliced sweet onions
- 2 tomatoes, sliced
- 4 cups shredded lettuce

Directions:
1. Place the quinoa in a pot with 2 cups of salted water. Bring to a boil. Lower the heat and simmer covered for 15 minutes. Turn the heat off and let sit for 5 minutes. Using a fork, fluff the quinoa and set aside. In a small bowl, whisk the vinegar, olive oil, dill, salt, and pepper; set aside. In a serving plate, combine onions, tomatoes, quinoa, and lettuce. Pour in the dressing and toss to coat.

Nutrition Info:

- Per Serving: Calories: 380;Fat: 11g;Protein: 12g;Carbs: 58g.

Fantastic Green Salad

Servings: 4
Cooking Time: 10 Minutes
Ingredients:

- 1 head Iceberg lettuce
- 8 asparagus, chopped
- 2 seedless cucumbers, sliced
- 1 zucchini, cut into ribbons
- 1 carrot, cut into ribbons
- 1 avocado, sliced
- ½ cup green dressing
- 2 scallions, thinly sliced

Directions:
1. Share the lettuce into 4 bowls and add in some asparagus, cucumber, zucchini, carrot, and avocado. Sprinkle each bowl with 2 tbsp of dressing. Serve topped with scallions.

Nutrition Info:

- Per Serving: Calories: 255;Fat: 21g;Protein: 4g;Carbs: 15g.

Squash Salad

Servings: 4
Cooking Time: 20 Minutes
Ingredients:

- 2 lb green squash, cubed
- 2 tbsp olive oil
- Sea salt and pepper to taste
- 3 oz fennel, sliced
- 2 oz chopped green onions
- 1 cup paleo mayonnaise
- 2 tbsp chives, chopped
- ¼ tbsp mustard powder
- 1 tbsp chopped dill

Directions:

1. Put a pan over medium heat and warm the olive oil. Fry in squash cubes until slightly softened but not browned, about 7 minutes. Allow the squash to cool. Mix the cooled squash, fennel slices, green onions, mayonnaise, chives, salt, pepper, and mustard powder in a salad bowl. Garnish with dill and serve.

Nutrition Info:

- Per Serving: Calories: 365;Fat: 27g;Protein: 6g;Carbs: 29g.

Tempting Salad With Celery, Beet, And Sliced Apple

Servings: 4
Cooking Time: 0 Minutes
Ingredients:

- 2 green apples, cored and quartered
- 2 small beets, peeled and quartered
- 4 cups spinach
- 2 celery stalks, sliced thin
- ½ red onion, sliced thin
- ½ cup shredded carrots
- 1 tablespoon apple cider vinegar
- 1 tablespoon raw honey or maple syrup
- 3 tablespoons extra-virgin olive oil
- Sea salt
- Freshly ground black pepper
- ¼ cup pumpkin seeds

Directions:

1. Slice the apples and the beets using a mandoline or the slicing disk of a food processor.
2. Place the spinach on a large platter. Arrange the apples and beets over the spinach. Top with the celery, red onion, and carrots.
3. Whisk together the cider vinegar, honey, and olive oil in a small bowl. Season with salt and pepper.
4. Drizzle the dressing over the salad and garnish with the pumpkin seeds.

Nutrition Info:

- Per Serving: Calories: 239 ;Fat: 15g ;Protein: 4g ;Carbs: 27g.

Cashew & Raisin Salad

Servings: 4
Cooking Time: 15 Minutes
Ingredients:

- 3 cups haricots verts, trimmed and chopped
- 2 carrots, sliced
- 3 cups shredded cabbage
- 1/3 cup golden raisins
- ¼ cup roasted cashew
- 1 garlic clove, minced
- 1 medium shallot, chopped
- 1 ½ tsp grated fresh ginger
- 1/3 cup creamy peanut butter
- 2 tsp low-sodium soy sauce
- 2 tbsp fresh lemon juice
- Sea salt to taste
- ⅛ tsp ground cayenne
- ¾ cup coconut milk

Directions:

1. Place the haricots verts, carrots, and cabbage in a pot with water and steam for 5 minutes. Drain and transfer to a bowl. Add in raisins and cashew. Let cool. In a food processor, put the garlic, shallot, and ginger. Pulse until puréed. Add in peanut butter, soy sauce, lemon juice, salt, cayenne pepper. Blitz until smooth. Stir in coconut milk. Sprinkle the salad with the dressing and toss to coat.

Nutrition Info:

- Per Serving: Calories: 410;Fat: 31g;Protein: 40g;Carbs: 30g.

Savory Pasta Salad With Cannellini Beans

Servings: 4
Cooking Time: 35 Minutes
Ingredients:

- 8 oz whole-wheat pasta
- 1 tbsp olive oil
- 1 medium zucchini, sliced
- 2 garlic cloves, minced
- 2 large tomatoes, chopped
- 1 can cannellini beans
- 10 green olives, sliced
- ½ cup crumbled tofu
- Sea salt and pepper to taste

Directions:

1. Cook the pasta until al dente, 10 minutes. Drain and set aside. Heat olive oil in a skillet and sauté zucchini and garlic for 4 minutes. Stir in tomatoes, beans, salt, pepper, and olives. Cook until the tomatoes soften, 10 minutes. Mix in pasta. Allow warming for 1 minute. Stir in tofu.

Nutrition Info:

- Per Serving: Calories: 220;Fat: 7g;Protein: 8g;Carbs: 32g.

Authentic Caesar Salad

Servings: 4
Cooking Time: 0 Minutes
Ingredients:

- 2 romaine lettuce hearts, chopped
- One 14 ounces can hearts of palm, drained and sliced
- ½ cup sunflower seeds
- 1 recipe Almost Caesar Dressing
- Salt
- Freshly ground black pepper

Directions:

1. Combine the romaine lettuce, hearts of palm, and sunflower seeds in a large bowl.
2. To lightly coat the lettuce leaves, add enough dressing. Reserve any remaining dressing for another use.
3. Season the salad with salt and pepper, and serve.

Nutrition Info:

- Per Serving: Calories: 431 ;Fat: 42g ;Protein: 6g ;Carbs: 14g .

Beet & Cucumber Salad

Servings: 2
Cooking Time: 40 Minutes
Ingredients:

- 3 beets, peeled and sliced
- 1 tsp olive oil
- 1 cucumber, sliced
- 2 cups mixed greens
- 4 tbsp balsamic dressing
- 2 tbsp chopped almonds
- Sea salt to taste

Directions:

1. Preheat your oven to 390°F. In a bowl, stir the beets, oil, and salt. Toss to coat. Transfer to a baking dish and roast for 20 minutes, until golden brown. Once the beets are ready, divide between 2 plates and place a cucumber slice on each beet. Top with mixed greens. Pour over the dressing and garnish with almonds to serve.

Nutrition Info:

- Per Serving: Calories: 170;Fat: 8g;Protein: 6g;Carbs: 21g.

Hot Chickpea Salad

Servings: 4
Cooking Time: 30 Minutes
Ingredients:

- 1 tsp chili pepper flakes
- 1 avocado, chopped
- 1 bunch of kale, sliced
- 2 tsp lemon juice
- 2 tbsp extra-virgin olive oil
- Sea salt to taste
- 1 can chickpeas

Directions:

1. Add the kale to a large bowl. Sprinkle with salt, 1 tablespoon of olive oil, and lemon juice. Gently knead the kale leaves in the bowl for 5 minutes or until wilted and bright. Rip the leafy part of the kale off the stem, then discard the stem.
2. Warm the remaining olive oil in a nonstick skillet over medium heat. Add the chickpeas, chili pepper flakes, and salt and cook for 15 minutes or until the chickpeas are crispy. Transfer the kale to a large serving bowl, then top with chickpeas and avocado. Toss to combine and serve.

Nutrition Info:

- Per Serving: Calories: 360;Fat: 20g;Protein: 12g;Carbs: 35g.

Rich In Antioxidant Vegetable Slaw With Feta Cheese

Servings: 4 To 6
Cooking Time: 0 Minutes
Ingredients:

- ½ cup extra-virgin olive oil
- ½ cup apple cider vinegar
- 1 tablespoon raw honey or maple syrup
- 1 teaspoon Dijon mustard
- 1 teaspoon salt
- ¼ teaspoon black pepper, freshly ground
- 2 large broccoli stems, peeled and shredded
- 2 carrots, peeled and shredded
- ½ celery root bulb, peeled and shredded
- 1 large beet, peeled and shredded
- 2 zucchinis, shredded
- 1 small red onion, sliced thin
- ¼ cup fresh Italian parsley, chopped
- 3 ounces feta cheese, crumbled

Directions:

1. Whisk together the olive oil, cider vinegar, honey, Dijon mustard, salt, and pepper in a large bowl.
2. Add the broccoli, carrots, celery root, beets, zucchini, onion, and Italian parsley. Toss to coat the vegetables with the dressing.
3. Transfer the slaw to a serving bowl and garnish with the feta cheese.

Nutrition Info:

- Per Serving: Calories: 388 ;Fat: 30g ;Protein: 8g ;Carbs: 26g .

Soy-free Salad With Chopped Chicken And Apple

Servings: 2
Cooking Time: 0 Minutes
Ingredients:

- 2 cooked boneless, skinless chicken breasts, cut into ½-inch cubes
- ½ cup celery, chopped
- 1 large green apple, cored and coarsely chopped
- 1 romaine lettuce heart, chopped

- 3 scallions, chopped
- ½ cup canned chickpeas
- ½ cup Lemony Mustard Dressing

Directions:

1. In a large bowl, combine the chicken, celery, apple, romaine, scallions, and chickpeas.
2. Add the dressing and toss to mix.
3. Divide the salad among four serving bowls, top with the toasted walnuts (if using), and serve.

Nutrition Info:

- Per Serving: Calories: 860 ;Fat: 61g ;Protein: 45g ;Carbs: 39g .

Millet Salad With Olives & Cherries

Servings: 4
Cooking Time: 40 Minutes
Ingredients:

- ½ cup toasted pecans, chopped
- 1 cup millet
- 1 can navy beans
- 1 celery stalk, chopped
- 1 carrot, shredded
- 3 green onions, minced
- ½ cup chopped green olives
- ½ cup dried cherries
- ½ cup minced fresh parsley
- 1 garlic clove, pressed
- 3 tbsp sherry vinegar
- ¼ cup olive oil
- Sea salt and pepper to taste

Directions:

1. Cook the millet in salted water for 30 minutes. Remove to a bowl. Mix in beans, celery, carrot, green onions, olives, cherries, pecans, and parsley. Whisk the garlic, vinegar, olive oil, salt, and pepper until well mixed in another bowl. Pour over the millet mixture and toss coat. Serve.

Nutrition Info:

- Per Serving: Calories: 590;Fat: 27g;Protein: 9g;Carbs: 71g.

Warm Cod & Zucchini Salad

Servings: 2
Cooking Time: 25 Minutes
Ingredients:

- 2 cups mustard greens
- 1 skinless cod fillets
- ½ zucchini, sliced
- 1 tbsp balsamic vinegar
- 2 tbsp extra-virgin olive oil
- 2 thyme sprigs, torn
- 1 lemon, juiced

Directions:

1. Brush the cod fillet with olive oil and fry it in a pan over medium heat until browned. Remove and flake it. Sauté the zucchini and mustard greens in the same pan for 4-5 minutes.

Transfer to a plate and top with cod. Drizzle with lemon and sprinkle with thyme.

Nutrition Info:

- Per Serving: Calories: 530;Fat: 26g;Protein: 68g;Carbs: 5g.

Bulgur & Kale Salad

Servings: 4
Cooking Time: 30 Minutes
Ingredients:

- ½ cup chopped green beans, steamed
- 1 avocado, peeled and pitted
- 1 tbsp fresh lemon juice
- 1 small garlic clove, pressed
- 1 scallion, chopped
- Sea salt to taste
- 8 large kale leaves, chopped
- 16 cherry tomatoes, halved
- 1 red bell pepper, chopped
- 2 scallions, chopped
- 2 cups cooked bulgur

Directions:

1. In a food processor, place the avocado, lemon juice, garlic, scallion, salt, and ¼ cup water. Blend until smooth. Set aside the dressing. Put kale, green beans, cherry tomatoes, bell pepper, scallions, and bulgur in a serving bowl. Add in the dressing and toss to coat. Serve.

Nutrition Info:

- Per Serving: Calories: 200;Fat: 8g;Protein: 5g;Carbs: 30.3g.

Convenient Salad With Raspberry Vinaigrette, Spinach, And Walnut

Servings: 4
Cooking Time: 0 Minutes
Ingredients:

- 4 cups baby spinach, fresh
- ¼ cup walnut pieces
- ¼ cup raspberry vinaigrette

Directions:

1. Combine the spinach and walnuts in a medium bowl.
2. Toss with the vinaigrette and serve immediately.

Nutrition Info:

- Per Serving: Calories: 501 ;Fat: 50g ;Carbs: 9g ;Sugar: 2g ;Fiber: 5g ;Protein: 11g ;Sodium: 96mg

Complementary Spinach Salad

Servings: 4
Cooking Time: 0 Minutes
Ingredients:

- ¼ cup extra-virgin olive oil
- ¼ cup Dijon mustard
- 2 tablespoons lemon juice, freshly squeezed
- 1½ tablespoons maple syrup
- ¼ teaspoon sea salt, plus additional as needed

- 6 cups baby spinach leaves

Directions:

1. Combine the olive oil, Dijon mustard, lemon juice, maple syrup, and salt in a small jar. Cover and shake well to mix.

2. Taste, and adjust the seasoning if necessary.

3. Toss together the spinach and dressing in a large serving bowl.

Nutrition Info:

- Per Serving: Calories: 150 ;Fat: 14g ;Protein: 2g ;Carbs: 8g .

African Zucchini Salad

Servings: 2
Cooking Time: 20 Minutes
Ingredients:

- 1 lemon, half zested and juiced, half cut into wedges
- 1 tsp olive oil
- 1 zucchini, chopped
- ½ tsp ground cumin
- ½ tsp ground ginger
- ¼ tsp turmeric
- ¼ tsp ground nutmeg
- A pinch of sea salt
- 2 tbsp capers
- 1 tbsp chopped green olives
- 1 garlic clove, pressed
- 2 tbsp fresh mint, chopped
- 2 cups spinach, chopped

Directions:

1. Warm the olive oil in a skillet over medium heat. Place the zucchini and sauté for 10 minutes. Stir in cumin, ginger, turmeric, nutmeg, and salt. Pour in lemon zest, lemon juice, capers, garlic, and mint and cook for 2 minutes more. Divide the spinach between serving plates and top with zucchini mixture. Garnish with lemon and olives.

Nutrition Info:

- Per Serving: Calories: 50;Fat: 3g;Protein: 41g;Carbs: 5g.

Minty Melon & Cantaloupe Salad

Servings: 4
Cooking Time: 20 Minutes
Ingredients:

- 2 tbsp apple cider vinegar
- 3 tbsp olive oil
- Sea salt to taste
- ½ cantaloupe, cubed
- 1 honeydew melon, cubed
- 3 stalks celery, sliced
- ½ red onion, thinly sliced
- ¼ cup chopped fresh mint

Directions:

1. Whisk the apple cider vinegar, olive oil, and salt in a bowl. Add the honeydew, cantaloupe, celery, red onion, and mint and toss to combine. Serve and enjoy!

Nutrition Info:

- Per Serving: Calories: 220;Fat: 10g;Protein: 2g;Carbs: 32g.

Oily Salad With Celery And Kipper

Servings: 2
Cooking Time: 0 Minutes
Ingredients:

- 1 can kippers, cooked
- 1 celery stalk, chopped
- 1 tablespoon fresh parsley, chopped
- ½ cup low fat Greek yogurt
- 1 lemon, juiced
- 1 clove garlic, minced
- 1 onion, minced

Directions:

1. All of the ingredients must be combined apart from the kippers into a salad bowl.

2. Drain the kippers and then toss in the dressing mix.

3. Chill before serving for at least 20 minutes in the fridge.

Nutrition Info:

- Per Serving: Calories: 140 ;Fat: 2g ;Protein: 8g ;Carbs: 24g ;Sugar: 15g .

Summer Time Sizzling Green Salad With Salmon

Servings: 2
Cooking Time: 10 Minutes
Ingredients:

- 2 salmon fillets, skinless
- 2 cups of seasonal greens
- ½ cup zucchini, sliced
- 1 tablespoon balsamic vinegar
- 2 tablespoons extra virgin olive oil
- 2 sprigs thyme, torn from the stem
- 1 lemon, juiced

Directions:

1. Preheat the broiler to a medium-high heat.

2. For 10 minutes, broil the salmon in parchment paper with some oil, lemon, and pepper.

3. Slice the zucchini and sauté for 4-5 minutes with the oil in a pan on medium heat.

4. Build the salad by creating a bed of zucchini and topping it with flaked salmon.

5. Drizzle with balsamic vinegar and sprinkle with thyme.

Nutrition Info:

- Per Serving: Calories: 67 ;Fat: 6g ;Protein: 7g;Carbs: 3g .

Maple Walnut & Pear Salad

Servings: 4
Cooking Time: 10 Minutes
Ingredients:
- 4 cored pears, chopped
- ¼ cup walnuts, chopped
- 2 tbsp maple syrup
- 2 tbsp balsamic vinegar
- 2 tbsp extra-virgin olive oil

Directions:
1. Mix the pears and walnuts in a bowl. In another bowl, combine the maple syrup, balsamic vinegar, and olive oil, pour it over pears, and toss to coat. Serve immediately.

Nutrition Info:
- Per Serving: Calories: 280;Fat: 14g;Protein: 4g;Carbs: 43g.

Refreshing Slaw With Maple Dressing

Servings: 4
Cooking Time: 25 Minutes
Ingredients:
- ½ cup roasted pumpkin seeds
- 2 tbsp lime juice
- ¼ cup olive oil
- 3 tbsp pure maple syrup
- 1 tsp ginger powder
- Sea salt to taste
- 2 carrots, shredded
- 1 jicama, shredded
- ½ peeled celeriac, shredded
- 1 cucumber, shredded
- 5 radishes, shredded
- 2 scallions, sliced

Directions:
1. Whisk the olive oil, maple syrup, lime juice, salt, and ginger powder in a bowl. Toss together the jicama, carrots, celeriac, cucumber, radishes, and scallions. Add the dressing and toss to coat. Top with pumpkin seeds.

Nutrition Info:
- Per Serving: Calories: 345;Fat: 20g;Protein: 8g;Carbs: 36g.

Diverse Salad With Shredded Root Vegetable

Servings: 4
Cooking Time: 0 Minutes
Ingredients:
- Dressing:
- ¼ cup olive oil
- 3 tablespoons pure maple syrup
- 2 tablespoons apple cider vinegar
- 1 teaspoon fresh ginger, grated
- Sea salt
- Slaw:
- 1 jicama, or 2 parsnips, peeled and shredded

- 2 carrots, shredded, or 1 cup pre-shredded packaged carrots
- ½ celeriac, peeled and shredded
- ¼ fennel bulb, shredded
- 5 radishes, shredded
- 2 scallions, white and green parts, peeled and thinly sliced
- ½ cup pumpkin seeds, roasted

Directions:
1. Whisk the olive oil, maple syrup, cider vinegar, and ginger in a small bowl until well blended. Season with sea salt and set it aside.
2. Toss together the jicama, carrots, celeriac, fennel, radishes, and scallions in a large bowl.
3. Add the dressing and toss to coat.
4. Top the slaw with the pumpkin seeds and serve.

Nutrition Info:
- Per Serving: Calories: 343 ;Fat: 21g ;Protein: 7g;Carbs: 36g .

Easy Pineapple & Jicama Salad

Servings: 6
Cooking Time: 15 Minutes
Ingredients:
- 1 jicama, peeled and grated
- 1 peeled pineapple, sliced
- ¼ cup non-dairy milk
- 2 tbsp fresh basil, chopped
- 1 large scallion, chopped
- Sea salt to taste
- 1 ½ tbsp tahini
- Arugula for serving
- Chopped cashews

Directions:
1. Place jicama in a bowl. In a food processor, put the pineapple and enough milk. Blitz until puréed. Add in basil, scallions, tahini, and salt. Pour over the jicama and cover. Transfer to the fridge and marinate for 1 hour. Place a bed of arugula on a plate and top with the salad. Serve garnished with cashews.

Nutrition Info:
- Per Serving: Calories: 175;Fat: 5g;Protein: 2g;Carbs: 33g.

Lemony Ditalini Salad With Chickpeas

Servings: 4
Cooking Time: 25 Minutes
Ingredients:
- ¼ cup olive oil
- 2 tbsp lemon juice
- A pinch of sea salt
- 1 ½ cups canned chickpeas
- 2 cups cooked ditalini pasta
- 2 cups spinach, chopped
- 1 cup chopped cucumber

- ¼ red onion, finely diced

Directions:

1. Mix the olive oil, lemon juice, and salt in a bowl. Stir in chickpeas and ditalini pasta. Add spinach, cucumber, and red onion and stir to combine. Serve and enjoy!

Nutrition Info:

- Per Serving: Calories: 505;Fat: 19g;Protein: 18g;Carbs: 69g.

Date & Carrot Salad With Pistachios

Servings: 6
Cooking Time: 10 Minutes
Ingredients:

- 4 carrots, shredded
- ½ cup cilantro, chopped
- 1/3 cup pistachios, chopped
- ¼ tsp red pepper flakes
- 3 scallions, sliced
- 4 Medjool dates, chopped
- ½ cup tahini lime dressing

Directions:

1. Place the carrots, cilantro, pistachios, red pepper flakes, scallions, and dates in a bowl and toss to combine. Drizzle with tahini lime dressing. Serve right away.

Nutrition Info:

- Per Serving: Calories: 100;Fat: 3g;Protein: 2g;Carbs: 20g.

Freshly-made Fennel Salad With Tuna Steak

Servings: 2
Cooking Time: 25 Minutes
Ingredients:

- 2 tuna steaks, 1 inch thick each
- 2 tablespoon olive oil,
- 1 tablespoon olive oil
- 1 teaspoon black peppercorns, crushed
- 1 teaspoon fennel seeds, crushed
- 1 fennel bulb, trimmed and sliced
- ½ cup water
- 1 lemon, juiced
- 1 teaspoon fresh parsley, chopped

Directions:

1. Coat the fish with oil and then season with peppercorns and fennel seeds.
2. For 5 minutes, heat the oil on medium heat and sauté the fennel bulb slices until light brown, stir in the garlic and cook for 1 minute.
3. Add the water to the pan and cook for 10 minutes until the fennel is tender.
4. Stir in the lemon juice and lower heat to a simmer.
5. Heat another skillet and sauté the tuna steaks for about 2 to 3 minutes each side for medium-rare. Add 1 minute on each side for medium and 2 minutes on each side for medium-well.

6. Serve the fennel mix with the tuna steaks on top and garnish with the fresh parsley.

Nutrition Info:

- Per Serving: Calories: 463 ;Fat: 42g ;Protein: 4g ;Carbs: 24g.

Spinach Salad With Cranberries

Servings: 1
Cooking Time: 10 Minutes
Ingredients:

- 1 cup chopped fresh cranberries
- 1 tbsp apple cider vinegar
- 2 tsp olive oil
- 1 orange, sliced
- 1 cup spinach, chopped
- 2 tsp grated ginger

Directions:

1. Combine the vinegar and olive oil in a bowl. Add the cranberries, spinach, ginger, and orange and toss to coat. Chill before serving.

Nutrition Info:

- Per Serving: Calories: 300;Fat: 19g;Protein: 2g;Carbs: 30g.

Gratifying Healthy Sweet Potato Salad With Mustard And Tarragon

Servings: 2
Cooking Time: 30 Minutes
Ingredients:

- 2 medium-sized sweet potatoes, peeled and cubed
- 2½cup of low-fat Greek yogurt
- 2 tablespoons Dijon mustard
- 1 tablespoon tarragon, dried
- 1 beef tomato, finely chopped
- 2½ yellow pepper, finely chopped
- ½ red onion, finely chopped
- pinch of black pepper

Directions:

1. Boil water in a large pot on high heat.
2. Cook the potatoes in the pot for 20 minutes or until tender.
3. After draining, set aside to cool down.
4. In a serving bowl, combine Dijon mustard, plain yogurt, tarragon, peppers, tomatoes, and red onion.
5. Add the cooled potatoes and mix well then serve.

Nutrition Info:

- Per Serving: Calories: 260 ;Fat: 3g ;Protein: 12g ;Carbs: 50g.

Nourishing Vegetable Salad With Curry

Servings: 6
Cooking Time: 45 Minutes
Ingredients:
- 3 cups Brussels sprouts, halved
- 2 cups broccoli florets
- 5 cloves garlic, sliced
- 3 tablespoons avocado oil
- 1 teaspoon fish sauce
- 1 teaspoon Himalayan salt, fine
- 1 teaspoon black pepper, ground
- 1 teaspoon cumin, ground
- 1 teaspoon turmeric powder
- ½ teaspoon ginger powder
- ¼ cup Homemade Mayo

Directions:
1. Preheat the oven to 400°F.
2. On a sheet pan, spread evenly the Brussels sprouts, broccoli, and garlic. Drizzle with avocado oil and fish sauce and sprinkle the salt, pepper, cumin, turmeric, and ginger powder over them. Toss to combine, massaging the oil and seasonings into the Brussels and broccoli. Then spread them out again on the sheet pan. Wash your yellow hands so the turmeric doesn't stain.
3. For 40 minutes, roast the vegetables on the middle rack of the oven. Remove from the oven and let cool to room temperature.
4. Transfer the roasted vegetables to a bowl. Add the mayo and stir to combine. Store in the fridge for up to 5 days, until ready to serve or for meal prep.

Nutrition Info:
- Per Serving: Calories: 176 ;Fat: 17g ;Protein: 3g ;Carbs: 7g .

Minty Eggplant Salad

Servings: 2
Cooking Time: 45 Minutes
Ingredients:
- 1 lemon, half zested and juiced, half cut into wedges
- 1 tsp olive oil
- 1 eggplant, chopped
- ½ tsp ground cumin
- ½ tsp ground ginger
- ¼ tsp turmeric
- ¼ tsp ground nutmeg
- Sea salt to taste
- 2 tbsp capers
- 1 tbsp chopped green olives
- 1 garlic clove, pressed
- 2 tbsp fresh mint, chopped
- 2 cups watercress, chopped

Directions:
1. In a skillet over medium heat, warm the oil. Place the eggplant and cook for 5 minutes. Add in cumin, ginger,

turmeric, nutmeg, and salt. Cook for another 10 minutes. Stir in lemon zest, lemon juice, capers, olives, garlic, and mint. Cook for 1-2 minutes more. Place some watercress on each plate and top with the eggplant mixture. Serve.

Nutrition Info:
- Per Serving: Calories: 110;Fat: 3g;Protein: 44g;Carbs: 20g.

Pantry Salad With White Bean And Tuna

Servings: 4
Cooking Time: 0 Minutes
Ingredients:
- 4 cups arugula
- Two 5 ounces cans flaked white tuna, drained
- One 15 ounces can white beans, drained and rinsed
- ½ pint cherry tomatoes, halved lengthwise
- ½ red onion, finely chopped
- ½ cup pitted Kalamata olives
- ¼ cup extra-virgin olive oil
- 2 tablespoons freshly squeezed lemon juice
- Salt
- Freshly ground black pepper
- 2 ounces crumbled sheep's milk or goat's milk feta cheese

Directions:
1. Mix together the arugula, tuna, white beans, tomatoes, onion, olives, olive oil, and lemon juice in a large bowl. Season with salt and pepper.
2. Top the salad with the feta cheese before serving.

Nutrition Info:
- Per Serving: Calories: 373 ; Fat: 19g ; Protein: 29g;Carbs: 28g.

Spinach Salad With Blackberries & Pecans

Servings: 4
Cooking Time: 10 Minutes
Ingredients:
- 10 oz baby spinach
- 1 cup raisins
- 1 cup fresh blackberries
- ¼ red onion, thinly sliced
- ½ cup chopped pecans
- ¼ cup balsamic vinegar
- ¾ cup olive oil
- Sea salt and pepper to taste

Directions:
1. Combine the spinach, raisins, blackberries, red onion, and pecans in a bowl. In another bowl, mix the vinegar, olive oil, salt, and pepper. Pour over the salad and toss to coat. Serve immediately.

Nutrition Info:
- Per Serving: Calories: 600;Fat: 50g;Protein: 4g;Carbs: 40g.

Tangy Nutty Brussel Sprout Salad

Servings: 4
Cooking Time: 20 Minutes
Ingredients:

- 1 lb Brussels sprouts, grated
- 1 lemon, juiced and zested
- 4 tbsp olive oil
- 1 tsp chili paste
- 2 oz pecans
- 1 oz pumpkin seeds
- 1 oz sunflower seeds
- ½ tsp cumin powder
- Sea salt to taste

Directions:

1. Put Brussels sprouts in a salad bowl. In a small bowl, mix lemon juice, zest, half of the olive oil, salt, and pepper, and drizzle the dressing over the Brussels sprouts. Toss and allow the vegetable to marinate for 10 minutes. Warm the remaining olive oil in a pan. Stir in chili paste and toss the pecans, pumpkin seeds, sunflower seeds, cumin powder, and salt in the chili oil. Sauté on low heat for 3-4 minutes just to heat the nuts. Allow cooling. Pour the nuts and seeds mix in the salad bowl, toss, and serve.

Nutrition Info:

- Per Serving: Calories: 345;Fat: 29g;Protein: 21g;Carbs: 19g.

Crunchy Brussels Sprout Slaw

Servings: 4
Cooking Time: 0 Minutes
Ingredients:

- 1 pound Brussels sprouts, stem ends removed and sliced thin
- ½ red onion, sliced thin
- 1 apple, cored and sliced thin
- 1 teaspoon Dijon mustard
- 1 teaspoon salt
- 1 tablespoon raw honey or maple syrup
- 2 teaspoons apple cider vinegar
- 1 cup coconut milk yogurt, plain
- ½ cup toasted hazelnuts, chopped
- ½ cup pomegranate seeds

Directions:

1. Combine the Brussels sprouts, onion, and apple in a medium bowl.
2. Whisk together the Dijon mustard, salt, honey, cider vinegar, and yogurt in a small bowl.
3. Add the dressing to the Brussels sprouts and toss until evenly coated.
4. Garnish the salad with the hazelnuts and pomegranate seeds.

Nutrition Info:

- Per Serving: Calories: 189 ;Fat: 8g ;Protein: 6g ;Carbs: 29g .

Quick Insalata Caprese

Servings: 4
Cooking Time: 10 Minutes
Ingredients:

- 16 oz fresh mozzarella cheese, sliced
- 4 large tomatoes, sliced
- ¼ cup fresh basil leaves
- ¼ cup extra-virgin olive oil
- Sea salt and pepper to taste

Directions:

1. On a salad platter, layer alternating slices of tomatoes and mozzarella. Add a basil leaf between each slice. Season with olive oil, salt, and pepper. Serve right away.

Nutrition Info:

- Per Serving: Calories: 150;Fat: 15g;Protein: 1g;Carbs: 5g.

Thai Green Bean & Mango Salad

Servings: 4
Cooking Time: 15 Minutes
Ingredients:

- 1 mango, julienned
- 8 oz green beans, trimmed
- ½ cup chopped mint
- ½ cup chopped cilantro
- ½ cup chopped almonds
- 12 cherry tomatoes, halved
- 2 red Thai chiles, sliced
- 3 tbsp sugar-free soy sauce
- 2 tbsp raw honey
- ½ cup lime juice

Directions:

1. Steam the green beans for approximately 2 minutes or until crisp-tender. Drain and slice them in half crosswise. Combine red chilies, soy sauce, honey, and lime juice in a bowl and stir well. Combine the green beans with the remaining ingredients in a large serving bowl. Drizzle with the dressing, then toss to combine well. Serve.

Nutrition Info:

- Per Serving: Calories: 155;Fat: 1g;Protein: 5g;Carbs: 37g.

Apple & Spinach Salad With Walnuts

Servings: 4
Cooking Time: 20 Minutes
Ingredients:

- ¼ cup tahini
- 2 tbsp Dijon mustard
- 1 tbsp maple syrup
- 1 tbsp lemon juice
- ½ cup chopped walnuts
- 2 tsp low-sodium soy sauce
- 1 lb baby spinach
- 1 cored green apple, sliced
- Sea salt to taste

Directions:

1. Preheat your oven to 360°F. Line with parchment paper a baking sheet. In a bowl, mix the tahini, mustard, 1 tbsp maple syrup, lemon juice, and salt. Set aside the dressing.
2. In another bowl, combine the walnuts, soy sauce, and the remaining maple syrup. Spread evenly on the baking sheet and bake for 5 minutes, shaking once until crunchy. Allow cooling for 3 minutes. Combine the spinach and apples in a bowl. Pour over the dressing and toss to coat. Serve garnished with the walnut crunch.

Nutrition Info:

- Per Serving: Calories: 250;Fat: 15g;Protein: 8g;Carbs: 26g.

The Best Mediterranean Salad

Servings: 4
Cooking Time: 15 Minutes
Ingredients:

- 2 green onions, sliced
- 2 garlic cloves, minced
- 2 cups packed spinach
- 3 large tomatoes, diced
- 1 bunch radishes, sliced
- 1 peeled cucumber, diced
- 1 tbsp chopped fresh mint
- 1 tbsp chopped parsley
- 1 cup plain almond yogurt
- 1 tbsp apple cider vinegar
- 3 tbsp lemon juice
- 1 tbsp sumac
- 2 tbsp extra-virgin olive oil
- Sea salt and pepper to taste

Directions:

1. Place all the ingredients in a large salad bowl and toss to coat well. Serve immediately.

Nutrition Info:

- Per Serving: Calories: 200;Fat: 15g;Protein: 5g;Carbs: 15g.

Mediterranean Pasta Salad

Servings: 4
Cooking Time: 15 Minutes

Ingredients:

- ½ cup minced sun-dried tomatoes
- 2 roasted bell red peppers, chopped
- 8 oz whole-wheat pasta
- 1 can chickpeas
- ½ cup pitted black olives
- 1 jar dill pickles, sliced
- ½ cup frozen peas, thawed
- 1 tbsp capers
- 3 tsp dried chives
- ½ cup olive oil
- ¼ cup white wine vinegar
- ½ tsp dried basil
- 1 garlic clove, minced
- Sea salt and pepper to taste

Directions:

1. Cook the pasta in salted water for 8-10 minutes until al dente. Drain and remove to a bowl. Stir in chickpeas, black olives, sun-dried tomatoes, dill pickles, roasted peppers, peas, capers, and chives. In another bowl, whisk oil, white wine vinegar, basil, garlic, sugar, salt, and pepper. Pour over the pasta and toss to coat. Serve.

Nutrition Info:

- Per Serving: Calories: 590;Fat: 32g;Protein: 12g;Carbs: 67g.

Traditional Lebanese Salad

Servings: 4
Cooking Time: 25 Minutes
Ingredients:

- 1 cup cooked bulgur
- 1 cup boiling water
- Zest and juice of 1 lemon
- 1 garlic clove, pressed
- Sea salt to taste
- 1 tbsp olive oil
- ½ cucumber, sliced
- 1 tomato, sliced
- 1 cup fresh parsley, chopped
- ¼ cup fresh mint, chopped
- 2 scallions, chopped
- 4 tbsp sunflower seeds

Directions:

1. Mix lemon juice, lemon zest, garlic, salt, and olive oil in a bowl. Stir in cucumber, tomato, parsley, mint, and scallions. Toss to coat. Fluff the bulgur and stir it into the cucumber mix. Top with sunflower seeds and serve.

Nutrition Info:

- Per Serving: Calories: 140;Fat: 8g;Protein: 7g;Carbs: 14g.

Quinoa & Artichoke Salad With Almonds

Servings: 4
Cooking Time: 25 Minutes
Ingredients:
- 2 cans artichoke hearts
- ½ cup chopped almonds
- 2 cups cooked quinoa
- 1 cup chopped kale
- ½ cup chopped red onion
- 3 tbsp chopped parsley
- 1 lemon, zested and juiced
- 2 tbsp olive oil
- 1 tbsp balsamic vinegar
- 1 tsp garlic powder
- Sea salt to taste

Directions:
1. Combine quinoa, artichoke hearts, kale, red onion, almonds, parsley, lemon juice, lemon zest, olive oil, vinegar, salt, and garlic powder in a bowl and mix. Serve.

Nutrition Info:
- Per Serving: Calories: 400;Fat: 15g;Protein: 17g;Carbs: 55g.

Chapter 10. Desserts

Aunt's Apricot Tarte Tatin

Servings: 4
Cooking Time: 30 Minutes + Cooling Time
Ingredients:
- 4 eggs
- ¼ cup almond flour
- 3 tbsp whole-wheat flour
- ½ tsp sea salt
- ¼ cup cold almond butter, crumbled
- 3 tbsp pure maple syrup
- 4 tbsp melted almond butter
- 3 tsp pure maple syrup
- 1 tsp vanilla extract
- 1 lemon, juiced
- 12 pitted apricots, halved
- ½ cup coconut cream
- 4 fresh basil leaves

Directions:
1. Preheat your oven to 350ºF. Grease a large pie pan with cooking spray. In a large bowl, combine the flours and salt. Add the melted almond butter, and using an electric hand mixer, whisk until crumbly. Pour in the eggs and maple syrup and mix until smooth dough forms. Flatten the dough on a flat surface, cover with plastic wrap, and refrigerate for 1 hour. Dust a working surface with almond flour, remove the dough onto the surface, and using a rolling pin, flatten the dough into a 1-inch diameter circle. Set aside. In a large bowl, mix the almond butter, maple syrup, vanilla, and lemon juice. Add the apricots to the mixture and coat well.
2. Arrange the apricots (open side down) in the pie pan and lay the dough on top. Press to fit and cut off the dough hanging on the edges. Bake in the oven for 35 to 40 minutes or until golden brown and puffed up. Remove the pie pan from the oven, allow cooling for 5 minutes, and run a butter knife around the edges of the pastry. Invert the dessert onto a large plate, spread the coconut cream on top, and garnish with basil leaves. Serve sliced.

Nutrition Info:
- Per Serving: Calories: 535;Fat: 38g;Protein: 5g;Carbs: 49g.

Pumpkin & Mango Lemon Cake

Servings: 6
Cooking Time: 60 Minutes
Ingredients:
- 1 ½ cups whole-grain flour
- ¾ cup pure date sugar
- ¼ cup tapioca starch
- 1 tsp baking soda
- ½ tsp salt
- ½ tsp baking powder
- ½ tsp ground cinnamon
- ½ tsp ground allspice
- ½ tsp ground ginger
- 1 cup pumpkin puree
- 2 tbsp olive oil
- 2 tsp grated lemon zest
- 1 mango, chopped

Directions:
1. Preheat your oven to 360ºF. In a bowl, mix flour, date sugar, tapioca starch, baking soda, salt, baking powder, cinnamon, allspice, and ginger. In another bowl, whisk pumpkin puree, oil, lemon zest, and 2 tbsp water until blend. Add in the mango. Pour the flour mixture into the pumpkin mixture and toss to coat. Pour the batter into a greased baking pan and bake for 45-50 minutes. Let cool.

Nutrition Info:
- Per Serving: Calories: 400;Fat: 23g;Protein: 10g;Carbs: 43g.

Impressive Parfait With Yogurt, Berry, And Walnut

Servings: 2
Cooking Time: 0 Minutes
Ingredients:

- 2 cups plain unsweetened yogurt, or plain unsweetened coconut yogurt or almond yogurt
- 2 tablespoons honey
- 1 cup blueberries, fresh
- 1 cup raspberries, fresh
- ½ cup walnut pieces

Directions:

1. Whisk the yogurt and honey in a medium bowl. Spoon into 2 serving bowls.
2. Top each with ½ cup blueberries, ½ cup raspberries, and ¼ cup walnut pieces.

Nutrition Info:

- Per Serving: Calories: 505 ;Fat: 22g ;Protein: 23g ;Carbs: 56g .

Avocado-chocolate Mousse

Servings: 4
Cooking Time: 15 Minutes
Ingredients:

- 1 cup raspberries
- 2 peeled, pitted avocados
- ¼ cup almond butter
- ¼ cup lite coconut milk
- ¼ cup cocoa powder
- ¼ cup pure maple syrup
- A pinch of sea salt

Directions:

1. Place the avocados, almond butter, coconut milk, cocoa powder, maple syrup, and salt in a food processor and pulse until smooth. Spoon the mixture into individual serving glasses. Place in the refrigerator for at least 1 hour. Decorate with raspberries just before serving.

Nutrition Info:

- Per Serving: Calories: 270;Fat: 20g;Protein: 7g;Carbs: 24g.

Poached Clove With Pears

Servings: 4
Cooking Time: 15 Minutes
Ingredients:

- 4 cups water
- 2 cups apple juice, unsweetened
- ¼ cup raw honey
- 1 teaspoon whole cloves
- ½ teaspoon whole cardamom seeds
- 1 teaspoon pure vanilla extract
- 4 pears, carefully peeled, halved lengthwise leaving the stem on one side, core removed

Directions:

1. Combine the water, apple juice, honey, cloves, cardamom, and vanilla in a large saucepan over medium heat. Bring the mixture to a boil. Reduce the heat to low and simmer for 5 minutes.
2. Add the pear halves to the simmering liquid and cover the saucepan. Simmer the pears for about 10 minutes, turning several times until they are very tender.
3. Carefully remove with a slotted spoon the pears from the liquid and serve warm or cooled.

Nutrition Info:

- Per Serving: Calories: 242 ;Fat: g ;Fat: 15g;Protein: 46g;Carbs: 63g.

Coconut Chocolate Truffles

Servings: 6
Cooking Time:1 Hour 15 Minutes
Ingredients:

- 1 cup raw cashews, soaked
- ¾ cup pitted cherries
- 2 tbsp coconut oil
- 1 cup shredded coconut
- 2 tbsp cocoa powder

Directions:

1. Line a baking sheet with parchment paper and set aside. Blend cashews, cherries, coconut oil, half of the shredded coconut, and cocoa powder in a food processor until ingredients are evenly mixed. Spread the remaining shredded coconut on a dish. Mold the mixture into 12 truffle shapes. Roll the truffles in the coconut dish, shaking off any excess, then arrange on the prepared baking sheet. Refrigerate for 1 hour. Serve and enjoy!

Nutrition Info:

- Per Serving: Calories: 320;Fat: 28g;Protein: 6g;Carbs: 18g.

Delectable Honeyed Apple Cinnamon Compote

Servings: 4
Cooking Time: 10 Minutes
Ingredients:

- 6 apples, peeled, cored, and chopped
- ¼ cup apple juice
- ¼ cup honey
- 1 teaspoon cinnamon, ground
- pinch sea salt

Directions:

1. Combine the apples, apple juice, honey, cinnamon, and salt in a large pot over medium-high heat. Simmer for 10 minutes while stirring occasionally until the apples are quite chunky and saucy.

Nutrition Info:

- Per Serving: Calories: 247 ;Protein: 1g ;Carbs: 66g .

Easy Maple Rice Pudding

Servings: 4
Cooking Time: 30 Minutes
Ingredients:
- 1 cup short-grain brown rice
- 1 ¾ cups non-dairy milk
- 4 tbsp pure maple syrup
- 1 tsp vanilla extract
- A pinch of salt
- ¼ cup dates, chopped

Directions:
1. In a pot over medium heat, place the rice, milk, 1 ½ cups of water, maple, vanilla, and salt. Bring to a boil, then reduce the heat. Cook for 20 minutes, stirring occasionally. Mix in dates and cook for another 5 minutes. Serve chilled in cups.

Nutrition Info:
- Per Serving: Calories: 1100;Fat: 96g;Protein: 4g;Carbs: 60g.

Interesting Snack Bars With Date And Pecan

Servings: 4
Cooking Time: 40 Minutes
Ingredients:
- 4 cups of dates, pitted and chopped
- 3 cups pecans

Directions:
1. Preheat the oven to 350°F.
2. Put the dates in a bowl and cover them with water.
3. Leave for 20 minutes then blitz the pecans in a food processor until they form a breadcrumb texture.
4. Drain the water from the dates then add to the processor until the nuts and fruit create a dough that easily needs together with your hands.
5. Line a baking sheet with parchment paper and then spread the dough onto the pan into a layer 2 inches thick.
6. Bake for 35 to 40 minutes or until cooked through and crispy on the top.
7. Remove to cool and slice into bars to serve.

Nutrition Info:
- Per Serving: Calories: 928 ;Fat: 54g ;Protein: 10g ;Carbs: 121g .

Delicious Nutmeg Muffins With Vanilla And Blueberries

Servings: 4
Cooking Time: 20 Minutes
Ingredients:
- 3 free range egg whites
- 1/10 cup chickpea flour
- 1 tablespoon coconut flour
- 1 teaspoon baking powder
- 1 tablespoon nutmeg, grated
- 1 teaspoon vanilla extract
- 1 teaspoon stevia
- ½ cup fresh blueberries

Directions:
1. Preheat the oven to 325°F.
2. In a mixing bowl, mix all of the ingredients.
3. Divide the batter into 4 and spoon into a muffin tin.
4. Bake in the oven for 15 to 20 minutes or until cooked through.
5. Your knife should pull out clean from the middle of the muffins once done.
6. Allow to cool on a wire rack before serving.

Nutrition Info:
- Per Serving: Calories: 63 ;Fat: 1g ;Protein: 4g ;Carbs: 10g .

Natural Crispy Seasonal Fruits

Servings: 8
Cooking Time: 30 To 40 Minutes
Ingredients:
- 2 cups rolled oats, 200 g
- 1 ½ cups gluten-free flour, 180g
- ¾ cup firmly packed brown sugar, 150g
- ½ teaspoon cinnamon, ground
- ¼ teaspoon nutmeg, ground
- ¼ teaspoon kosher salt
- ½ cup (4 ½ ounces) unsalted butter, cut into 8 pieces
- 2 to 3 pounds apples or pears, peeled, cored, and chopped, or other seasonal fruit
- 1 to 2 teaspoons raw cane sugar
- Greek yogurt
- Honey

Directions:
1. Preheat the oven to 350°F. Line a baking sheet with parchment paper, and place eight 1-cup (240-ml) ramekins on the prepared sheet.
2. In a large bowl, combine the oats, flour, brown sugar, cinnamon, nutmeg, and salt. Add the butter and use a pastry blender or fork to cut it into pea-size pieces. Refrigerate until ready to use.
3. In a medium bowl, place the fruit and taste, adding the raw cane sugar only if needed to sweeten. Fill each ramekin to the top with fruit, then sprinkle with 3 tablespoons of oat mixture. Bake until the tops are brown and bubbly for 30 to 40 minutes. Set aside to cool for 20 minutes.
4. Top with a dollop of Greek yogurt, drizzle with honey, and serve.

Nutrition Info:
- Per Serving: Calories: 294 ;Fat: 10g ;Protein: 5g ;Carbs: 58g .

Layered Raspberry & Tofu Cups

Servings: 4
Cooking Time: 60 Minutes
Ingredients:
- ½ cup raw cashews
- 3 tbsp pure date sugar
- ½ cup soy milk
- ¾ cup tofu
- 1 tsp vanilla extract
- 2 cups sliced raspberries
- 1 tsp fresh lemon juice
- Fresh mint leaves

Directions:
1. Grind the cashews and 3 tbsp of date sugar in a blender until a fine powder is obtained. Pour in soy milk and blitz until smooth. Add in tofu and vanilla and pulse until creamy. Remove to a bowl and refrigerate covered for 30 minutes. In a bowl, mix the raspberries, lemon juice, and remaining date sugar. Let sit for 20 minutes. Assemble by alternating into small cups, one layer of raspberries, and one cashew cream layer, ending with the cashew cream. Serve garnished with mint leaves.

Nutrition Info:
- Per Serving: Calories: 390;Fat: 18g;Protein: 9g;Carbs: 54g.

Sherry-lime Mango Dessert

Servings: 4
Cooking Time: 15 Minutes
Ingredients:
- 3 ripe mangoes, cubed
- ¼ cup pure date sugar
- 2 tbsp fresh lime juice
- ½ cup Sherry wine
- Fresh mint sprigs

Directions:
1. Arrange the mango cubes on a baking sheet. Sprinkle with some dates and let sit covered for 30 minutes. Sprinkle with lime juice and sherry wine. Refrigerate for 1 hour. Remove from the fridge and let sit for a few minutes at room temperature. Serve topped with mint.

Nutrition Info:
- Per Serving: Calories: 80;Fat: 1g;Protein: 1g;Carbs: 18g.

Oat & Fruit Cobbler

Servings: 6
Cooking Time: 30 Minutes
Ingredients:
- 1 tsp coconut oil
- 2 tbsp lemon juice
- 2 cups peaches, sliced
- 2 cups nectarines, sliced
- ¼ cup coconut oil, melted
- ¾ cup rolled oats
- ¾ cup almond flour
- ¼ cup coconut sugar
- ½ tsp vanilla extract
- 1 tsp ground cinnamon
- A pinch of salt

Directions:
1. Preheat the oven to 425°F. Warm 1 tsp of coconut oil in a skillet over medium heat. Place the lemon juice, peaches, and nectarine and cook. Place the almond flour, oats, coconut sugar, the coconut oil, cinnamon, vanilla, and salt in a bowl and stir to form a dry dough. Pour 1 tbsp of water to get more moisture. Break the dough into chunks and scatter over the fruit. Bake for 20 minutes.

Nutrition Info:
- Per Serving: Calories: 195;Fat: 8g;Protein: 4g;Carbs: 16g.

Spiced Chai With Baked Apples

Servings: 5
Cooking Time: 2 To 3 Hours
Ingredients:
- 5 apples
- ½ cup water
- ½ cup pecans, crushed
- ¼ cup coconut oil, melted
- 1 teaspoon cinnamon, ground
- ½ teaspoon ginger, ground
- ¼ teaspoon cardamom, ground
- ¼ teaspoon cloves, ground

Directions:
1. Core each apple and peel off a thin strip from the top of each.
2. Add the water to the slow cooker. Gently place each apple upright along the bottom.
3. Stir together in a small bowl the pecans, coconut oil, cinnamon, ginger, cardamom, and cloves. Drizzle the mixture over the tops of the apples.
4. Cover the cooker and set to high. Cook for 2 to 3 hours until the apples soften then serve.

Nutrition Info:
- Per Serving: Calories: 217 ;Fat: 12g ;Protein: 16g;Carbs: 30g .

Pleasant Sorbet With Lime

Servings: 4
Cooking Time: 0 Minutes
Ingredients:
- 1 cup water, 240ml
- ½ cup raw cane sugar
- 1 cup lime juice, 240ml plus grated zest from ½ lime

Directions:
1. Fill a medium bowl with ice water. In a small saucepan, combine the 1 cup water and sugar. Warm over low heat until the sugar is dissolved. Remove the simple syrup from the heat, place the pan in the ice-water bath, and stir to chill rapidly.

2. In a medium bowl, combine the lime juice with 1 cup (240 ml) of the simple syrup. Whisk in the lime zest. Freeze the sorbet in an ice-cream maker according to the manufacturer's instructions. Transfer the ice cream to a freezer-safe container and place in the freezer for 3 hours to set, or store for up to 2 weeks.

Nutrition Info:
- Per Serving: Calories: 26 ;Fat: 15g;Protein: 46g;Carbs: 7g .

Yogurt & Berry Ice Cream

Servings: 4
Cooking Time: 3 Hours 5 Minutes
Ingredients:
- 1 cup blueberries
- 1 cup strawberries
- 2 cups whole milk yogurt
- 1 tsp lemon juice
- 2 tbsp honey

Directions:
1. Place the blueberries, strawberries, milk, ¼ of water, lemon juice, and honey in a food processor and pulse until smooth. Pour it into molds and transfer to the freezer for 3 hours. Serve right away.

Nutrition Info:
- Per Serving: Calories: 142;Fat: 5g;Protein: 5g;Carbs: 25g.

Coconut Chocolate Barks

Servings: 4
Cooking Time: 35 Minutes
Ingredients:
- 1/3 cup coconut oil, melted
- ¼ cup almond butter, melted
- 2 tbsp coconut flakes.
- 1 tsp pure maple syrup
- A pinch of sea salt
- ¼ cup cocoa nibs

Directions:
1. Line a baking tray with baking paper and set aside. In a medium bowl, mix the coconut oil, almond butter, coconut flakes, maple syrup, and fold in the rock salt and cocoa nibs. Pour and spread the mixture on the baking sheet, chill in the refrigerator for 20 minutes or until firm. Remove the dessert, break into shards, and enjoy. Preserve extras in the refrigerator.

Nutrition Info:
- Per Serving: Calories: 280;Fat: 28g;Protein: 4g;Carbs: 9g.

Beneficial Clumps With Coconut And Chocolate

Servings: 12 To 16
Cooking Time: 5 Minutes
Ingredients:
- ¼ cup cacao powder

- ¼ cup maple syrup
- 3 tablespoons coconut oil
- 1 tablespoon cacao butter
- ½ cup shredded coconut, unsweetened
- Pinch salt

Directions:
1. Create a makeshift double boiler. Fill a small pot with a few inches of water and place a metal bowl on top of the pot. Bring the water to a boil.
2. Into the bowl, put the cacao powder, maple syrup, coconut oil, and cacao butter. Use oven mitts when handling the bowl.
3. Stir the chocolate mixture until it melts for 5 minutes.
4. Remove the bowl with the mitts from the top of the pot. Stir in the shredded coconut.
5. Pour the chocolate mixture into candy molds.
6. Refrigerate or freeze until set.

Nutrition Info:
- Per Serving: Calories: 91 ;Fat: 8g ;Protein: 1g ;Carbs: 6g.

Baked Apples Filled With Nuts

Servings: 4
Cooking Time: 35 Minutes + Cooling Time
Ingredients:
- 4 gala apples
- 3 tbsp pure maple syrup
- 4 tbsp almond flour
- 6 tbsp pure date sugar
- 6 tbsp cubed almond butter
- 1 cup chopped mixed nuts

Directions:
1. Preheat your oven the 400ºF. Slice off the top of the apples and use a melon baller or spoon to scoop out the cores of the apples. In a bowl, mix the maple syrup, almond flour, date sugar, butter, and nuts. Spoon the mixture into the apples and then bake in the oven for 25 minutes or until the nuts are golden brown on top and the apples soft. Let the apples cool. Serve.

Nutrition Info:
- Per Serving: Calories: 580;Fat: 44g;Protein: 4g;Carbs: 52g.

Flavourful Glazed Maple Pears And Hazelnuts

Servings: 4
Cooking Time: 20 Minutes
Ingredients:
- 4 pears, peeled, cored, and quartered lengthwise
- 1 cup apple juice
- ½ cup pure maple syrup
- 1 tablespoon fresh ginger, grated
- ¼ cup hazelnuts, chopped

Directions:
1. Combine the pears and apple juice in a large pot over medium-high heat. Bring to a simmer and reduce the heat to

medium-low. Cover and simmer for 15 to 20 minutes until the pears becomes soft.

2. Combine in a small saucepan over medium-high heat the maple syrup and ginger while the pears poach. Bring to a simmer while stirring. Remove the pan from the heat and let the syrup rest.

3. Remove the pears using a slotted spoon from the poaching liquid and brush with maple syrup. Serve topped with the hazelnuts.

Nutrition Info:

- Per Serving: Calories: 286 ;Fat: 3g ;Protein: 2g ;Carbs: 67g .

Apples Stuffed With Pecans & Dates

Servings: 4
Cooking Time: 40 Minutes
Ingredients:

- 4 cored apples, halved lengthwise
- ½ cup chopped pecans
- 4 pitted dates, chopped
- 1 tbsp almond butter
- 1 tbsp pure maple syrup
- ¼ tsp ground cinnamon

Directions:

1. Preheat your oven to 360°F. Mix the pecans, dates, almond butter, maple syrup, and cinnamon in a bowl. Arrange the apple on a greased baking pan and fill them with the pecan mixture. Pour 1 tbsp of water into the baking pan. Bake for 30-40 minutes, until soft and lightly browned. Serve warm or cold.

Nutrition Info:

- Per Serving: Calories: 240;Fat: 12g;Protein: 2g;Carbs: 36g.

Chocolate & Avocado Fudge

Servings: 4
Cooking Time: 3 Hours 15 Minutes
Ingredients:

- ¼ cup coconut oil
- 1 ½ cup chocolate chips
- 1 avocado, peeled and pitted
- ½ tsp sea salt

Directions:

1. Line a baking pan with parchment paper. Melt the coconut oil and chocolate in a double broiler. Remove to a blender and let cool slightly. Add in avocado and pulse until smooth. Pour it into the baking pan and sprinkle with salt. Transfer to the fridge and let cool for 3 hours. Slice into 16 pieces and serve.

Nutrition Info:

- Per Serving: Calories: 122;Fat: 40g;Protein: 1g;Carbs: 10g.

Peanut Butter Truffles

Servings: 6
Cooking Time: 15 Minutes
Ingredients:

- 1 lemon, zested
- ¾ cup creamy peanut butter
- 2 tbsp almond butter, softened
- 1 ¾ cups powdered sugar
- ¼ cup cocoa powder
- ½ tsp vanilla extract

Directions:

1. Mix the peanut butter, butter, powdered sugar, cocoa powder, lemon zest, and vanilla in a bowl until well combined. Make 12 balls out of the mixture and transfer them to a lined with parchment paper tray. Let chill.

Nutrition Info:

- Per Serving: Calories: 150;Fat: 9g;Protein: 2g;Carbs: 18g.

Walnut Pears With Maple Glaze

Servings: 4
Cooking Time: 30 Minutes
Ingredients:

- 4 pears, peeled, cored, and quartered lengthwise
- 1 cup apple juice
- ½ cup pure maple syrup
- 1 tbsp grated fresh ginger
- ¼ cup walnuts, chopped

Directions:

1. Place the pears and apple juice in a pot over medium heat and bring to a simmer. Then low the heat and cook covered for 15-20 minutes until tender. Place the maple syrup and ginger in a saucepan and bring to a simmer. Turn the heat off and let it rest. Transfer the pears to a plate and drizzle with maple syrup. Scatter with walnuts.

Nutrition Info:

- Per Serving: Calories: 290;Fat: 4g;Protein: 8g;Carbs: 68g.

Berry Macedonia With Mint

Servings: 4
Cooking Time: 20 Minutes
Ingredients:

- ¼ cup lemon juice
- 4 tsp maple syrup
- 2 cups chopped pears
- 2 cups chopped strawberries
- 3 cups mixed berries
- 8 fresh mint leaves

Directions:

1. Chop half of the mint leaves; reserve. In a large bowl, combine together pears, strawberries, raspberries, blackberries, and half of the mint leaves. Divide the mixture between 4 small cups. Top with lemon juice, maple syrup, and mint leaves and serve chilled.

Nutrition Info:

- Per Serving: Calories: 520;Fat: 10g;Protein: 5g;Carbs: 108g.

Cinnamon Pumpkin Pie

Servings: 4
Cooking Time:70 Minutes + Cooling Time
Ingredients:

* For the piecrust:
* 4 eggs, beaten
* 1/3 cup whole-wheat flour
* ½ tsp salt
* ¼ cup cold almond butter
* 3 tbsp pure malt syrup
* For the filling:
* ¼ cup pure maple syrup
* ¼ cup pure date sugar
* 1 tsp cinnamon powder
* ½ tsp ginger powder
* 1/8 tsp clove powder
* 1 can pumpkin purée
* 1 cup almond milk

Directions:

1. Preheat your oven to 350ºF. In a bowl, combine flour and salt. Add the almond butter and whisk until crumbly. Pour in crust's eggs, maple syrup, vanilla, and mix until smooth dough forms. Flatten, cover with plastic wrap, and refrigerate for 1 hour.
2. Dust a working surface with flour, remove the dough onto the surface and flatten it into a 1-inch diameter circle. Lay the dough on a greased pie pan and press to fit the shape of the pan. Use a knife to trim the edges of the pan. Lay a parchment paper on the dough, pour on some baking beans and bake for 15-20 minutes. Remove, pour out the baking beans, and allow cooling. In a bowl, whisk the maple syrup, date sugar, cinnamon powder, ginger powder, clove powder, pumpkin puree, and almond milk. Pour the mixture onto the piecrust and bake for 35-40 minutes. Let cool completely. Serve sliced.

Nutrition Info:

* Per Serving: Calories: 590;Fat: 36g;Protein: 12g;Carbs: 61g.

Mixed Berry Yogurt Ice Pops

Servings: 6
Cooking Time: 5 Minutes + Chilling Time
Ingredients:

* 2/3 cup avocado pulp
* 2/3 cup berries
* 1 cup dairy-free yogurt
* ½ cup coconut cream
* 1 tsp vanilla extract

Directions:

1. Pour the avocado pulp, berries, dairy-free yogurt, coconut cream, and vanilla extract. Process until smooth. Pour into ice pop sleeves and freeze for 8 or more hours. Enjoy the ice pops when ready.

Nutrition Info:

* Per Serving: Calories: 145;Fat: 12g;Protein: 3g;Carbs: 9g.

Lemony Lavender With Strawberry Compote

Servings: 4
Cooking Time: 30 Minutes
Ingredients:

* 2 cups strawberries, halved
* juice and zest a lemon
* 2 tablespoons raw honey
* 1 tablespoon lavender extract

Directions:

1. Into a saucepan, put all of the ingredients together and then simmer on a very low heat until the honey has been dissolved for 15 to 20 minutes.
2. Add the strawberries when the sauce starts to thicken and simmer for 5 to 10 minutes.
3. Serve warm right away or allow to cool and drizzle over yogurt later on.

Nutrition Info:

* Per Serving: Calories: 67 ;Fat: 2g;Protein: 1g ;Carbs: 15g .

Kiwi & Peanut Bars

Servings: 4
Cooking Time: 5 Minutes
Ingredients:

* 2 kiwis, mashed
* 1 tbsp maple syrup
* ½ tsp vanilla extract
* 2 cups rolled oats
* ½ tsp sea salt
* ¼ cup chopped peanuts

Directions:

1. Preheat your oven to 360ºF. In a bowl, add kiwi, maple syrup, and vanilla and stir. Mix in oats, salt, and peanuts. Pour into a greased baking dish and bake for 25-30 minutes until crisp. Let cool. Slice into bars to serve.

Nutrition Info:

* Per Serving: Calories: 225;Fat: 10g;Protein: 13g;Carbs: 41g.

Thick Coconut Rice With Blueberries

Servings: 4
Cooking Time: 10 Minutes
Ingredients:

* One 14 ounces can coconut milk, full-fat
* 1 cup blueberries, fresh
* ¼ cup sugar
* 1 teaspoon ginger, ground
* pinch sea salt
* 2 cups brown rice, cooked

Directions:

1. Combine the coconut milk, blueberries, sugar, ginger, and salt in a large pot over medium-high heat. Cook for 7 minutes and stir constantly until the blueberries become soft.
2. Stir in the rice. Cook for 3 minutes while stirring until the rice is heated through.

Nutrition Info:
- Per Serving: Calories: 469 ;Fat: 25g ;Protein: 6g ;Carbs: 60g .

Effortless Chocolate Fondue

Servings: 4 To 6
Cooking Time: 5 Minutes
Ingredients:
- ½ cup cacao powder
- ¼ cup coconut oil
- ¼ cup maple syrup, or raw honey
- 4 cups fresh fruit for dipping, sliced or cut into bite-size pieces

Directions:
1. Create a makeshift double boiler. Fill a small pot with a few inches of water and place a metal bowl on top of the pot. Bring the water to a boil.
2. Into the bowl, put the cacao powder, coconut oil, and maple syrup. Use oven mitts when handling the bowl.
3. Stir the chocolate mixture until it melts for 5 minutes. Transfer to a serving bowl or individual bowls for dipping.

Nutrition Info:
- Per Serving: Calories: 452 ;Fat: 16g ;Protein: 6g ;Carbs: 83g .

Mid Afternoon Grilled Banana And Homemade Nut Butter

Servings: 2
Cooking Time: 5 Minutes
Ingredients:
- 2 bananas
- 1 cup almonds

Directions:
1. Peel bananas and cut lengthways with a knife down the center to form a banana split.
2. Blend the almonds until smooth to form your own nut butter.
3. Spread almond butter along the middle of the bananas and broil for 3 to 4 minutes on a medium heat until browned.
4. Serve immediately.

Nutrition Info:
- Per Serving: Calories: 3 ;Fat: 5g;Protein: 6g;Carbs: 2g

Silky Smooth Vegan Chocolate Pots Decrème

Servings: 4 To 6
Cooking Time: 5 Minutes
Ingredients:
- 1 pound silken tofu, drained
- 2 teaspoons vanilla extract
- Kosher salt

- 1 ½ cups semi sweet vegan chocolate chips, 250g
- 1 tsp maple
- Chopped strawberries or blueberries

Directions:
1. Bring 2 inch water to a simmer in a medium saucepan.
2. In a blender, place the tofu, vanilla, and ¼ teaspoon salt and puree on low speed until smooth. Scrape down the sides with a spatula if necessary.
3. Place the chocolate chips in a medium heatproof bowl that will fit in the saucepan over the simmering water without touching it when the water is simmering. Turn the heat to low and melt the chocolate, stirring, until smooth for 2 to 3 minutes.
4. Allow the chocolate to cool slightly then pour into the blender. Purée until smooth, scraping down the sides if necessary, until the tofu and chocolate are combined. Taste and add the maple syrup if preferred. Taste once more and add a pinch of salt if necessary.
5. Divide the mixture evenly among six ½ cup ramekins. Garnish with berries before serving.

Nutrition Info:
- Per Serving: Calories: 318 ;Fat: 23g ;Protein: 20g ;Carbs: 13g .

Spiced Supreme Orange

Servings: 2
Cooking Time: 15 Minutes
Ingredients:
- ½ cup water
- 1 tablespoon raw honey
- 1 lemon
- 1 small cinnamon stick
- 1 clove
- 2 oranges, peeled and sectioned
- 1 sprig fresh mint

Directions:
1. Add all of the ingredients except the oranges to a saucepan.
2. Cook over a medium heat until thickened for 10 to 15 minutes.
3. Add the oranges, and then simmer for a minute.
4. Transfer all ingredients to a bowl or container and place in the fridge, marinate for 2 hours or preferably overnight.
5. Drain orange slices and garnish with a little fresher mint to serve.
6. Best served with low fat Greek yogurt for summer or warmed through in the winter.

Nutrition Info:
- Per Serving: Calories: 128 ;Fat: 3g ;Protein: 12g;Carbs: 27g .

Pistachios & Chocolate Popsicles

Servings: 4
Cooking Time: 5 Minutes + Cooling Time
Ingredients:

- 2 oz dark chocolate, melted
- 1 ½ cups oat milk
- 1 tbsp cocoa powder
- 3 tbsp pure date syrup
- 1 tsp vanilla extract
- 2 tbsp pistachios, chopped

Directions:
1. In a blender, add chocolate, oat milk, cocoa powder, date syrup, vanilla, pistachios, and process until smooth. Divide the mixture into popsicle molds and freeze for 3 hours. Dip the popsicle molds in warm water to loosen the popsicles and pull out the popsicles.

Nutrition Info:

- Per Serving: Calories: 120;Fat: 3g;Protein: 6g;Carbs: 24g.

Great Pudding With Chocolate And Avocado

Servings: 4
Cooking Time: 0 Minutes
Ingredients:

- 12 Medjool dates, pitted
- 2 avocados, halved and pitted
- ½ cup cacao powder
- 1 cup coconut milk, divided

Directions:
1. Combine the dates, avocado flesh, cacao powder, and ¾ cup of coconut milk in a food processor. Blend until smooth. Add the remaining ¼ cup of coconut milk if the pudding is too thick and blend well.
2. Refrigerate for an hour before serving.

Nutrition Info:

- Per Serving: Calories: 488 ;Fat: 36g ;Protein: 6g ;Carbs: 48g .

Cinnamon Faux Rice Pudding

Servings: 6
Cooking Time: 25 Minutes
Ingredients:

- 1 ¼ cups coconut cream
- 1 tsp vanilla extract
- 1 tsp cinnamon powder
- 1 cup mashed tofu
- 2 oz fresh strawberries

Directions:
1. Pour the coconut cream into a bowl and whisk until a soft peak forms. Mix in the vanilla and cinnamon. Lightly fold in the coconut cream and refrigerate for 10 to 15 minutes to set. Top with the strawberries and serve.

Nutrition Info:

- Per Serving: Calories: 215;Fat: 19g;Protein: 4g;Carbs: 12g.

Tropical Baked Fruit With Nut Pudding

Servings: 4
Cooking Time: 1 Hour
Ingredients:

- 15 apricots
- 10 prunes
- 6 free range eggs
- 3 cups water
- 1 cup raw pecans/walnuts
- 2 tablespoons pure vanilla extract
- 2 broken cinnamon sticks

Directions:
1. Preheat the oven to 350°F.
2. Boil the water on a high heat and then add the apricots, prunes, and cinnamon sticks before turning down the heat and simmering for 30 minutes in a large saucepan.
3. Allow to cool.
4. Remove the cinnamon sticks and blend mixture, add in the eggs and vanilla until smooth.
5. Add mixture to a glass oven dish and top with the nuts.
6. Oven bake for 30 minutes.
7. Cool and serve.

Nutrition Info:

- Per Serving: Calories: 195 ;Fat: 13g ;Protein: 3g ;Carbs: 16g .

Hearty Gelato With Chocolate And Cinnamon

Servings: 4 To 6
Cooking Time: 0 Minutes
Ingredients:

- 2 teaspoon cornstarch
- 3 cups Almond Milk or whole milk, 720 ml
- ¼ cup raw cane sugar, 50 g
- ¼ teaspoon kosher salt
- 4 ounces dark chocolate (70 percent cacao), coarsely chopped
- 1 teaspoon cinnamon, ground
- ½ teaspoon vanilla extract
- Chocolate shavings, crushed walnuts, or crushed fresh raspberries

Directions:
1. In a small bowl, put the cornstarch, add 1 tablespoon of almond milk and stir with a fork to dissolve the cornstarch.
2. Into a medium saucepan, pour the rest of the almond milk. Bring to a simmer over medium heat, then turn lower the heat. Whisk in the cornstarch mixture, sugar, and salt to dissolve. Add the chocolate and cinnamon and whisk until the mixture is completely smooth. Cook while whisking until the mixture starts to thicken for 5 minutes.

3. Pour the milk mixture through a fine-mesh strainer into a large bowl. Stir in the vanilla. Refrigerate until chilled for 3 hours.

4. Whisk the chilled mixture. Freeze in an ice-cream maker according to the manufacturer's instructions. The gelato is ready when it has the consistency of soft-serve ice cream. Transfer to an airtight container and freeze for up to 1 week.

5. To serve, scoop into serving bowls and garnish as desired.

Nutrition Info:

- Per Serving: Calories: 354 ;Fat: 18g ;Protein: 8g ;Carbs: 42g .

Mint Ice Cream

Servings: 4
Cooking Time: 10 Minutes + Chilling Time
Ingredients:

- 2 avocados, pitted
- 1 ¼ cups coconut cream
- ½ tsp vanilla extract
- 2 tbsp stevia
- 2 tsp chopped mint leaves

Directions:

1. Into a blender, spoon the avocado pulps, pour in the coconut cream, vanilla extract, stevia, and mint leaves. Process until smooth. Pour the mixture into your ice cream maker and freeze according to the manufacturer's instructions. Scoop the ice cream into bowls. Serve.

Nutrition Info:

- Per Serving: Calories: 410;Fat: 41g;Protein: 5g;Carbs: 14g.

Comfort Cobbler With Blueberry And Peach

Servings: 4 To 6
Cooking Time: 2 Hours
Ingredients:

- 5 tablespoons coconut oil, divided
- 3 large peaches, peeled and sliced
- 2 cups blueberries, frozen
- 1 cup almond flour
- 1 cup rolled oats
- 1 tablespoon maple syrup
- 1 tablespoon coconut sugar
- 1 teaspoon cinnamon, ground
- ½ teaspoon vanilla extract
- Pinch ground nutmeg

Directions:

1. Coat the bottom of the slow cooker with 1 tablespoon of coconut oil.

2. Arrange the peaches and blueberries along the bottom of the slow cooker.

3. Stir together in a small bowl the almond flour, oats, remaining 4 tablespoons of coconut oil, maple syrup, coconut sugar, cinnamon, vanilla, and nutmeg until a coarse

mixture form. Gently crumble the topping over the fruit in the slow cooker.

4. Cover the cooker and set to high. Cook for 2 hours and serve.

Nutrition Info:

- Per Serving: Calories: 516 ;Fat: 34g Protein: 10g ;;Carbs: 49g.

Raisin Oatmeal Biscuits

Servings: 6
Cooking Time: 20 Minutes
Ingredients:

- ½ cup almond butter
- 1 cup date sugar
- ¼ cup pineapple juice
- 1 cup whole-grain flour
- 1 tsp baking powder
- ½ tsp salt
- 1 tsp vanilla extract
- 1 cup old-fashioned oats
- ½ cup dark chocolate chips
- ½ cup raisins

Directions:

1. Preheat your oven to 370ºF. Beat the almond butter and date sugar in a bowl until creamy and fluffy. Pour in the juice and blend. Mix in flour, baking powder, salt, and vanilla. Stir in oats, chocolate chips, and raisins. Spread the dough on a baking sheet and bake for 15 minutes. Let completely cool on a rack. Serve and enjoy!

Nutrition Info:

- Per Serving: Calories: 385;Fat: 17g;Protein: 6g;Carbs: 60g.

Oatmeal Chocolate Cookies

Servings: 2
Cooking Time: 30 Minutes
Ingredients:

- ¼ cup whole wheat flour
- ¼ cup oats
- 1 tbsp olive oil
- 2 tbsp packed brown sugar
- ½ tsp vanilla extract
- 1 tbsp honey
- 2 tbsp coconut milk
- 2 tsp coconut oil
- ⅛ tsp sea salt
- 3 tbsp dark chocolate chips

Directions:

1. Combine all of the ingredients in a large bowl. Line a baking pan with parchment paper. Make lemon-sized cookies out of the mixture and flatten them onto the lined pan. Add some water to your Instant Pot and lower the trivet Add the baking pan to your pot. Cook for 15 minutes on "Manual" on high pressure. Release the pressure quickly, carefully open the lid and serve warm.

Nutrition Info:

- Per Serving: Calories: 415;Fat: 20g;Protein: 6g;Carbs: 60g.

Cardamom Coconut Fat Bombs

Servings: 6
Cooking Time: 10 Minutes
Ingredients:
- ¼ tsp green cardamom powder
- ½ cup grated coconut
- 3 oz almond butter, softened
- ½ tsp vanilla extract
- ¼ tsp cinnamon powder

Directions:
1. Pour the grated coconut into a skillet and roast until lightly brown. Set aside to cool. In a bowl, combine butter, half of the coconut, cardamom, vanilla, and cinnamon. Form balls from the mixture and roll each one in the remaining coconut. Refrigerate until ready to serve.

Nutrition Info:
- Per Serving: Calories: 110;Fat: 12g;Protein: 1g;Carbs: 1g.

Sweet And Special Spiced Pecans

Servings: 4
Cooking Time: 17 Minutes
Ingredients:
- 1 cup pecan halves
- ¼ cup brown sugar, packed
- 3 tablespoons unsalted butter, melted
- 1 teaspoon cinnamon, ground
- ½ teaspoon nutmeg, ground
- ¼ teaspoon sea salt

Directions:
1. Preheat the oven to 350°F.
2. Line a rimmed baking sheet with parchment paper.
3. Toss in a medium bowl together with the pecans, brown sugar, butter, cinnamon, nutmeg, and salt to combine. Spread the nuts in a single layer on the prepared sheet.
4. Bake for 15 to 17 minutes until the nuts are fragrant.

Nutrition Info:
- Per Serving: Calories: 323 ;Fat: 30g ;Protein: 3g ;Carbs: 14g .

Party Matcha & Hazelnut Cheesecake

Servings: 4
Cooking Time: 20 Minutes + Cooling Time
Ingredients:
- 2 tbsp toasted hazelnuts, chopped
- 2/3 cup toasted rolled oats
- ¼ cup almond butter, melted
- 3 tbsp pure date sugar
- 6 oz coconut cream
- ¼ cup almond milk
- 1 tbsp matcha powder
- ¼ cup just-boiled water
- 3 tsp agar agar powder

Directions:
1. Process the oats, butter, and date sugar in a blender until smooth. Pour the mixture into a greased springform pan and press the mixture onto the bottom of the pan. Refrigerate for 30 minutes until firm while you make the filling. In a large bowl, using an electric mixer, whisk the coconut cream cheese until smooth. Beat in the almond milk and mix in the matcha powder until smooth.
2. Mix the boiled water and agar agar until dissolved and whisk this mixture into the creamy mix. Fold in the hazelnuts until well distributed. Remove the cake pan from the fridge and pour in the cream mixture. Shake the pan to ensure smooth layering on top. Refrigerate further for at least 3 hours. Take out the cake pan, release the cake, slice, and serve.

Nutrition Info:
- Per Serving: Calories: 650;Fat: 59g;Protein: 14g;Carbs: 26g.

Melon Chocolate Pudding

Servings: 4
Cooking Time: 25 Minutes
Ingredients:
- 1 cup cubed melon
- 4 tbsp non-dairy milk
- 2 tbsp cocoa powder
- 2 tbsp pure date sugar
- ½ ripe avocado

Directions:
1. Blitz the milk, cocoa powder, sugar, and avocado in a blender until smooth. Mash the melon with a fork in a bowl. Mix in the cocoa mixture and serve.

Nutrition Info:
- Per Serving: Calories: 85;Fat: 5g;Protein: 2g;Carbs: 12g.

Chocolate Peppermint Mousse

Servings: 4
Cooking Time: 10 Minutes + Chilling Time
Ingredients:
- ¼ cup stevia, divided
- 4 oz cream cheese, softened
- 3 tbsp cocoa powder
- ¾ tsp peppermint extract
- ½ tsp vanilla extract
- 1/3 cup coconut cream

Directions:
1. Put 2 tablespoons of stevia, cream cheese, and cocoa powder in a blender. Add the peppermint extract, ¼ cup of warm water, and process until smooth. In a bowl, whip vanilla extract, coconut cream, and the remaining stevia using a whisk. Fetch out 5-6 tablespoons for garnishing. Fold in the cocoa mixture until thoroughly combined. Spoon the mousse into serving cups and chill in the fridge for 30 minutes. Garnish with the reserved whipped cream and serve.

Nutrition Info:
- Per Serving: Calories: 315;Fat: 30g;Protein: 5g;Carbs: 14g.

Cinnamon Tropical Cobbler

Servings: 6
Cooking Time: 45 Minutes
Ingredients:
- 3 apples, shredded
- 2 ripe pineapples, chopped
- 2 tsp lemon juice
- ½ cup pure date sugar
- 2 tbsp arrowroot
- 1 tsp ground cinnamon
- ½ tsp ground allspice
- 1 cup whole-grain flour
- 1 ½ tsp baking powder
- ¼ tsp sea salt
- 2 tbsp peanut butter
- ½ cup soy milk

Directions:
1. Preheat your oven to 390ºF. Arrange apples and pineapples on a greased baking pan. Drizzle with lemon juice, arrowroot, cinnamon, and allspice. In a bowl, combine flour, date sugar, baking powder, and salt. Stir in the peanut butter with a fork until the batter resembles crumbs. Mix in soy milk. Spread the mixture over the fruit and bake for 30 minutes. Serve and enjoy!

Nutrition Info:
- Per Serving: Calories: 190;Fat: 2g;Protein: 4g;Carbs: 41g.

Greek Cheesecake With Blueberries

Servings: 6
Cooking Time: 90 Minutes + Chilling Time
Ingredients:
- 2 oz almond butter
- 1 ¼ cups almond flour
- 3 tbsp stevia
- 1 tsp vanilla extract
- 3 eggs
- 2 cups Greek yogurt
- ½ cup coconut cream
- 1 tsp lemon zest
- 2 oz fresh blueberries

Directions:
1. Preheat oven to 350ºF. To make the crust, put the almond butter in a skillet over low heat until nutty in flavor. Turn the heat off and stir in almond flour, 2 tbsp of stevia, and half of vanilla until a dough forms. Press the mixture into a greased baking pan. Bake for 8 minutes.
2. In a bowl, combine yogurt, coconut cream, remaining stevia, lemon zest, remaining vanilla extract, and eggs. Remove the crust from the oven and pour the mixture on top. Use a spatula to layer evenly. Bake the cake for 15 minutes at 400ºF. Then, reduce the heat to 230ºF and bake for 45-60 minutes. Cool completely. Refrigerate overnight and scatter the blueberries on top. Serve.

Nutrition Info:
- Per Serving: Calories: 425;Fat: 40g;Protein: 8g;Carbs: 12g.

Poppy-granola Balls With Chocolate

Servings: 6
Cooking Time: 25 Minutes + Chilling Time
Ingredients:
- ½ cup granola
- ¼ cup pure date sugar
- ½ cup golden raisins
- ½ cup sunflower seeds
- ¼ cup poppy seeds
- 1 ½ cups almond butter
- 2 cups dark chocolate chips

Directions:
1. Blend the granola, date sugar, raisins, sunflower seeds, and poppy seeds in a food processor. Stir in the almond butter and pulse until a smooth dough is formed. Leave in the fridge overnight. Shape small balls out of the mixture. Set aside. Melt the chocolate in the microwave oven. Dip the balls into the melted chocolate and place on a baking sheet. Chill in the fridge until firm.

Nutrition Info:
- Per Serving: Calories: 540;Fat: 43g;Protein: 17g;Carbs: 31g.

Apple & Berry Parfait

Servings: 4
Cooking Time: 15 Minutes
Ingredients:
- 2 tbsp pistachios, chopped
- 1 can coconut milk
- 2 tbsp honey
- 4 cups mixed berries
- 1 peeled apple, chopped

Directions:
1. Put the coconut milk in the refrigerator to chill overnight. The next day, open the tin and scoop the solids have collected on top into a mixing bowl. Set aside the water. Add the honey to the coconut milk and whisk well. Divide half of the mixture between 4 glasses. Top with half of the fruit. Spoon over the remaining coconut mixture and finish with the remaining fruit. Chill the parfaits until needed. Sprinkle with pistachios before serving.

Nutrition Info:
- Per Serving: Calories: 390;Fat: 22g;Protein: 10g;Carbs: 47g.

Coconut & Chocolate Cake

Servings: 4
Cooking Time: 40 Minutes + Cooling Time
Ingredients:
- 2/3 cup almond flour
- ¼ cup almond butter, melted
- 2 cups chocolate bars, cubed
- 2 ½ cups coconut cream
- Fresh berries for topping

Directions:
1. Mix the almond flour and almond butter in a medium bowl and pour the mixture into a greased springform pan. Use the spoon to spread and press the mixture into the pan. Place in the refrigerator to firm for 30 minutes.
2. Meanwhile, pour the chocolate in a safe microwave bowl and melt for 1 minute stirring every 30 seconds. Remove from the microwave and mix in the coconut cream and maple syrup. Remove the cake pan from the oven, pour the chocolate mixture on top, and shake the pan and even the layer. Chill further for 4 to 6 hours. Take out the pan from the fridge, release the cake and garnish with the raspberries or strawberries. Slice and serve.

Nutrition Info:
- Per Serving: Calories: 985;Fat: 62g;Protein: 9g;Carbs: 108g.

Wonderful Whipped Goat Cheese With Dark Berries

Servings: 4
Cooking Time: 0 Minutes
Ingredients:
- 5 oz goat cheese, at room temperature
- 1 ½ tablespoon honey, plus more for serving
- 1 tablespoon lemon juice
- ½ teaspoon orange zest, grated
- Kosher salt
- 2 cups blueberries, 240g
- 2 cups blackberries, 240g
- ¼ cup pistachios, chopped and 30g

Directions:
1. In a medium bowl, place the goat cheese, honey, lemon juice, orange zest, and a pinch of salt. Whisk until the goat cheese is fluffy and smooth.
2. Divide the goat cheese mixture among bowls or wine glasses, reserving four spoonsful. Top each portion with berries, pistachios, and a spoonful of the whipped goat cheese. Drizzle with additional honey. Serve immediately.

Nutrition Info:
- Per Serving: Calories: 523 ;Fat: 17g ;Protein: 15g ;Carbs: 85g .

Maple Fruit Crumble

Servings: 4
Cooking Time: 25 Minutes
Ingredients:
- 3 cups chopped apricots
- 3 cups chopped mangoes
- 4 tbsp pure maple syrup
- 1 cup gluten-free rolled oats
- ½ cup shredded coconut
- 2 tbsp coconut oil

Directions:
1. Preheat your oven to 360ºF. Place the apricots, mangoes, and 2 tbsp of maple syrup in a round baking dish. In a food processor, put the oats, coconut, coconut oil, and remaining maple syrup. Blend until combined. Pour over the fruit. Bake for 20-25 minutes. Allow cooling. Serve.

Nutrition Info:
- Per Serving: Calories: 480;Fat: 10g;Protein: 9g;Carbs: 110g.

Coconut Chia Pudding

Servings: 4
Cooking Time: 30 Minutes
Ingredients:
- 1 orange, zested and juiced
- 1 can coconut milk
- 2 pitted dates
- 1 tbsp chia seeds

Directions:
1. In a blender, put the orange juice, orange zest, coconut milk, dates, and chia seeds. Blitz until smooth. Transfer to a bowl and put it in the fridge for 20 minutes. Top with berries, whipped cream, or toasted coconut and serve.

Nutrition Info:
- Per Serving: Calories: 30;Fat: 1g;Protein: 1g;Carbs: 7g.

Southern Apple Cobbler With Raspberries

Servings: 4
Cooking Time: 50 Minutes
Ingredients:
- 3 apples, chopped
- 2 tbsp pure date sugar
- 1 cup fresh raspberries
- 2 tbsp almond butter
- ½ cup whole-wheat flour
- 1 cup toasted rolled oats
- 2 tbsp pure date sugar
- 1 tsp cinnamon powder

Directions:
1. Preheat your oven to 350ºF and grease a baking dish with some almond butter. Add apples, date sugar, and 3 tbsp of water to a pot. Cook over low heat until the date sugar melts and then mix in the raspberries. Cook until the fruits soften, 10 minutes. Pour and spread the fruit mixture into the baking dish and set aside.
2. In a blender, add the almond butter, flour, oats, date sugar, and cinnamon powder. Pulse a few times until crumbly. Spoon and spread the mixture on the fruit mix until evenly layered. Bake in the oven for 25 to 30 minutes or

until golden brown on top. Remove the dessert, allow cooling for 2 minutes, and serve.

Nutrition Info:
- Per Serving: Calories: 270;Fat: 5g;Protein: 5g;Carbs: 59g.

Tofu & Almond Pancakes

Servings: 6
Cooking Time: 15 Minutes
Ingredients:
- 1 ½ cups almond milk
- 1 cup almond flour
- 1 cup firm tofu, crumbled
- 3 tbsp almond butter, melted
- 2 tbsp pure date sugar
- 1 ½ tsp pure vanilla extract
- ½ tsp baking powder
- ⅛ tsp sea salt

Directions:
1. Blitz almond milk, tofu, almond butter, sugar, vanilla, baking powder, and salt in a blender until smooth. Heat a pan and coat with oil. Scoop a ladle of batter at the center and spread all over. Cook for 3-4 minutes until golden, turning once. Transfer to a plate and repeat the process until no batter is left. Serve and enjoy!

Nutrition Info:
- Per Serving: Calories: 170;Fat: 12g;Protein: 4g;Carbs: 13g.

Blueberry & Almond Greek Yogurt

Servings: 4
Cooking Time: 5 Minutes
Ingredients:
- 3 cups plain greek yogurt
- 1 ½ cups blueberries
- ¾ cup almonds, chopped
- ½ cup honey

Directions:
1. Divide the greek yogurt between four bowls and top each with blueberries, almonds, and honey. Serve and enjoy!

Nutrition Info:
- Per Serving: Calories: 460;Fat: 19g;Protein: 4g;Carbs: 63g.

A Different Pumpkin Pie

Servings: 4
Cooking Time: 30 Minutes
Ingredients:
- 1 lb butternut squash, diced
- 1 egg
- 2 tbsp honey
- ½ cup coconut milk
- ½ tsp cinnamon
- ½ tbsp arrowroot
- A pinch of sea salt

Directions:

1. Pour the water inside your Instant Pot and insert a trivet. Place the butternut squash in a steamer basket and put it on the trivet. Seal the lid and cook for 4 minutes on "Manual". Whisk all of the remaining ingredients in a bowl. Once the cooking is completed, perform a quick pressure release and drain the squash. Then, transfer to the milk mixture. Pour the batter into a greased baking dish. Place inside the Instant Pot. Seal the lid and cook for 10 minutes on "Manual". Once it goes off, let the pressure release naturally for 5 minutes. Then perform a quick pressure release. Very carefully remove the pan. Let it cool a few minutes before serving.

Nutrition Info:
- Per Serving: Calories: 170;Fat: 2g;Protein: 3g;Carbs: 40g.

Poached Pears With Green Tea

Servings: 4
Cooking Time: 15 Minutes
Ingredients:
- 4 pears, peeled, cored, and quartered lengthwise
- 2 cups green tea, strongly brewed
- ¼ cup honey
- 1 tablespoon fresh ginger, grated

Directions:
1. Combine the pears, tea, honey, and ginger in a large pot over medium-high heat. Bring to a simmer. Lower the heat to medium-low, cover, and simmer for 15 minutes until the pears soften. Serve the pears with the poaching liquid spooned over the top.

Nutrition Info:
- Per Serving: Calories: 190 ;Fat: 6g;Protein: 23g;Carbs: 50g .

Stunning Lemon Cake With Almond, Pistachio, Citrus Salad, And Coconut Whipped Cream

Servings: 6 To 8
Cooking Time: 40 To 45 Minutes
Ingredients:
- Cake:
- 1 ¼ cup raw almonds or almond meal, 240g
- ½ cup pistachios, 70g
- ½ teaspoon salt
- 6 eggs, separated
- 1 ¼ cup raw cane sugar, 250g
- 1 tablespoon lemon zest, grated
- 1 teaspoon orange zest, grated
- 1 teaspoon vanilla extract
- ¼ teaspoon almond extract
- Coconut Whipped Cream:
- One 13 ½ ounces can coconut milk, full-fat
- 1 tablespoon confectioner's sugar
- Citrus Salad:
- 2 oranges, sectioned
- 2 grapefruits, sectioned

- 1 tablespoon mint leaves, cut into strips
- 1 tablespoon honey, plus more as needed

Directions:

1. Make the cake. Preheat the oven to 350°F. Coat a 9-inch round springform pan with nonstick cooking spray.

2. Combine in a food processor the almonds, pistachios, and salt and pulse until finely ground. Combine the egg yolks and 1 cup (200 g) of the raw cane sugar in a large bowl. Beat until light and fluffy for 2 minutes. Add the lemon zest, orange zest, vanilla, and almond extract and beat until incorporated.

3. Beat the egg whites and the remaining ¼ cup (50 g) raw cane sugar on high speed until glossy in a clean bowl of a stand mixer fitted with the whisk attachment, stiff peaks form.

4. Alternate folding the egg whites and the almond mixture into the egg yolk mixture using a spatula, starting and ending with the egg whites. Pour into the prepared pan. Bake until a toothpick inserted into the center of the cake comes out clean and the top is golden brown for 40 to 45 minutes. Allow the cake to cool completely.

5. Make the coconut whipped cream. Chill the can of coconut milk, upside down, in the refrigerator overnight. Turn right-side up and open the can with a can opener. The water will be on the top. Pour carefully out the water and reserve for another use, only the coconut cream remains. Place the cream in a stand mixer fitted with the whisk attachment. Add the confectioner's sugar and whip on high speed until light and fluffy for 3 to 4 minutes.

6. Make the citrus salad. In a medium bowl, combine the orange and grapefruit sections with the mint and honey. Taste for sweetness and add more honey if necessary.

7. Remove the sides of the springform pan and transfer the cake to a serving platter. Spread the coconut cream into an even layer over the cake. Cut the cake into wedges, then top with the citrus salad and serve.

Nutrition Info:

- Per Serving: Calories: 334 ;Fat: 12g ;Protein: 12g ;Carbs: 43g .

Homemade Goji Berry Chocolate Granita

Servings: 4
Cooking Time: 5 Minutes

Ingredients:

- 1 pear, chopped
- 1 tbsp almond butter
- 2 tbsp fresh mint, minced
- ¼ cup non-dairy milk
- 3 tbsp dark chocolate chips
- 2 tbsp goji berries

Directions:

1. In your food processor, place the almond butter, pear, and mint. Pulse until smooth. Pour in the milk while keep blending. Add in chocolate chips and berries. Divide the mixture between glasses and serve. Serve chilled.

Nutrition Info:

- Per Serving: Calories: 235;Fat: 27g;Protein: 1g;Carbs: 0g.

Scrumptious Fruity Dark Chocolate Mousse

Servings: 2
Cooking Time: 5 Minutes

Ingredients:

- 1 cup strawberries, sliced
- ¼ cup free range egg whites
- 4 squares dark cooking chocolate
- 1 small banana, sliced
- ½ cup blueberries
- 2 tablespoons water

Directions:

1. Melt the dark chocolate over a bowl of boiling water on a low heat on the stove.

2. Add the water and egg whites to the melted chocolate and mix well to reach a thick consistency.

3. Spoon the batter out onto a small plate.

4. Put in the freezer for 30 minutes.

5. Garnish with the strawberries, banana and blueberries to serve.

Nutrition Info:

- Per Serving: Calories: 95 ;Protein: 4g ;Carbs: 20g .

Craving Peanut Butter Balls

Servings: 15
Cooking Time: 0 Minutes

Ingredients:

- ¾ cup creamy peanut butter
- 2 tablespoons unsalted butter, softened
- 1¾ cups powdered sugar
- ¼ cup cocoa powder, unsweetened
- ½ teaspoon vanilla extract

Directions:

1. Stir together in a medium bowl the peanut butter, butter, powdered sugar, cocoa powder, and vanilla until well combined.

2. Roll the mixture into about 15 (1-inch) balls and place them on a parchment paper-lined tray. Chill or serve immediately.

Nutrition Info:

- Per Serving: Calories: 147 ;Fat: 8g ;Protein: 4g ;Carbs: 17g ;.

Walnut Chocolate Squares

Servings: 6
Cooking Time: 10 Minutes

Ingredients:

- 4 oz dark chocolate
- 4 tbsp peanut butter
- 1 pinch of sea salt
- ¼ cup walnut butter
- ½ tsp vanilla extract

- ¼ cup chopped walnuts

Directions:

1. Pour the chocolate and peanut butter into a safe microwave bowl and melt in the microwave for 1-2 minutes. Remove the bowl from the microwave and mix in salt, walnut butter, and vanilla. Pour the batter into a greased baking dish and use a spatula to spread out into a rectangle. Top with walnuts and chill in the refrigerator. Once set, cut into squares. Serve while firming.

Nutrition Info:

- Per Serving: Calories: 245;Fat: 26g;Protein: 2g;Carbs: 2g.

Lemon Blackberry Cake

Servings: 4
Cooking Time: 45 Minutes
Ingredients:

- 4 peeled peaches, sliced
- 2 cups fresh blackberries
- 1 tbsp arrowroot
- ¾ cup pure date sugar
- 2 tsp fresh lemon juice
- 1 tsp ground cinnamon
- ½ cup whole-grain flour
- ½ cup old-fashioned oats
- 3 tbsp almond butter

Directions:

1. Preheat your oven to 370ºF. In a bowl, mix the peaches, blackberries, arrowroot, ¼ cup of sugar, lemon juice, and ½ tsp of cinnamon. Pour the batter into the pan. Set aside. In a bowl, stir the flour, oats, almond butter, remaining cup of sugar, and remaining cinnamon. Blend until crumbly. Drizzle the topping over the fruit. Bake for 30-40 minutes until browned. Serve.

Nutrition Info:

- Per Serving: Calories: 370;Fat: 10g;Protein: 6g;Carbs: 73g.

Nutty Date Cake

Servings: 4
Cooking Time:1 Hour 30 Minutes
Ingredients:

- ½ cup cold almond butter, cut into pieces
- 1 egg, beaten
- ½ cup whole-wheat flour
- ¼ cup chopped nuts
- 1 tsp baking powder
- 1 tsp baking soda
- 1 tsp cinnamon powder
- 1 tsp salt
- 1/3 cup dates, chopped
- ½ cup pure date sugar
- 1 tsp vanilla extract
- ¼ cup pure date syrup

Directions:

1. Preheat your oven to 350ºF. In a food processor, add the flour, nuts, baking powder, baking soda, cinnamon powder, and salt. Blend until well combined. Add 1/3 cup of water, almond butter, dates, date sugar, and vanilla. Process until smooth with tiny pieces of dates evident.

2. Pour the batter into a greased baking dish. Bake in the oven for 1 hour and 10 minutes or until a toothpick inserted comes out clean. Remove the dish from the oven, invert the cake onto a serving platter to cool, drizzle with the date syrup, slice, and serve.

Nutrition Info:

- Per Serving: Calories: 440;Fat: 28g;Protein: 8g;Carbs: 48g.

Chocolate Campanelle With Hazelnuts

Servings: 4
Cooking Time: 10 Minutes
Ingredients:

- ½ cup chopped toasted hazelnuts
- ¼ cup dark chocolate chips
- 8 oz campanelle pasta
- 3 tbsp almond butter
- ¼ cup maple syrup

Directions:

1. Pulse the hazelnuts and chocolate pieces in a food processor until crumbly. Set aside. Place the campanelle pasta in a pot with boiling salted water. Cook for 8-10 minutes until al dente, stirring often. Drain and back to the pot. Stir in almond butter and maple syrup and stir until the butter is melted. Serve garnished with chocolate-hazelnut mixture.

Nutrition Info:

- Per Serving: Calories: 360;Fat: 20g;Protein: 4g;Carbs: 44g.

Elegant Panna Cotta With Honey And Blackberry-lime Sauce

Servings: 6
Cooking Time: 5 Minutes
Ingredients:

- 2 ½ cups canned unsweetened coconut milk, 600ml
- 2 teaspoons gelatin
- ¼ cup honey, 60ml
- 1 vanilla bean, split and seeds scraped
- Kosher salt
- Blackberry-Lime Sauce:
- 2 cups blackberries, 240g
- Finely grated zest of ½ lime, plus 2 teaspoons lime juice
- 1 teaspoon raw cane sugar

Directions:

1. In a small bowl, place ½ cup (120 ml) of coconut milk. Sprinkle the gelatin over the top and allow it to sit for 2 minutes.

2. Place the remaining 2 cups (480 ml) coconut milk, honey, vanilla bean with its seeds, and a pinch of salt in a medium saucepan. Warm over low heat while whisking until

bubbles form around the edge of the pan. Remove from the heat and let the mixture steep for 5 minutes.

3. Pour the coconut milk mixture through a fine-mesh strainer into a large bowl. Discard the vanilla bean. Whisk slowly the gelatin mixture into the warm coconut mixture until there are no lumps of gelatin. Divide evenly among six ½ cup ramekins or wine glasses. Cover and refrigerate until set for 4 hours or overnight.

4. Make the blackberry-lime sauce. In a medium bowl, place the blackberries, lime zest, lime juice, and sugar. Gently mash using a fork or pastry blender the berries, leaving some large pieces of berry while allowing some of the juices to make a sauce. Set aside for 10 minutes, or cover and refrigerate up to overnight.

5. Spoon the sauce over each chilled panna cotta. Serve immediately.

Nutrition Info:

- Per Serving: Calories: 357 ;Fat: 24g ;Protein: 4g ;Carbs: 39g .

Healthy Brownies With Cacao

Servings: 4 To 6
Cooking Time: 2 ½ To 3 Hours
Ingredients:

- 3 tablespoons coconut oil, divided
- 1 cup almond butter
- 1 cup cacao powder, unsweetened
- ½ cup coconut sugar
- 2 large eggs
- 2 ripe bananas
- 2 teaspoons vanilla extract
- 1 teaspoon baking soda
- ½ teaspoon sea salt

Directions:

1. Coat the bottom of the slow cooker with 1 tablespoon of coconut oil.

2. Combine in a medium bowl the almond butter, cacao powder, coconut sugar, eggs, bananas, vanilla, baking soda, and salt. Mash the bananas and stir well until the batter forms. Pour the batter into the slow cooker.

3. Cover the cooker and set to low. Cook for 2½ to 3 hours until firm to a light touch and gooey in the middle then serve.

Nutrition Info:

- Per Serving: Calories: 779 ;Fat: 51g ;Protein: 18g ;Carbs: 68g .

Easiest Pressure-cooked Raspberry Curd

Servings: 4
Cooking Time: 25 Minutes + Chilling Time
Ingredients:

- 12 oz raspberries
- 2 tbsp almond butter
- Juice of ½ lemon

- 1 cup packed brown sugar
- 2 egg yolks

Directions:

1. Combine the raspberries, sugar, and lemon juice in your Instant Pot. Close the lid and cook for a 1 on "Manual". Release the pressure naturally for 5 minutes. Puree the raspberries and discard the seeds. Whisk the yolks in a bowl. Combine the yolks with the hot raspberry puree. Pour the mixture into your pot. Cook with the lid off for a minute on "Sauté". Stir in the butter and cook for a couple more minutes, until thick. Transfer to a container with a lid. Refrigerate for at least an hour before serving.

Nutrition Info:

- Per Serving: Calories: 250;Fat: 7g;Protein: 2g;Carbs: 50g.

Mango Chocolate Fudge

Servings: 3
Cooking Time: 10 Minutes + Chilling Time
Ingredients:

- 1 mango, pureed
- ¾ cup dark chocolate chips
- 4 cups pure date sugar

Directions:

1. Microwave the chocolate until melted. Add in the pureed mango and date sugar and stir to combine. Spread on a lined with waxed paper baking pan and chill in the fridge for 2 hours. Take out the fudge and lay on a cutting board. Slice into small pieces and serve.

Nutrition Info:

- Per Serving: Calories: 730;Fat: 1g;Protein: 2g;Carbs: 182g.

Vanilla Cookies With Poppy Seeds

Servings: 3
Cooking Time: 15 Minutes
Ingredients:

- ¾ cup almond butter
- ½ cup pure date sugar
- 1 tsp pure vanilla extract
- 2 tbsp pure maple syrup
- 2 cups whole-grain flour
- ¾ cup poppy seeds, toasted

Directions:

1. Beat the butter and sugar in a bowl until creamy and fluffy. Add in vanilla, and maple syrup, blend. Stir in flour and poppy seeds. Wrap the dough in a cylinder and cover it with plastic foil. Let chill in the fridge.

2. Preheat your oven to 330ºF. Cut the dough into thin circles and arrange on a baking sheet. Bake for 12 minutes until light brown. Let completely cool. Serve.

Nutrition Info:

- Per Serving: Calories: 965;Fat: 63g;Protein: 17g;Carbs: 93g.

21 day meal plan

Day 1
Breakfast: Amazing Banana Oat Pancakes 14
Lunch: Baked Basil Chicken 36
Dinner: Baked Mustard Beans 83

Day 2
Breakfast: Cranberry & Chia Pudding 14
Lunch: Port Wine Garlicky Lamb 36
Dinner: Baked Tempeh & Brussels Sprouts 83

Day 3
Breakfast: Pear & Kale Smoothie 14
Lunch: Korean Chicken Thighs 37
Dinner: Challenging Grain-free Fritters 83

Day 4
Breakfast: Chocolate-blueberry Smoothie 14
Lunch: Spicy Lime Pork Tenderloins 36
Dinner: Pasta Primavera With Cherry Tomatoes 83

Day 5
Breakfast: Maple Coconut Pancakes 15
Lunch: Authentic Chicken Curry With Coconut 37
Dinner: Tomato & Alfredo Penne 84

Day 6
Breakfast: Mango Green Tea Smoothie 15
Lunch: Rosemary Turkey With Mushrooms 37
Dinner: Feels Like Autumn Loaf With Root Vegetable 84

Day 7
Breakfast: Turkey Scotch Eggs 15
Lunch: Hot & Spicy Shredded Chicken 37
Dinner: Restorative Stew With Lentil And Corn 84

Day 8
Breakfast: Veggie Panini 15
Lunch: Sicilian Chicken Bake 38
Dinner: Versatile Zucchini Patties 84

Day 9
Breakfast: Tropical French Toasts16
Lunch: Cumin Lamb Meatballs With Aioli 38
Dinner: Mushroom & Green Bean Biryani 85

Day 10
Breakfast: Flaky Eggs With Cabbage16
Lunch: Cute Tiny Chicken Burgers 38
Dinner: Grilled Tempeh With Green Beans 85

Day 11
Breakfast: Sausage With Turkey And Berries 16
Lunch: Potted Rump Steak 38
Dinner: White Salad With Walnut Pesto 85

Day 12
Breakfast: Sunflower Seed Granola 16
Lunch: Creamy Beef Tenderloin Marsala 39
Dinner: Zucchini & Pepper Hash With Fried Eggs 85

Day 13
Breakfast: Cherry & Coconut Oatmeal With Chia 17
Lunch: Ground Turkey & Spinach Stir-fry 39
Dinner: Health Supportive Vegetable Curry 86

Day 14
Breakfast: Orange-bran Cups With Dates 17
Lunch: Worth It Glazed Chicken Thighs With Cauliflower 39
Dinner: Mushroom Lettuce Wraps 86

Day 15
Breakfast: Strawberry & Pecan Breakfast 17
Lunch: Sumac Chicken Thighs 39
Dinner: Spicy Moong Beans 86

Day 16
Breakfast: Spicy Quinoa Bowl With Black Beans 17
Lunch: Sweet Gingery & Garlicky Chicken Thighs 40
Dinner: Satisfying Mushroom Risotto 86

Day 17
Breakfast: Thyme Pumpkin Stir-fry 18
Lunch: Thyme Pork Loin Bake 40
Dinner: Savoy Cabbage Rolls With Tofu 87

Day 18
Breakfast: Sweet Kiwi Oatmeal Bars 18
Lunch: Spicy Beef Fajitas 40
Dinner: Tuscan-style Asparagus Frittata 87

Day 19
Breakfast: Terrific Pancakes With Coconut And Banana 18
Lunch: Chicken A La Tuscana 41
Dinner: Hot Quinoa Florentine 87

Day 20
Breakfast: Blackberry Waffles 18
Lunch: Tomato & Lentil Lamb Ragù 41
Dinner: Tempeh & Vegetable Stir-fry 87

Day 21
Breakfast: Sweet Potato, Tomato, & Onion Frittata 19
Lunch: Magical Ramen And Pork Char Siu 41
Dinner: Kale Pizza With Grilled Zucchini 88

INDEX

A

B

135

Cherry Tomato

Cherry Tomato & Basil Chicken Casserole 45
Sicilian Chicken Bake 38
Sautéed Cherry Tomatoes With Scrambled Herb 25
Seitan & Spinach Salad A La Puttanesca 101
Bulgur & Kale Salad 110
Thai Green Bean & Mango Salad 115
Tuscan-style Asparagus Frittata 87
Tomato & Alfredo Penne 84
Pasta Primavera With Cherry Tomatoes 83

Chia Seeds

Cranberry & Chia Pudding 14
Delightful Coconut With Cherries And Chia Seeds 20

Chicken Breast

The Best General Tso's Chicken 50
Basic Poached Wrapped Chicken 48
Good For The Bones Stir Fried Sesame Chicken 51
Sweet Balsamic Chicken 47
Italian-style Chicken 47
Mumbai-inspired Chicken 47
Hot & Spicy Shredded Chicken 37
Chicken Piccata 51
Sicilian Chicken Bake 38
Mexican Burrito Brunch 27
Refreshingly Spicy Chicken Salad With Cumin And Mango 104
Soy-free Salad With Chopped Chicken And Apple 109
Chicken & Vegetable Stew With Barley 74

Chicken Drumstick

Jerk Chicken Drumsticks 51

Chicken Thighs

Dairy Free Chicken Alfredo 45
Baked Basil Chicken 36
Authentic Chicken Curry With Coconut 37
Worth It Glazed Chicken Thighs With Cauliflower 39
Sweet Gingery & Garlicky Chicken Thighs 40
Sumac Chicken Thighs 39
Cherry Tomato & Basil Chicken Casserole 45
Korean Chicken Thighs 37
Miso Chicken With Sesame 42

Chickpea

Superb Salad With Chickpea 104
Hot Chickpea Salad 109
Chickpea & Celery Salad 105
Lemony Ditalini Salad With Chickpeas 112
Quinoa & Chickpea Pot 93
Mediterranean Chickpeas With Vegetables 88

Chocolate

Coconut & Chocolate Cake 129
Chocolate & Avocado Fudge 122
Hearty Gelato With Chocolate And Cinnamon 125
Walnut Chocolate Squares 131
Silky Smooth Vegan Chocolate Pots Decrème 124
Scrumptious Fruity Dark Chocolate Mousse 131
Pistachios & Chocolate Popsicles 125
Chocolate Campanelle With Hazelnuts 132
Poppy-granola Balls With Chocolate 128

Coconut Flour

Crispy Coconut Prawns 60
Battered Bite Size Shrimp With Gluten-free Coconut 56
Mediterranean Coconut Pancakes 25
Maple Coconut Pancakes 15
Terrific Pancakes With Coconut And Banana 18

Coconut Milk

Authentic Chicken Curry With Coconut 37
Creamy Dressing With Sesame 32
Must-have Ranch Dressing 35
Delicate Rice With Coconut And Berries 21
Cherry & Coconut Oatmeal With Chia 17
Lovable Smoothie With Coconut And Ginger 29
Coconut Chia Pudding 129
Thick Coconut Rice With Blueberries 123
Great Pudding With Chocolate And Avocado 125

Cod Fillet

Dense Oven Roasted Cod And Shiitake Mushrooms 54
Baked Cod Fillets With Mushroom 56
Tropical-style Cod 54
Spicy Aromatic Bowl Of Cod 58
Warm Cod & Zucchini Salad 110

Cremini Mushroom

Sicilian Chicken Bake 38
Broccoli Stuffed Cremini Mushrooms 94
Comforting Soup With Riced Cauliflower, Cremini Mushrooms, And Baby Spinach 69

Cucumber

Beet & Cucumber Salad 109
Effortless Half-sour Pickled Salad 107
Summer Salad 106

D

Daikon

Cumin Salmon With Daikon Relish 52
Daikon Salad With Caramelized Onion 106
Daikon & Sweet Potato Soup 71

Dill Pickle

Seared Trout With Greek Yogurt Sauce 66

K

Kale

Crusty And Nutty Tilapia With Kale 52

Baked Tilapia With Chili Kale 62

Delicious Pesto With Kale 32

Pear & Kale Smoothie 14

Amazing Breakfast Bowl With Kale, Pickled Red Onions, And Carne Molida 22

Pleasant And Tender Salad With Kale 103

Bulgur & Kale Salad 110

Frittata With Kale & Seeds 91

Rich In Nutrients Noodles With Tahini And Kale 96

Kale Pizza With Grilled Zucchini 88

Extraordinary Creamy Green Soup 78

Kiwi

Sweet Kiwi Oatmeal Bars 18

Kiwi & Peanut Bars 123

L

Lamb

Robust Herbed Lamb With Zucchini Boats 43

Tomato & Lentil Lamb Ragù 41

Mustardy Leg Of Lamb 42

Delightful Stuffed Lamb With Peppers 45

Port Wine Garlicky Lamb 36

Cumin Lamb Meatballs With Aioli 38

Smoky Lamb Souvlaki 48

Port Wine Garlicky Lamb 36

Lettuce

Lettuce-wrapped Beef Roast 49

Lettuce & Tomato Salad With Quinoa 107

M

Mango

Mango Green Tea Smoothie 15

Mango Rice Pudding 24

Vegetarian Mango Smoothie With Green Tea And Turmeric 29

Avocado Salad With Mango & Almonds 106

Thai Green Bean & Mango Salad 115

Maple Fruit Crumble 129

Sherry-lime Mango Dessert 120

Mango Chocolate Fudge 133

Mozzarella Cheese

Quick Insalata Caprese 115

Savoury Pasta With Sun-dried Tomato And Nut 89

O

Orange

Rosemary Salmon With Orange Glaze 61

Bell Pepper & Quinoa Salad 102

Orange Berry Salad 102

Spiced Supreme Orange 124

P

Parmesan Cheese

Veggie Panini 15

Parsnip

Parsnip & Tilapia Bake 65

Diverse Salad With Shredded Root Vegetable 112

Fennel & Parsnip Bisque 68

Peach

Feels Like Summer Chutney With Mint 35

Fragrant Peach Butter 33

Fresh Peach Smoothie 21

Comfort Cobbler With Blueberry And Peach 126

Pear

Matcha Smoothie With Pear & Ginger 19

Pear & Kale Smoothie 14

Smoothie That Can Soothe Inflammation 29

Irresistible Pear And Walnut Salad 105

Maple Walnut & Pear Salad 112

Hazelnut & Pear Salad 103

Flavourful Glazed Maple Pears And Hazelnuts 121

Walnut Pears With Maple Glaze 122

Homemade Goji Berry Chocolate Granita 131

Poached Clove With Pears 118

Poached Pears With Green Tea 130

Natural Crispy Seasonal Fruits 119

Pecan

Southern Trout With Crusty Pecan 53

Sweet And Special Spiced Pecans 127

Interesting Snack Bars With Date And Pecan 119

Pineapple

Simple Tacos With Fish And Pineapple Salsa 56

Minty Juice With Pineapple And Cucumber 30

Easy Pineapple & Jicama Salad 112

Cinnamon Tropical Cobbler 128

Pork Chop

Classic Pork Chops And Creamy Green Beans 44

Pork Tenderloin

Ragù Dish With Pork 46

Magical Ramen And Pork Char Siu 41

Chili Pork Ragout 44

Spicy Lime Pork Tenderloins 37

Fiery Pork Loin With Lime 48

Pecan-dusted Pork Tenderloin Slices 48

Portobello Mushroom
Basil & Tofu Stuffed Portobello Mushrooms 93
Prawn
Crispy Coconut Prawns 60
Prune
Tropical Baked Fruit With Nut Pudding 125
Pumpkin
Thyme Pumpkin Stir-fry 18
Marinated Tempah And Spaghetti Squash 97
Cayenne Pumpkin Soup 76
Roasted-pumpkin Soup 71
Pumpkin Seed
Pecan & Pumpkin Seed Oat Jars 21
Tangy Nutty Brussel Sprout Salad 115

R

Radish
Coleslaw & Spinach Salad With Grapefruit 102
Refreshing Slaw With Maple Dressing 112
Diverse Salad With Shredded Root Vegetable 112
Radish & Tomato Salad 100
Warm Chili Pumpkin Soup 81
Red Bell Pepper
Gingered Beef Stir-fry With Peppers 46
Bell Pepper & Quinoa Salad 102
Peppery Soup With Tomato 79
Red Cabbage
Chinese-style Cabbage Salad 106
Rice Milk
Chocolate-blueberry Smoothie 14

S

Sardine
Sardine & Butter Bean Meal 57
Famous Herbaceous Sardines With Citrus 57
Scallop
Tarragon Scallops 57
Scallops & Mussels Cauliflower Paella 59
Scallops With Capers 59
Saucy And Natural Flavoured Golden Seared Scallops With Wilted Bacon Spinach 65
Extraordinary Scallops With Lime And Cilantro 60
Sea Scallops In Citrus Dressing 63
Sea Scallop
Scallops With Capers 59
Sea Scallops In Citrus Dressing 63
Shiitake Mushroom
Dense Oven Roasted Cod And Shiitake Mushrooms 54

Baked Cod Fillets With Mushroom 56
Mushroom Curry Soup 81
Shiitake Mushroom Soup 72
Shrimp
Shrimp With Spiralized Veggies 57
Battered Bite Size Shrimp With Gluten-free Coconut 56
Shrimp & Egg Risotto 60
Lemony Spanish Shrimp With Parsley 67
Southwest Shrimp Soup 77
Smoked Mackerel
Beetroot Salad With Mackerel 105
Smoked Salmon
Childhood Favourite Salmon Zoodle Casserole 55
Scrambled Eggs With Smoked Salmon 22
Snow Pea
Melt-in-your-mouth Chicken & Rice 50
Tropical Salad 107
Spaghetti Squash
Marinated Tempah And Spaghetti Squash 97
Steel-Cut Oat
Maple Banana Oats 20
Sweet Onion
Herby Green Whole Chicken 46
Daikon Salad With Caramelized Onion 106
Lettuce & Tomato Salad With Quinoa 107

T

Tilapia Fillet
Parsnip & Tilapia Bake 65
Crusty And Nutty Tilapia With Kale 52
Almond-crusted Tilapia 61
Tofu
Scrambled Tofu With Garlic, Onions, And Mung Bean Sprouts 14
Hot And Spicy Scrambled Tofu And Spinach 96
Basil & Tofu Stuffed Portobello Mushrooms 93
Tofu & Almond Pancakes 130
Layered Raspberry & Tofu Cups 120
Brussels Sprouts & Tofu Soup 80
Trout
Seared Trout With Greek Yogurt Sauce 66
Mediterranean Trout 65
Trout Fillets With Almond Crust 59
Southern Trout With Crusty Pecan 53
Hazelnut Crusted Trout Fillets 66
Tuna
Hawaiian Tuna 63
Nostalgic Tuna And Avocado Salad Sandwiches 67

Freshly-made Fennel Salad With Tuna Steak 113
Pantry Salad With White Bean And Tuna 144

Turkey

Ground Turkey & Spinach Stir-fry 39
Holiday Turkey 42
Rosemary Turkey With Mushrooms 37
Lemon & Caper Turkey Scaloppine 50
Smoked Turkey 42
Turkey Stuffed Bell Peppers 49
Tasteful Hash With Sweet Potato And Ground Turkey 17
Sausage With Turkey And Berries 16
Turkey Scotch Eggs 15
French Peasant Turkey Stew 78
Meatball Soup With Vegetables 68

W

Walnut

Irresistible Pear And Walnut Salad 105
Maple Walnut & Pear Salad 112
White Salad With Walnut Pesto 85

White Bean

Pantry Salad With White Bean And Tuna 114
Cabbage & Bean Stir-fry 93
Italian Bean Soup 82

Rosemary White Bean Soup 73

White Fish Fillet

Lovage Fish Soup 75

Y

Yellow Squash

Shrimp With Spiralized Veggies 57

Z

Zucchini

Robust Herbed Lamb With Zucchini Boats 43
Italian-style Chicken 47
Shrimp With Spiralized Veggies 57
Zesty Frittata With Sweet Potato And Zucchini 26
African Zucchini Salad 111
Warm Cod & Zucchini Salad 110
Zucchini & Bell Pepper Salad With Beans 104
Rich In Antioxidant Vegetable Slaw With Feta Cheese 109
Versatile Zucchini Patties 84
Zoodle Bolognese 97
Zucchini & Pepper Hash With Fried Eggs 85
Soft Zucchini With White Beans And Olives Stuffing 89
Hot Lentil Soup With Zucchini 78
Green Bean & Zucchini Velouté 81

CPSIA information can be obtained
at www.ICGtesting.com
Printed in the USA
BVHW010934280422
635364BV00021B/477